ŚRĪ CAITANYA-CARITĀMṚTA

BOOKS by
His Divine Grace A.C. Bhaktivedanta Swami Prabhupāda

Bhagavad-gītā As It Is
Śrīmad-Bhāgavatam, Cantos 1-5 (15 Vols.)
Śrī Caitanya-caritāmṛta (17 Vols.)
Teachings of Lord Caitanya
The Nectar of Devotion
Śrī Īśopaniṣad
Easy Journey to Other Planets
Kṛṣṇa Consciousness: The Topmost Yoga System
Kṛṣṇa, The Supreme Personality of Godhead (3 Vols.)
Transcendental Teachings of Prahlād Mahārāja
Kṛṣṇa, the Reservoir of Pleasure
The Perfection of Yoga
Beyond Birth and Death
On the Way to Kṛṣṇa
Rāja-vidyā: The King of Knowledge
Elevation to Kṛṣṇa Consciousness
Kṛṣṇa Consciousness: The Matchless Gift
Back to Godhead Magazine (Founder)

A complete catalogue is available upon request

International Society for Krishna Consciousness
3764 Watseka Avenue
Los Angeles, California 90034

All Glory to Śrī Guru and Gaurāṅga

Śrī Caitanya-caritāmṛta

of Kṛṣṇadāsa Kavirāja Gosvāmī

Antya-līlā
Volume Four

"Śrī Caitanya Mahāprabhu's Ecstatic Love of Godhead"

with the original Bengali text, Roman transliterations, synonyms, translation and elaborate purports

by

HIS DIVINE GRACE
A.C. Bhaktivedanta Swami Prabhupāda
Founder-Ācārya of the International Society for Krishna Consciousness

THE BHAKTIVEDANTA BOOK TRUST
New York · Los Angeles · London · Bombay

Readers interested in the subject matter of this book
are invited by the International Society for Krishna Consciousness
to correspond with its Secretary.

International Society for Krishna Consciousness
3764 Watseka Avenue
Los Angeles, California 90034

Library of Congress Catalogue Card Number: 73-93206
International Standard Book Number: 0-912776-76-5

First printing, 1975: 20,000 copies

Printed in the United States of America

Contents

Introduction

Śrī Caitanya-caritāmṛta is the principal work on the life and teachings of Śrī Kṛṣṇa Caitanya. Śrī Caitanya is the pioneer of a great social and religious movement which began in India a little less than five hundred years ago and which has directly and indirectly influenced the subsequent course of religious and philosophical thinking not only in India but in the recent West as well.

Caitanya Mahāprabhu is regarded as a figure of great historical significance. However, our conventional method of historical analysis—that of seeing a man as a product of his times—fails here. Śrī Caitanya is a personality who transcends the limited scope of historical settings.

At a time when, in the West, man was directing his explorative spirit toward studying the structure of the physical universe and circumnavigating the world in search of new oceans and continents, Śrī Kṛṣṇa Caitanya, in the East, was inaugurating and masterminding a revolution directed inward, toward a scientific understanding of the highest knowledge of man's spiritual nature.

The chief historical sources for the life of Śrī Kṛṣṇa Caitanya are the *kaḍacās* (diaries) kept by Murāri Gupta and Svarūpa Dāmodara Gosvāmī. Murāri Gupta, a physician and close associate of Śrī Caitanya's, recorded extensive notes on the first twenty-four years of Śrī Caitanya's life, culminating in his initiation into the renounced order, *sannyāsa*. The events of the rest of Caitanya Mahāprabhu's forty-eight years are recorded in the diary of Svarūpa Dāmodora Gosvāmī, another of Caitanya Mahāprabhu's intimate associates.

Śrī Caitanya-caritāmṛta is divided into three sections called *līlās,* which literally means "pastimes"—*Ādi-līlā* (the early period), *Madhya-līlā* (the middle period) and *Antya-līlā* (the final period). The notes of Murāri Gupta form the basis of the *Ādi-līlā,* and Svarūpa Dāmodara's diary provides the details for the *Madhya-* and *Antya-līlās.*

The first twelve of the seventeen chapters of *Ādi-līlā* constitute the preface for the entire work. By referring to Vedic scriptural evidence, this preface establishes Śrī Caitanya as the *avatāra* (incarnation) of Kṛṣṇa (God) for the age of Kali—the current epoch, beginning five thousand years ago and characterized by materialism, hypocrisy and dissension. In these descriptions, Caitanya Mahāprabhu, who is identical with Lord Kṛṣṇa, descends to liberally grant pure love of God to the fallen souls of this degraded age by propagating *saṅkīrtana*—literally, "congregational glorification of God"—especially by organizing massive public chanting of the *mahā-mantra* (Great Chant for Deliverance). The esoteric purpose of Lord Caitanya's appearance in the world is revealed, his co-*avatāras* and principal devotees are described and his teachings are summarized. The remaining portion of *Ādi-līlā,* chapters thirteen through seventeen, briefly recounts his divine birth and his life until he accepted the renounced order. This includes his childhood miracles, schooling, marriage and early philosophical confrontations, as well as his organization of a widespread *saṅkīrtana* movement and his civil disobedience against the repression of the Mohammedan government.

The subject of *Madhya-līlā,* the longest of the three divisions, is a detailed narration of Lord Caitanya's extensive and eventful travels throughout India as a renounced mendicant, teacher, philosopher, spiritual preceptor and mystic. During this period of six years, Śrī Caitanya transmits his teachings to his principal disciples. He debates and converts many of the most renowned philosophers and theologians of his time, including Śaṅkarites, Buddhists and Muslims, and incorporates their many thousands of followers and disciples into his own burgeoning numbers. A dramatic account of Caitanya Mahāprabhu's miraculous activities at the giant Jagannātha Cart Festival in Orissa is also included in this section.

Antya-līlā concerns the last eighteen years of Śrī Caitanya's manifest presence, spent in semiseclusion near the famous Jagannātha temple at Jagannātha Purī in Orissa. During these final years, Śrī Caitanya drifted deeper and deeper into trances of spiritual ecstasy unparalleled in all of religious and literary history, Eastern or Western. Śrī Caitanya's perpetual and ever-increasing religious beatitude, graphically described in the eyewitness accounts of Svarūpa Dāmodara Gosvāmī, his constant companion during this period, clearly defy the investigative and descriptive abilities of modern psychologists and phenomenologists of religious experience.

The author of this great classic, Kṛṣṇadāsa Kavirāja Gosvāmī, born in the year 1507, was a disciple of Raghunātha dāsa Gosvāmī, a confidential follower of Caitanya Mahāprabhu. Raghunātha dāsa, a renowned ascetic saint, heard and memorized all the activities of Caitanya Mahāprabhu told to him by Svarūpa Dāmodara. After the passing away of Śrī Caitanya and Svarūpa Dāmodara, Raghunātha dāsa, unable to bear the pain of separation from these objects of his complete devotion, traveled to Vṛndāvana, intending to commit suicide by jumping from Govardhana Hill. In Vṛndāvana, however, he encountered Rūpa Gosvāmī and Sanātana Gosvāmī, the most confidential disciples of Caitanya Mahāprabhu. They convinced him to give up his plan of suicide and impelled him to reveal to them the spiritually inspiring events of Lord Caitanya's later life. Kṛṣṇadāsa Kavirāja Gosvāmī was also residing in Vṛndāvana at this time, and Raghunātha dāsa Gosvāmī endowed him with a full comprehension of the transcendental life of Śrī Caitanya.

By this time, several biographical works had already been written on the life of Śrī Caitanya by contemporary and near-contemporary scholars and devotees. These included *Śrī Caitanya-carita* by Murāri Gupta, *Caitanya-maṅgala* by Locana dāsa Ṭhākura and *Caitanya-bhāgavata.* This latter text, a work by Vṛndāvana dāsa Ṭhākura, who was then considered the principal authority on Śrī Caitanya's life, was highly revered. While composing his important work, Vṛndāvana dāsa, fearing that it would become too voluminous, avoided elaborately describing many of the events of Śrī Caitanya's life, particulary the later ones. Anxious to hear of these later pastimes, the devotees of Vṛndāvana requested Kṛṣṇadāsa Kavirāja Gosvāmī, whom they respected as a great saint, to compose a book to narrate these episodes in detail. Upon this request, and with the permission and blessings of the Madana-mohana Deity of Vṛndāvana, he began compiling *Śrī Caitanya-caritāmṛta,* which, due to its biographical excellence and thorough exposition of Lord Caitanya's profound philosophy and teachings, is regarded as the most significant of biographical works on Śrī Caitanya.

He commenced work on the text while in his late nineties and in failing health, as he vividly describes in the text itself: "I have now become too old and disturbed in invalidity. While writing, my hands tremble. I cannot remember anything, nor can I see or hear properly. Still I write, and this is a great wonder." That he nevertheless completed, under such debilitating conditions, the greatest literary gem of medieval India is surely one of the wonders of literary history.

This English translation and commentary is the work of His Divine Grace A. C. Bhaktivedanta Swami Prabhupāda, the world's most distinguished teacher of Indian religious and philosophical thought. His commentary is based upon two Bengali commentaries, one by his teacher Śrīla Bhaktisiddhānta Sarasvatī Gosvāmī, the eminent Vedic scholar who predicted, "The time will come when the people of the world will learn Bengali to read *Śrī Caitanya-caritāmṛta,*" and the other by Śrīla Bhaktisiddhānta's father, Bhaktivinoda Ṭhākura.

His Divine Grace A. C. Bhaktivedanta Swami Prabhupāda is himself a disciplic descendant of Śrī Caitanya Mahāprabhu, and he is the first scholar to execute systematic English translations of the major works of Śrī Caitanya's followers. His consummate Bengali and Sanskrit scholarship and intimate familiarity with the precepts of Śrī Kṛṣṇa Caitanya are a fitting combination that eminently qualifies him to present this important classic to the English-speaking world. The ease and clarity with which he expounds upon difficult philosophical concepts lures even a reader totally unfamiliar with Indian religious tradition into a genuine understanding and appreciation of this profound and monumental work.

The entire text, with commentary, presented in seventeen lavishly illustrated volumes by the Bhaktivedanta Book Trust, represents a contribution of major importance to the intellectual, cultural and spiritual life of contemporary man.

—The Publishers

His Divine Grace
A. C. Bhaktivedanta Swami Prabhupāda
Founder-Ācārya of the International Society for Krishna Consciousness

In Purī, the *bhajana-kuṭira* (place of worship) of Śrīla Haridāsa Ṭhākura, who received the title *nāmācārya* (the preacher of the glories of the holy name) from Śrī Caitanya Mahāprabhu. At this site he would chant the holy name of Kṛṣṇa 300,000 times a day without fail.

The *samādhi* (tomb) of Śrīla Haridāsa Ṭhākura in Purī. On the wall there is an inscription by Śrīla Bhaktivinoda Ṭhākura: "He reasons ill who tells that Vaiṣṇavas die when thou art living still in sound! The Vaiṣṇavas die to live, and living try to spread the holy name around!" There was no end to the transcendental qualities of Haridāsa Ṭhākura.

The Siṁha-dvāra gate of the Jagannātha Purī temple, where Śrī Caitanya Mahāprabhu was found lying unconscious in ecstatic love of Godhead. (*p.222*)

The temple and Deity of Śrī Ṭoṭa Gopīnātha in Purī. At this sacred place, Śrī Caitanya Mahāprabhu concluded His manifested pastimes in this material world.

PLATE ONE

"As He described the transcendental attributes of Haridāsa Ṭhākura, Śrī Caitanya Mahāprabhu seemed to possess five mouths. The more He described, the more His happiness increased. After hearing of the transcendental qualities of Haridāsa Ṭhākura, all the devotees present were struck with wonder. They all offered their respectful obeisances to the lotus feet of Haridāsa Ṭhākura. Haridāsa Ṭhākura made Śrī Caitanya Mahāprabhu sit down in front of him, and then he fixed his eyes, like two bumblebees, on the lotus face of the Lord. He held the lotus feet of Śrī Caitanya Mahāprabhu on his heart and then took the dust of the feet of all the devotees present and put it on his head. He began to chant the holy name of Śrī Kṛṣṇa Caitanya again and again. As he drank the sweetness of the face of the Lord, tears constantly glided down from his eyes." (*pp.24-25*)

PLATE TWO

"The devotees, in great happiness, started for Jagannātha Purī, congregationally chanting the holy name of the Lord. One day when the party was being checked by a toll collector, the devotees were allowed to pass, and Śivānanda Sena remained behind alone to pay the taxes. The party went into a village and waited beneath a tree because no one but Śivānanda Sena could arrange for their residential quarters. Nityānanda Prabhu meanwhile became very hungry and upset. Because He had not yet obtained a suitable residence, He began calling Śivānanda Sena ill names. 'Śivānanda Sena has not arranged for My residence,' He complained, 'and I am so hungry I could die. Because he has not come, I curse his three sons to die.' Hearing this curse, Śivānanda Sena's wife began to cry. Just then, Śivānanda returned from the toll station. Crying, his wife informed him, 'Lord Nityānanda has cursed our sons to die because His quarters have not been provided.' Śivānanda Sena replied, 'You crazy woman! Why are you needlessly crying? Let my three sons die for all the inconveniences we have caused Nityānanda Prabhu.' After saying this, Śivānanda Sena went to Nityānanda Prabhu, who then stood up and kicked him." (*pp.57-62*)

PLATE THREE

"When ten days had passed, Govinda again told Śrī Caitanya Mahāprabhu, 'It is the desire of Jagadānanda Paṇḍita that Your Lordship accept the oil.' When the Lord heard this, He angrily said, 'Why not keep a masseur to massage me? Have I taken *sannyāsa* for such happiness? Accepting this oil would bring Me ruination, and all of you would laugh. If someone passing on the road smelled this oil on My head, he would think Me a *dārī sannyāsī,* a tantric *sannyāsī* who keeps women.' Hearing these words of Śrī Caitanya Mahāprabhu, Govinda remained silent. The next morning Jagadānanda went to see the Lord. Śrī Caitanya Mahāprabhu said to Jagadānanda Paṇḍita, 'My dear Paṇḍita, you have brought Me some oil from Bengal, but since I am in the renounced order, I cannot accept it. Deliver the oil to the temple of Jagannātha so that it may be burned in the lamps. Thus your labor in preparing the oil will be fruitful.' Jagadānanda Paṇḍita replied, 'Who tells You all these false stories? I never brought any oil from Bengal.' After saying this, Jagadānanda Paṇḍita took the jug of oil from the room and threw it down before Śrī Caitanya Mahāprabhu in the courtyard and broke it." (*pp.99-103*)

PLATE FOUR

"One day while He was resting, Śrī Caitanya Mahāprabhu dreamed He saw Kṛṣṇa performing His *rāsa* dance. Śrī Caitanya Mahāprabhu saw Lord Kṛṣṇa standing with His beautiful body curved in three places, holding His flute to His lips. Wearing yellow garments and garlands of forest flowers, He was enchanting even to Cupid. The *gopīs* were dancing in a circle, and in the middle of that circle, Kṛṣṇa, the son of Mahārāja Nanda, danced with Rādhārāṇī. Seeing this, Śrī Caitanya Mahāprabhu was overwhelmed with the transcendental mellow of the *rāsa* dance, and He thought, 'Now I am with Kṛṣṇa in Vṛndāvana.' " (*pp.195-196*)

PLATE FIVE

"Śrī Caitanya Mahāprabhu performed His customary daily duties, and at the usual time He went to see Lord Jagannātha in the temple. As He viewed Lord Jagannātha from behind the Garuḍa column, hundreds and thousands of people in front of Him were seeing the Deity. Suddenly, a woman from Orissa, unable to see Lord Jagannātha because of the crowd, climbed the column of Garuḍa, placing her foot on Śrī Caitanya Mahāprabhu's shoulder. When he saw this, Caitanya Mahāprabhu's personal secretary, Govinda, hastily got her down from her position. Śrī Caitanya Mahāprabhu, however, chastised him for this. Śrī Caitanya Mahāprabhu said to Govinda, 'O *ādi-vasyā* (uncivilized man), do not forbid this woman to climb the Garuḍa-stambha. Let her see Lord Jagannātha to her satisfaction.'" (*pp.197-199*)

PLATE SIX

"When Svarūpa Dāmodara entered the room, he found the three doors locked, but Śrī Caitanya Mahāprabhu had gone. All the devotees were very anxious when they saw that the Lord was not in His room. They wandered about searching for Him with a warning lamp. After searching for some time, they came upon Śrī Caitanya Mahāprabhu lying in a corner by the northern side of the Siṁha-dvāra gate. At first they were overjoyed to see Him, but when they saw His condition, all the devotees, headed by Svarūpa Dāmodara Gosvāmī, were very anxious. Śrī Caitanya Mahāprabhu was lying unconscious, and His body had become elongated to five or six cubits (eight or nine feet). There was no breath from His nostrils. . . .When they saw this, Svarūpa Dāmodara Gosvāmī and all the other devotees began to chant the holy name of Kṛṣṇa very loudly into Śrī Caitanya Mahāprabhu's ear." (*pp.221-225*)

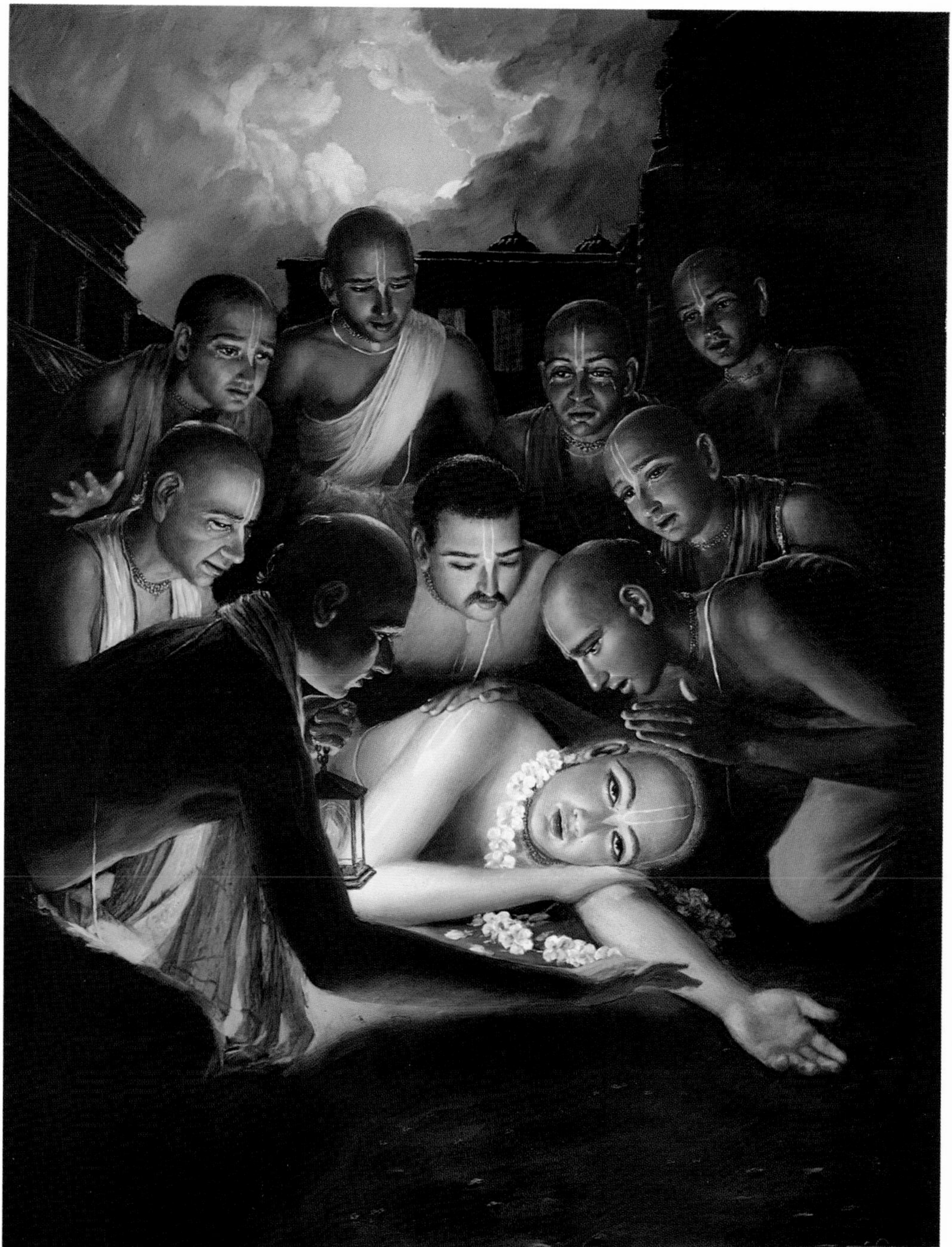
परीक्षित दास

PLATE SEVEN

"One day, while Śrī Caitanya Mahāprabhu was going to the sea to bathe, He suddenly saw a sand dune named Caṭaka-parvata. Śrī Caitanya Mahāprabhu mistook the sand dune for Govardhana Hill and ran toward it. Śrī Caitanya Mahāprabhu ran toward the sand dune as fast as the wind. Govinda ran after Him, but he could not approach Him. First one devotee shouted loudly, and then a tumultuous uproar arose as all the devotees stood up and began to run after the Lord. Svarūpa Dāmodara Gosvāmī, Jagadānanda Paṇḍita, Gadādhara Paṇḍita, Rāmāi, Nandāi and Śaṅkara Paṇḍita are some of the devotees who ran after Śrī Caitanya Mahāprabhu. Paramānanda Purī and Brahmānanda Bhāratī also went toward the beach, and Bhāgavan Ācārya, who was lame, followed them very slowly." (*pp.231-234*)

PLATE EIGHT

"When Śrī Caitanya Mahāprabhu saw all the Vaiṣṇavas, He returned to partial external consciousness and spoke to Svarūpa Dāmodara. Śrī Caitanya Mahāprabhu said, 'Who has brought Me here from Govardhana Hill? I was seeing Lord Kṛṣṇa's pastimes, but now I cannot see them. Today I went from here to Govardhana Hill to find out if Kṛṣṇa was tending His cows there. I saw Lord Kṛṣṇa climbing Govardhana Hill and playing His flute, surrounded on all sides by grazing cows. Hearing the vibration of Kṛṣṇa's flute, Śrīmatī Rādhārāṇī and all Her *gopī* friends came there to meet Him. They were all very nicely dressed. When Kṛṣṇa and Śrīmatī Rādhārāṇī entered a cave together, the other *gopīs* asked Me to pick some flowers. Just then, all of you made a tumultuous sound and carried Me from there to this place. Why have you brought Me here, causing Me unnecessary pain? I had a chance to see Kṛṣṇa's pastimes, but I could not see them.' " (*pp.240-243*)

PLATE NINE

"Lord Caitanya mistook a garden for Vṛndāvana and very quickly entered it. Absorbed in ecstatic love of Kṛṣṇa, He wandered through the garden in the mood of the *gopīs*. After Kṛṣṇa disappeared with Rādhārāṇī during the *rāsa* dance, the *gopīs* wandered in the forest looking for Him. The *gopīs* said, 'O *cūta* tree, *priyāla* tree, *panasa, āsana* and *kovidāra!* O *jambū* tree, O *arka* tree, O *bel, bakula* and mango! O *kadamba* tree, O *nīpa* tree and all other trees living on the bank of the Yamunā for the welfare of others, please let us know where Kṛṣṇa has gone. We have lost our minds and are almost dead. O *tulasī!* O *mālatī!* O *yūthī, mādhavī* and *mallikā!* Kṛṣṇa is very dear to you. Therefore He must have come near you. You are all just like dear friends to us. Kindly tell us which way Kṛṣṇa has gone and save our lives!' " (*pp.266-272*)

CHAPTER 11

The Passing of Haridāsa Ṭhākura

The summary of the chapter is given by Śrīla Bhaktivinoda Ṭhākura in his *Amṛta-pravāha-bhāṣya* as follows. In this chapter, Brahma Haridāsa Ṭhākura gave up his body with the consent of Śrī Caitanya Mahāprabhu, and the Lord Himself personally performed the funeral ceremony and carried the body to the sea. He personally entombed the body, covered it with sand, and erected a platform on the site. After taking bath in the sea, He personally begged *prasāda* of Jagannātha from shopkeepers and distributed *prasāda* to the assembled devotees.

TEXT 1

নমামি হরিদাসং তং চৈতন্যং তঞ্চ তৎপ্রভুম্ ।
সংস্থিতামপি যন্মূর্তিং স্বাঙ্কে কৃত্বা ননর্ত যঃ ॥ ১ ॥

namāmi haridāsaṁ taṁ
caitanyaṁ taṁ ca tat-prabhum
saṁsthitām api yan-mūrtiṁ
svāṅke kṛtvā nanarta yaḥ

SYNONYMS

namāmi—I offer my respectful obeisances; *haridāsam*—unto Haridāsa Ṭhākura; *tam*—him; *caitanyam*—unto Lord Caitanya; *tam*—Him; *ca*—also; *tat-prabhum*—his master; *saṁsthitām*—dead; *api*—certainly; *yat*—whose; *mūrtim*—bodily form; *sva-aṅke*—on His lap; *kṛtvā*—keeping; *nanarta*—danced; *yaḥ*—He who.

TRANSLATION

Let me offer my respectful obeisances unto Haridāsa Ṭhākura and his master, Śrī Caitanya Mahāprabhu, who danced with the body of Haridāsa Ṭhākura on His lap.

TEXT 2

জয় জয় শ্রীচৈতন্য জয় দয়াময় ।
জয়াদ্বৈতপ্রিয় নিত্যানন্দপ্রিয় জয় ॥ ২ ॥

jaya jaya śrī-caitanya jaya dayāmaya
jayādvaita-priya nityānanda-priya jaya

SYNONYMS

jaya jaya—all glories; *śrī-caitanya*—to Lord Śrī Caitanya Mahāprabhu; *jaya*—all glories; *dayā-maya*—to the most merciful; *jaya*—all glories; *advaita-priya*—to the dear master of Advaita Ācārya; *nityānanda-priya*—to Śrī Caitanya Mahāprabhu, who is very dear to Lord Nityānanda; *jaya*—all glories.

TRANSLATION

All glories to Lord Śrī Caitanya Mahāprabhu, who is very merciful and who is very dear to Advaita Ācārya and Lord Nityānanda.

TEXT 3

জয় শ্রীনিবাসেশ্বর হরিদাসনাথ ।
জয় গদাধরপ্রিয় স্বরূপ-প্রাণনাথ ॥ ৩ ॥

jaya śrīnivāseśvara haridāsa-nātha
jaya gadādhara-priya svarūpa-prāṇa-nātha

SYNONYMS

jaya—all glories; *śrīnivāsa-īśvara*—to the master of Śrīnivāsa; *haridāsa-nātha*—the master of Haridāsa Ṭhākura; *jaya*—all glories; *gadādhara-priya*—to the dear master of Gadādhara; *svarūpa-prāṇa-nātha*—the master of the life of Svarūpa Dāmodara.

TRANSLATION

All glories to the master of Śrīnivāsa Ṭhākura! All glories to the master of Haridāsa Ṭhākura! All glories to the dear master of Gadādhara Paṇḍita! All glories to the master of the life of Svarūpa Dāmodara!

TEXT 4

জয় কাশীপ্রিয় জগদানন্দ-প্রাণেশ্বর ।
জয় রূপ-সনাতন-রঘুনাথেশ্বর ॥ ৪ ॥

jaya kāśī-priya jagadānanda-prāṇeśvara
jaya rūpa-sanātana-raghunātheśvara

SYNONYMS

jaya—all glories; *kāśī-priya*—to Lord Śrī Caitanya, who is very dear to Kāśī Miśra; *jagadānanda-prāṇa-īśvara*—the Lord of the life of Jagadānanda Paṇḍita; *jaya*—all glories; *rūpa-sanātana-raghunātha-īśvara*—to the Lord of Rūpa Gosvāmī, Sanātana Gosvāmī and Raghunātha dāsa Gosvāmī.

TRANSLATION

All glories to Lord Śrī Caitanya, who is very dear to Kāśī Miśra. He is the Lord of the life of Jagadānanda and the Lord of Rūpa Gosvāmī, Sanātana Gosvāmī and Raghunātha dāsa Gosvāmī.

TEXT 5

জয় গৌরদেহ কৃষ্ণ স্বয়ং ভগবান্ ।
কৃপা করি' দেহ' প্রভু, নিজ-পদ-দান ॥ ৫ ॥

jaya gaura-deha kṛṣṇa svayaṁ bhagavān
kṛpā kari' deha' prabhu, nija-pada-dāna

SYNONYMS

jaya—all glories; *gaura-deha*—to the transcendental body of Śrī Caitanya Mahāprabhu; *kṛṣṇa*—Lord Kṛṣṇa; *svayam*—personally; *bhagavān*—the Supreme Personality of Godhead; *kṛpā kari'*—being merciful; *deha'*—please give; *prabhu*—my Lord; *nija-pada-dāna*—shelter at Your lotus feet.

TRANSLATION

All glories to the transcendental form of Śrī Caitanya Mahāprabhu, who is Kṛṣṇa Himself, the Supreme Personality of Godhead. My dear Lord, kindly give me shelter at Your lotus feet by Your causeless mercy.

TEXT 6

জয় নিত্যানন্দচন্দ্র জয় চৈতন্যের প্রাণ ।
তোমার চরণারবিন্দে ভক্তি দেহ' দান ॥ ৬ ॥

jaya nityānanda-candra jaya caitanyera prāṇa
tomāra caraṇāravinde bhakti deha' dāna

SYNONYMS

jaya—all glories; *nityānanda-candra*—to Lord Nityānanda Prabhu; *jaya*—all glories; *caitanyera prāṇa*—to the life and soul of Śrī Caitanya Mahāprabhu; *tomāra caraṇa-aravinde*—at Your lotus feet; *bhakti*—devotional service; *deha'*—please give; *dāna*—the gift.

TRANSLATION

All glories to Lord Nityānanda, who is the life and soul of Śrī Caitanya Mahāprabhu. My dear Lord, kindly give me engagement in devotional service at Your lotus feet.

TEXT 7

জয় জয়াদ্বৈতচন্দ্র চৈতন্যের আর্য ।
স্বচরণে ভক্তি দেহ' জয়াদ্বৈতাচার্য ॥ ৭ ॥

jaya jayādvaita-candra caitanyera ārya
sva-caraṇe bhakti deha' jayādvaitācārya

SYNONYMS

jaya jaya—all glories; *advaita-candra*—to Advaita Ācārya; *caitanyera ārya*—respected by the Lord; *sva-caraṇe*—at Your lotus feet; *bhakti deha'*—please give devotional service; *jaya*—all glories; *advaita-ācārya*—to Advaita Ācārya.

TRANSLATION

All glories to Advaita Ācārya, who is treated by Śrī Caitanya Mahāprabhu as superior due to His age and respectability. Please give me engagement in devotional service at Your lotus feet.

TEXT 8

জয় গৌরভক্তগণ, – গৌর যাঁর প্রাণ ।
সব ভক্ত মিলি' মোরে ভক্তি দেহ' দান ॥ ৮ ॥

jaya gaura-bhakta-gaṇa,——gaura yāṅra prāṇa
saba bhakta mili' more bhakti deha' dāna

SYNONYMS

jaya—all glories; *gaura-bhakta-gaṇa*—to the devotees of Śrī Caitanya Mahāprabhu; *gaura*—Lord Caitanya; *yāṅra*—of whom; *prāṇa*—the life and soul; *saba*—all; *bhakta*—devotees; *mili'*—together; *more*—to me; *bhakti*—devotional service; *deha' dāna*—kindly give the charity.

TRANSLATION

All glories to all the devotees of Śrī Caitanya Mahāprabhu, for the Lord is their life and soul. All of you, kindly bestow devotional service upon me.

TEXT 9

জয় রূপ, সনাতন, জীব, রঘুনাথ।
রঘুনাথ, গোপাল,—ছয় মোর নাথ॥ ৯॥

jaya rūpa, sanātana, jīva, raghunātha
raghunātha, gopāla,——chaya mora nātha

SYNONYMS

jaya—all glories; *rūpa*—to Rūpa Gosvāmī; *sanātana*—Sanātana Gosvāmī; *jīva*—Jīva Gosvāmī; *raghunātha*—Raghunātha dāsa Gosvāmī; *raghunātha*—Raghunātha Bhaṭṭa Gosvāmī; *gopāla*—Gopāla Bhaṭṭa Gosvāmī; *chaya*—six; *mora*—my; *nātha*—lords.

TRANSLATION

All glories to Rūpa Gosvāmī, Sanātana Gosvāmī, Jīva Gosvāmī, Raghunātha dāsa Gosvāmī, Raghunātha Bhaṭṭa Gosvāmī, and Gopāla Bhaṭṭa Gosvāmī, the six Gosvāmīs of Vṛndāvana. They are all my masters.

TEXT 10

এ-সব প্রসাদে লিখি চৈতন্য-লীলা-গুণ।
যৈছে তৈছে লিখি, করি আপন পাবন॥ ১০॥

e-saba prasāde likhi caitanya-līlā-guṇa
yaiche taiche likhi, kari āpana pāvana

SYNONYMS

e-saba—of all these; *prasāde*—by the mercy; *likhi*—I am writing; *caitanya-līlā-guṇa*—the attributes and pastimes of Śrī Caitanya Mahāprabhu; *yaiche taiche*—somehow or other; *likhi*—I am writing; *kari*—I do; *āpana pāvana*—purifying myself.

TRANSLATION

I am writing this narration of the pastimes and attributes of the Lord by the mercy of Śrī Caitanya Mahāprabhu and His associates. I do not know how to write properly, but I am purifying myself by writing this description.

TEXT 11

এইমত মহাপ্রভুর নীলাচলে বাস ।
সঙ্গে ভক্তগণ লঞা কীর্তন-বিলাস ॥ ১১ ॥

ei-mata mahāprabhura nīlācale vāsa
saṅge bhakta-gaṇa lañā kīrtana-vilāsa

SYNONYMS

ei-mata—in this way; *mahāprabhura*—of Śrī Caitanya Mahāprabhu; *nīlācale vāsa*—residence at Jagannātha Purī; *saṅge*—along; *bhakta-gaṇa lañā*—taking His devotees; *kīrtana-vilāsa*—enjoyment of performance of congregational chanting.

TRANSLATION

Śrī Caitanya Mahāprabhu thus resided at Jagannātha Purī with His personal devotees and enjoyed the congregational chanting of the Hare Kṛṣṇa mahā-mantra.

TEXT 12

দিনে নৃত্য-কীর্তন, ঈশ্বর-দরশন ।
রাত্র্যে রায়-স্বরূপ-সনে রস-আস্বাদন ॥ ১২ ॥

dine nṛtya-kīrtana, īśvara-daraśana
rātrye rāya-svarūpa-sane rasa-āsvādana

SYNONYMS

dine—during the daytime; *nṛtya-kīrtana*—dancing and chanting; *īśvara-daraśana*—visiting the temple of Lord Jagannātha; *rātrye*—at night; *rāya*—Rāmānanda Rāya; *svarūpa*—Svarūpa Dāmodara Gosvāmī; *sane*—with; *rasa-āsvādana*—tasting the transcendental mellows.

TRANSLATION

In the daytime Śrī Caitanya Mahāprabhu engaged in dancing and chanting and in seeing the temple of Lord Jagannātha. At night, in the company of His most confidential devotees, such as Rāmānanda Rāya and Svarūpa Dāmodara Gosvāmī, He tasted the nectar of the transcendental mellows of Lord Śrī Kṛṣṇa's pastimes.

TEXT 13

এইমত মহাপ্রভুর সুখে কাল যায় ।
কৃষ্ণের বিরহ-বিকার অঙ্গে নানা হয় ॥ ১৩ ॥

ei-mata mahāprabhura sukhe kāla yāya
kṛṣṇera viraha-vikāra aṅge nānā haya

SYNONYMS

ei-mata—in this way; *mahāprabhura*—of Śrī Caitanya Mahāprabhu; *sukhe*—in happiness; *kāla yāya*—time passes; *kṛṣṇera*—of Lord Kṛṣṇa; *viraha*—from separation; *vikāra*—transformations; *aṅge*—on the body; *nānā*—various; *haya*—there are.

TRANSLATION

Śrī Caitanya Mahāprabhu very happily passed His days in this way at Nīlācala, Jagannātha Purī. Feeling separation from Kṛṣṇa, He exhibited many transcendental symptoms all over His body.

TEXT 14

দিনে দিনে বাড়ে বিকার, রাত্র্যে অতিশয় ।
চিন্তা, উদ্বেগ, প্রলাপাদি যত শাস্ত্রে কয় ॥ ১৪ ॥

dine dine bāḍe vikāra, rātrye atiśaya
cintā, udvega, pralāpādi yata śāstre kaya

SYNONYMS

dine dine—day after day; *bāḍe*—increase; *vikāra*—transformations; *rātrye atiśaya*—especially at night; *cintā*—anxiety; *udvega*—agitation; *pralāpa*—talking like a madman; *ādi*—and so on; *yata*—as many as; *śāstre kaya*—are mentioned in the *śāstras.*

TRANSLATION

Day after day the symptoms increased, and at night they increased even more. All these symptoms, such as transcendental anxiety, agitation, and talking like a madman, were present, just as they are described in the śāstras.

TEXT 15

স্বরূপ গোসাঞি, আর রামানন্দ-রায় ।
রাত্রি-দিনে করে দোঁহে প্রভুর সহায় ॥ ১৫ ॥

svarūpa gosāñi, āra rāmānanda-rāya
rātri-dine kare doṅhe prabhura sahāya

SYNONYMS

svarūpa gosāñi—Svarūpa Dāmodara Gosvāmī; *āra*—and; *rāmānanda-rāya*—Rāmānanda Rāya; *rātri-dine*—day and night; *kare*—do; *doṅhe*—both of them; *prabhura*—of Śrī Caitanya Mahāprabhu; *sahāya*—help.

TRANSLATION

Svarūpa Dāmodara Gosvāmī and Rāmānanda Rāya, the chief assistants in Śrī Caitanya Mahāprabhu's pastimes, remained with Him both day and night.

TEXT 16

একদিন গোবিন্দ মহাপ্রসাদ লঞা ।
হরিদাসে দিতে গেলা আনন্দিত হঞা ॥ ১৬ ॥

eka-dina govinda mahā-prasāda lañā
haridāse dite gelā ānandita hañā

SYNONYMS

eka-dina—one day; *govinda*—the personal servant of Lord Caitanya Mahāprabhu; *mahā-prasāda lañā*—taking *mahā-prasāda; haridāse dite*—to deliver to Haridāsa; *gelā*—went; *ānandita hañā*—in great jubilation.

TRANSLATION

One day Govinda, the personal servant of Śrī Caitanya Mahāprabhu, went in great jubilation to deliver the remnants of Lord Jagannātha's food to Haridāsa Ṭhākura.

TEXT 17

দেখে,—হরিদাস ঠাকুর করিয়াছে শয়ন ।
মন্দ মন্দ করিতেছে সংখ্যা-সঙ্কীর্তন ॥ ১৭ ॥

dekhe,——haridāsa ṭhākura kariyāche śayana
manda manda kariteche saṅkhyā-saṅkīrtana

SYNONYMS

dekhe—he saw; *haridāsa ṭhākura*—Haridāsa Ṭhākura; *kariyāche śayana*—was lying down; *manda manda*—very slowly; *kariteche*—he was doing; *saṅkhyā-saṅkīrtana*—chanting the fixed number of rounds.

TRANSLATION

When Govinda came to Haridāsa, he saw that Haridāsa Ṭhākura was lying on his back and chanting his rounds very slowly.

TEXT 18

গোবিন্দ কহে,—'উঠ আসি' করহ ভোজন'।
হরিদাস কহে,—আজি করিমু লঙ্ঘন ॥ ১৮ ॥

govinda kahe,——'uṭha āsi' karaha bhojana'
haridāsa kahe,——āji karimu laṅghana

SYNONYMS

govinda kahe—Govinda said; *uṭha*—please get up; *āsi'*—coming; *karaha bhojana*—take your *prasāda; haridāsa kahe*—Haridāsa replied; *āji*—today; *karimu laṅghana*—I shall observe fasting.

TRANSLATION

"Please rise and take your mahā-prasāda," Govinda said. Haridāsa Ṭhākura replied, "Today I shall observe fasting.

TEXT 19

সংখ্যা-কীর্তন পূরে নাহি, কেমতে খাইব ?
মহাপ্রসাদ আনিয়াছ, কেমতে উপেক্ষিব ?" ১৯ ॥

saṅkhyā-kīrtana pūre nāhi, ke-mate khāiba?
mahā-prasāda āniyācha, ke-mate upekṣiba?

SYNONYMS

saṅkhyā-kīrtana—the fixed amount of chanting; *pūre nāhi*—is not complete; *ke-mate khāiba*—how shall I eat; *mahā-prasāda āniyācha*—you have brought the *mahā-prasāda; ke-mate upekṣiba*—how shall I neglect.

TRANSLATION

"I have not finished chanting my regular number of rounds. How, then, can I eat? But you have brought mahā-prasāda, and how can I neglect it?"

TEXT 20

এত বলি' মহাপ্রসাদ করিলা বন্দন।
এক রঞ্চ লঞা তার করিলা ভক্ষণ ॥ ২০ ॥

eta bali' mahā-prasāda karilā vandana
eka rañca lañā tāra karilā bhakṣaṇa

SYNONYMS

eta bali'—saying this; *mahā-prasāda*—to the *mahā-prasāda; karilā vandana*—he offered respect; *eka rañca*—one fractional part; *lañā*—taking; *tāra karilā bhakṣaṇa*—ate it.

TRANSLATION

Saying this, he offered prayers to the mahā-prasāda, took a little portion, and ate it.

PURPORT

Mahā-prasāda is nondifferent from Kṛṣṇa. Therefore, instead of eating *mahā-prasāda,* one should honor it. It is said here, *karilā vandana,* "he offered prayers." When taking *mahā-prasāda,* one should not consider the food ordinary preparations. *Prasāda* means favor. One should consider *mahā-prasāda* a favor of Kṛṣṇa. As stated by Śrīla Bhaktivinoda Ṭhākura, *kṛṣṇa baḍa dayāmaya karibāre jihvā jaya svaprasāda-anna dilā bhāi.* Kṛṣṇa is very kind. In this material world we are all very attached to tasting various types of food. Therefore, Kṛṣṇa eats many nice varieties of food and offers the food back to the devotees, so that not only are one's demands for various tastes satisfied, but by eating *prasāda* he makes advancement in spiritual life. Therefore, we should never consider ordinary food on an equal level with *mahā-prasāda.*

TEXT 21

আর দিন মহাপ্রভু তাঁর ঠাঞি আইলা ।
সুস্থ হও, হরিদাস—বলি' তাঁরে পুছিলা ॥ ২১ ॥

āra dina mahāprabhu tāṅra ṭhāñi āilā
sustha hao, haridāsa——bali' tāṅre puchilā

SYNONYMS

āra dina—the next day; *mahāprabhu*—Śrī Caitanya Mahāprabhu; *tāṅra ṭhāñi*—to his place; *āilā*—came; *su-stha hao*—are you all right; *haridāsa*—O Haridāsa; *bali'*—saying; *tāṅre*—unto him; *puchilā*—inquired.

TRANSLATION

The next day, Śrī Caitanya Mahāprabhu went to Haridāsa's place and inquired from him, "Haridāsa, are you well?"

TEXT 22

নমস্কার করি' তেঁহো কৈলা নিবেদন ।
শরীর সুস্থ হয় মোর, অসুস্থ বুদ্ধি-মন ॥ ২২ ॥

namaskāra kari' teṅho kailā nivedana
śarīra sustha haya mora, asustha buddhi-mana

SYNONYMS

namaskāra kari'—after offering obeisances; *teṅho*—he, Haridāsa Ṭhākura; *kailā nivedana*—submitted; *śarīra*—body; *su-stha*—all right; *haya*—is; *mora*—my; *asu-stha*—not in a healthy condition; *buddhi-mana*—my mind and intelligence.

TRANSLATION

Haridāsa offered his obeisances to the Lord and replied, "My body is all right, but my mind and intelligence are not well."

TEXT 23

প্রভু কহে,—'কোন্ ব্যাধি, কহ ত' নির্ণয় ?'
তেঁহো কহে, —'সংখ্যা-কীর্তন না পূরয়' ॥ ২৩ ॥

prabhu kahe,——'kon vyādhi, kaha ta' nirṇaya?'
teṅho kahe,——'saṅkhyā-kīrtana nā pūraya'

SYNONYMS

prabhu kahe—Śrī Caitanya Mahāprabhu said; *kon vyādhi*—what disease; *kaha ta' nirṇaya*—can you ascertain; *teṅho kahe*—he said; *saṅkhyā-kīrtana*—fixed amount of chanting; *nā pūraya*—has not become complete.

TRANSLATION

Śrī Caitanya Mahāprabhu further inquired from Haridāsa, "Can you ascertain what your disease is?" Haridāsa Ṭhākura replied, "My disease is that I cannot complete my rounds."

PURPORT

If one cannot complete the fixed number of rounds he is assigned, he should be considered to be in a diseased condition of spiritual life. Śrīla Haridāsa Ṭhākura is called *nāmācārya*. Of course, we cannot imitate Haridāsa Ṭhākura, but everyone must chant a prescribed number of rounds. In our Kṛṣṇa consciousness movement we have fixed sixteen rounds as the minimum so that the Westerners will not feel burdened. These sixteen rounds must be chanted, and chanted loudly, so that one can hear himself and others.

TEXT 24

প্রভু কহে,—"বৃদ্ধ হইলা 'সংখ্যা' অল্প কর ।
সিদ্ধ-দেহ তুমি, সাধনে আগ্রহ কেনে কর ? ২৪ ॥

prabhu kahe,——"vṛddha ha-ilā 'saṅkhyā' alpa kara
siddha-deha tumi, sādhane āgraha kene kara?

SYNONYMS

prabhu kahe—Lord Śrī Caitanya Mahāprabhu said; *vṛddha ha-ilā*—you have become old; *saṅkhyā alpa kara*—reduce your number; *siddha-deha tumi*—you are already liberated; *sādhane*—in the regulative principles; *āgraha kene kara*—why are you eager.

TRANSLATION

"Now that you have become old," the Lord said, "you may reduce the number of rounds you chant daily. You are already liberated, and therefore you need not follow the regulative principles very strictly.

PURPORT

Unless one has come to the platform of spontaneous love of God, he must follow the regulative principles. Ṭhākura Haridāsa was the living example of how to follow the regulative principles. Similarly, Raghunātha dāsa Gosvāmī was also such a living example. In the *Ṣaḍ-gosvāmy-aṣṭaka* it is stated: *saṅkhyā-pūrvaka-nāma-gāna-natibhiḥ kālāvasānīkṛtau.* The Gosvāmīs, especially Raghunātha dāsa Gosvāmī, strictly followed all the regulative principles. The first regulative principle is that one must chant the Hare Kṛṣṇa *mahā-mantra* loudly enough so that he can hear himself, and one must vow to chant a fixed number of rounds. Not only was Raghunātha dāsa Gosvāmī chanting a fixed number of rounds, but he had also taken a vow to bow down many times and offer obeisances to the Lord.

TEXT 25

লোক নিস্তারিতে এই তোমার 'অবতার' ।
নামের মহিমা লোকে করিলা প্রচার ॥ ২৫ ॥

loka nistārite ei tomāra 'avatāra'
nāmera mahimā loke karilā pracāra

SYNONYMS

loka nistārite—to deliver the people in general; *ei*—this; *tomāra avatāra*—your incarnation; *nāmera mahimā*—the glories of the holy name; *loke*—in this world; *karilā pracāra*—you have preached.

TRANSLATION

"Your role in this incarnation is to deliver the people in general. You have sufficiently preached the glories of the holy name in this world."

PURPORT

Haridāsa Ṭhākura is known as *nāmācārya* because it is he who preached the glories of chanting *hari-nāma,* the holy name of God. By using the words *tomāra avatāra* ("your incarnation"), Śrī Caitanya Mahāprabhu confirms that Haridāsa Ṭhākura is the incarnation of Lord Brahmā. Śrīla Bhaktisiddhānta Sarasvatī Ṭhākura says that advanced devotees help the Supreme Personality of Godhead in His mission and that such devotees or personal associates incarnate by the will of the Supreme Lord. The Supreme Lord incarnates by His own will, and, by His will, competent devotees also incarnate to help Him in His mission. Haridāsa Ṭhākura is thus the incarnation of Lord Brahmā, and other devotees are likewise incarnations who help in the prosecution of the Lord's mission.

TEXT 26

এবে অল্প সংখ্যা করি' কর সঙ্কীর্তন ।"
হরিদাস কহে,—"শুন মোর সত্য নিবেদন ॥ ২৬ ॥

ebe alpa saṅkhyā kari' kara saṅkīrtana"
haridāsa kahe,——"śuna mora satya nivedana

SYNONYMS

ebe—now; *alpa saṅkhyā*—a reduced number of chanting; *kari'*—doing; *kara saṅkīrtana*—chant the Hare Kṛṣṇa *mahā-mantra; haridāsa kahe*—Haridāsa Ṭhākura replied; *śuna*—kindly hear; *mora*—my; *satya*—real; *nivedana*—submission.

TRANSLATION

The Lord concluded, "Now, therefore, please reduce the fixed number of times you chant the Hare Kṛṣṇa mahā-mantra." Haridāsa Ṭhākura replied, "Kindly hear my real plea.

TEXT 27

হীন-জাতি জন্ম মোর নিন্দ্য-কলেবর ।
হীনকর্মে রত মুঞি অধম পামর ॥ ২৭ ॥

hīna-jāti janma mora nindya-kalevara
hīna-karme rata muñi adhama pāmara

SYNONYMS

hīna-jāti—in a low family; *janma mora*—my birth; *nindya*—abominable; *kalevara*—body; *hīna-karme*—in low activities; *rata muñi*—I am fully engaged; *adhama*—the lowest of men; *pāmara*—most condemned.

TRANSLATION

"I was born in an inferior family, and my body is most abominable. I always engage in low work. Therefore, I am the lowest, most condemned of men.

TEXT 28

অদৃশ্য, অস্পৃশ্য মোরে অঙ্গীকার কৈলা ।
রৌরব হইতে কাড়ি' মোরে বৈকুণ্ঠে চড়াইলা ॥২৮॥

adṛśya, aspṛśya more aṅgīkāra kailā
raurava ha-ite kāḍi' more vaikuṇṭhe caḍāilā

SYNONYMS

adṛśya—unseeable; *aspṛśya*—untouchable; *more*—me; *aṅgīkāra kailā*—You have accepted; *raurava ha-ite*—from a hellish condition; *kāḍi'*—taking away; *more*—me; *vaikuṇṭhe caḍāilā*—have raised to the Vaikuṇṭha platform.

TRANSLATION

"I am unseeable and untouchable, but You have accepted me as Your servant. This means that You have delivered me from a hellish condition and raised me to the Vaikuṇṭha platform.

TEXT 29

স্বতন্ত্র ঈশ্বর তুমি হও ইচ্ছাময় ।
জগৎ নাচাও, যারে যৈছে ইচ্ছা হয় ॥ ২৯ ॥

svatantra īśvara tumi hao icchāmaya
jagat nācāo, yāre yaiche icchā haya

SYNONYMS

svatantra—fully independent; *īśvara*—Supreme Personality of Godhead; *tumi*—You; *hao*—are; *icchā-maya*—free to act according to Your desire; *jagat*—the world; *nācāo*—You are causing to dance; *yāre*—which; *yaiche*—as; *icchā haya*—You like.

TRANSLATION

"My dear Lord, You are the fully independent Personality of Godhead. You act by Your own free will. You cause the whole world to dance and act as You like.

TEXT 30

অনেক নাচাইলা মোরে প্রসাদ করিয়া ।
বিপ্রের শ্রাদ্ধপাত্র খাইনু 'ম্লেচ্ছ' হঞা ॥ ৩০ ॥

aneka nācāilā more prasāda kariyā
viprera śrāddha-pātra khāinu 'mleccha' hañā

SYNONYMS

aneka—in many ways; *nācāilā*—You have made dance; *more*—me; *prasāda kariyā*—by Your mercy; *viprera*—of the *brāhmaṇas; śrāddha-pātra*—the dish of the *śrāddha* ceremony; *khāinu*—I have eaten; *mleccha hañā*—although born in a family of meateaters.

TRANSLATION

"My dear Lord, by Your mercy You have made me dance in many ways. For example, I was offered the śrāddha-pātra that should have been offered to first-class brāhmaṇas. I ate from it even though I was born in a family of meat-eaters.

PURPORT

Śrīla Bhaktisiddhānta Sarasvatī Ṭhākura, in his *Anubhāṣya,* quotes from the *Viṣṇu-smṛti* in reference to *śrāddha-pātra.*

brāhmaṇāpasadā hy ete
kathitāḥ paṅkti-dūṣakāḥ
etān vivarjayed yatnāt
śrāddha-karmaṇi paṇḍitaḥ

According to this verse, if one is born in a *brāhmaṇa* family but does not behave according to brahminical standards, he should not be offered the *śrāddha-pātra,* which is *prasāda* offered to the forefathers. Advaita Ācārya offered the *śrāddha-pātra* to Haridāsa Ṭhākura, not to a *brāhmaṇa* who had been born in a *brāhmaṇa* family. Although Haridāsa Ṭhākura was born in the family of meateaters, because he was an advanced devotee he was shown more respect than a first-class *brāhmaṇa.*

TEXT 31

এক বাঞ্ছা হয় মোর বহু দিন হৈতে ।
লীলা সম্বরিবে তুমি,—লয় মোর চিত্তে ॥ ৩১ ॥

eka vāñchā haya mora bahu dina haite
līlā samvaribe tumi——laya mora citte

SYNONYMS

eka vāñchā—one desire; *haya*—is; *mora*—my; *bahu dina*—a very long time; *haite*—since; *līlā*—Your activities; *samvaribe tumi*—You will close; *laya mora citte*—I am thinking.

TRANSLATION

"I have had one desire for a very long time. I think that quite soon, my Lord, You will bring to a close Your pastimes within this material world.

TEXT 32

সেই লীলা প্রভু মোরে কভু না দেখাইবা ।
আপনার আগে মোর শরীর পাড়িবা ॥ ৩২ ॥

sei līlā prabhu more kabhu nā dekhāibā
āpanāra āge mora śarīra pāḍibā

SYNONYMS

sei līlā—that pastime; *prabhu*—my Lord; *more*—unto me; *kabhu*—ever; *nā dekhāibā*—do not show; *āpanāra āge*—before You; *mora śarīra*—my body; *pāḍibā*—let fall down.

TRANSLATION

"I wish that You not show me this closing chapter of Your pastimes. Before that time comes, kindly let my body fall down in Your presence.

TEXT 33

হৃদয়ে ধরিমু তোমার কমল চরণ ।
নয়নে দেখিমু তোমার চাঁদ বদন ॥ ৩৩ ॥

hṛdaye dharimu tomāra kamala caraṇa
nayane dekhimu tomāra cāṅda vadana

SYNONYMS

hṛdaye—upon my heart; *dharimu*—I shall catch; *tomāra*—Your; *kamala caraṇa*—lotuslike feet; *nayane*—with my eyes; *dekhimu*—I shall see; *tomāra*—Your; *cāṅda vadana*—face like the moon.

TRANSLATION

"I wish to catch Your lotuslike feet upon my heart and see Your moonlike face.

TEXT 34

জিহ্বায় উচ্চারিমু তোমার 'কৃষ্ণচৈতন্য'-নাম।
এইমত মোর ইচ্ছা,—ছাড়িমু পরাণ ॥ ৩৪ ॥

jihvāya uccārimu tomāra 'kṛṣṇa-caitanya'-nāma
ei-mata mora icchā,——chāḍimu parāṇa

SYNONYMS

jihvāya—with my tongue; *uccārimu*—I shall chant; *tomāra*—Your; *kṛṣṇa-caitanya-nāma*—holy name of Lord Kṛṣṇa Caitanya; *ei-mata*—in this way; *mora icchā*—my desire; *chāḍimu parāṇa*—I shall give up life.

TRANSLATION

"With my tongue I shall chant Your holy name, 'Śrī Kṛṣṇa Caitanya!' That is my desire. Kindly let me give up my body in this way.

TEXT 35

মোর এই ইচ্ছা যদি তোমার প্রসাদে হয়।
এই নিবেদন মোর কর, দয়াময় ॥ ৩৫ ॥

mora ei icchā yadi tomāra prasāde haya
ei nivedana mora kara, dayāmaya

SYNONYMS

mora—my; *ei*—this; *icchā*—desire; *yadi*—if; *tomāra prasāde*—by Your mercy; *haya*—is; *ei nivedana*—this submission; *mora*—my; *kara*—just do; *dayā-maya*—O merciful one.

TRANSLATION

"O most merciful Lord, if by Your mercy it is possible, kindly grant my desire.

TEXT 36

এই নীচ দেহ মোর পড়ুক তব আগে ।
এই বাঞ্ছা-সিদ্ধি মোর তোমাতেই লাগে ॥" ৩৬ ॥

ei nīca deha mora paḍuka tava āge
ei vāñchā-siddhi mora tomātei lāge"

SYNONYMS

ei—this; *nīca*—lowborn; *deha*—body; *mora*—my; *paḍuka*—let it fall down; *tava āge*—in front of You; *ei*—this; *vāñchā-siddhi*—perfection of desire; *mora*—my; *tomātei*—by You; *lāge*—can become possible.

TRANSLATION

"Let this lowborn body fall down before You. You can make possible this perfection of all my desires."

TEXT 37

প্রভু কহে,—"হরিদাস, যে তুমি মাগিবে ।
কৃষ্ণ কৃপাময় তাহা অবশ্য করিবে ॥ ৩৭ ॥

prabhu kahe,—"haridāsa, ye tumi māgibe
kṛṣṇa kṛpāmaya tāhā avaśya karibe

SYNONYMS

prabhu kahe—Śrī Caitanya Mahāprabhu replied; *haridāsa*—My dear Haridāsa; *ye*—whatever; *tumi*—you; *māgibe*—request; *kṛṣṇa*—Lord Kṛṣṇa; *kṛpā-maya*—all-merciful; *tāhā*—that; *avaśya*—certainly; *karibe*—will execute.

TRANSLATION

Śrī Caitanya Mahāprabhu said, "My dear Haridāsa, Kṛṣṇa is so merciful that He must execute whatever you want.

TEXT 38

কিন্তু আমার যে কিছু সুখ, সব তোমা লঞা ।
তোমার যোগ্য নহে,—যাবে আমারে ছাড়িয়া ॥"৩৮॥

kintu āmāra ye kichu sukha, saba tomā lañā
tomāra yogya nahe,—yābe āmāre chāḍiyā"

SYNONYMS

kintu—but; *āmāra*—My; *ye*—whatever; *kichu*—any; *sukha*—happiness; *saba*—all; *tomā lañā*—because of your association; *tomāra*—for you; *yogya nahe*—it is not fit; *yābe*—you will go away; *āmāre chāḍiyā*—leaving Me aside.

TRANSLATION

"But whatever happiness is Mine is all due to your association. It is not fitting for you to go away and leave Me aside."

TEXT 39

চরণে ধরি' কহে হরিদাস,—"না করিহ 'মায়া'।
অবশ্য মো-অধমে, প্রভু, কর এই 'দয়া' ॥ ৩৯ ॥

caraṇe dhari' kahe haridāsa,——"nā kariha 'māyā'
avaśya mo-adhame, prabhu, kara ei 'dayā'

SYNONYMS

caraṇe—the lotus feet; *dhari'*—catching; *kahe*—said; *haridāsa*—Haridāsa Ṭhākura; *nā kariha māyā*—do not create an illusion; *avaśya*—certainly; *mo-adhame*—unto me, who am so fallen; *prabhu*—my Lord; *kara ei dayā*—show this mercy.

TRANSLATION

Catching the lotus feet of Śrī Caitanya Mahāprabhu, Haridāsa Ṭhākura said, "My Lord, do not create an illusion! Although I am so fallen, You must certainly show me this mercy!

TEXT 40

মোর শিরোমণি কত কত মহাশয়।
তোমার লীলার সহায় কোটিভক্ত হয় ॥ ৪০ ॥

mora śiromaṇi kata kata mahāśaya
tomāra līlāra sahāya koṭi-bhakta haya

SYNONYMS

mora—my; *śiromaṇi*—crown jewels; *kata kata*—many, many; *mahāśaya*—great persons; *tomāra līlāra*—in Your pastimes; *sahāya*—helpers; *koṭi-bhakta*—millions of devotees; *haya*—there are.

TRANSLATION

"My Lord, there are many respectable personalities, millions of devotees, who are fit to sit on my head. They are all helpful in Your pastimes.

TEXT 41

আমা-হেন যদি এক কীট মরি' গেল ।
এক পিপীলিকা মৈলে পৃথ্বীর কাহাঁ হানি হৈল ?৪১॥

āmā-hena yadi eka kīṭa mari' gela
eka pipīlikā maile pṛthvīra kāhāṅ hāni haila?

SYNONYMS

āmā-hena—like me; *yadi*—if; *eka*—one; *kīṭa*—insect; *mari' gela*—dies; *eka*—one; *pipīlikā*—ant; *maile*—if he dies; *pṛthvīra*—of the earth; *kāhāṅ*—where; *hāni haila*—is there any loss.

TRANSLATION

"My Lord, if an insignificant insect like me dies, what is the loss? If an ant dies, where is the loss to the material world?

TEXT 42

'ভকতবৎসল' প্রভু, তুমি, মুই 'ভক্তাভাস' ।
অবশ্য পূরাবে, প্রভু, মোর এই আশ ॥" ৪২ ॥

'bhakata-vatsala' prabhu, tumi, mui 'bhaktābhāsa'
avaśya pūrābe, prabhu, mora ei āśa"

SYNONYMS

bhakata-vatsala—always affectionate to devotees; *prabhu*—my Lord; *tumi*—You; *mui*—I; *bhakta-ābhāsa*—an imitation devotee; *avaśya*—certainly; *pūrābe*—You will fulfill; *prabhu*—my Lord; *mora*—my; *ei*—this; *āśa*—expectation.

TRANSLATION

"My Lord, You are always affectionate to Your devotees. I am just an imitation devotee, but nevertheless I wish that You fulfill my desire. That is my expectation."

TEXT 43

মধ্যাহ্ন করিতে প্রভু চলিলা আপনে ।
ঈশ্বর দেখিয়া কালি দিবেন দরশনে ॥ ৪৩ ॥

madhyāhna karite prabhu calilā āpane
īśvara dekhiyā kāli dibena daraśane

SYNONYMS

madhyāhna karite—to perform His noon duties; *prabhu*—Śrī Caitanya Mahāprabhu; *calilā āpane*—aroused Himself; *īśvara dekhiyā*—after visiting Lord Jagannātha; *kāli*—tomorrow; *dibena daraśane*—He would see Haridāsa Ṭhākura.

TRANSLATION

Because He had to perform His noon duties, Śrī Caitanya Mahāprabhu got up to leave, but it was settled that the following day, after He saw Lord Jagannātha, He would return to visit Haridāsa Ṭhākura.

TEXT 44

তবে মহাপ্রভু তাঁরে করি' আলিঙ্গন ।
মধ্যাহ্ন করিতে সমুদ্রে করিলা গমন ॥ ৪৪ ॥

tabe mahāprabhu tāṅre kari' āliṅgana
madhyāhna karite samudre karilā gamana

SYNONYMS

tabe—then; *mahāprabhu*—Śrī Caitanya Mahāprabhu; *tāṅre*—unto him (Haridāsa); *kari'*—doing; *āliṅgana*—embracing; *madhyāhna karite*—to perform His noon duties; *samudre*—toward the sea; *karilā gamana*—went.

TRANSLATION

After embracing him, Śrī Caitanya Mahāprabhu left to perform His noon duties and went to the sea to take His bath.

TEXT 45

প্রাতঃকালে ঈশ্বর দেখি' সব ভক্ত লঞা ।
হরিদাসে দেখিতে আইলা শীঘ্র করিয়া ॥ ৪৫ ॥

prātaḥ-kāle īśvara dekhi' saba bhakta lañā
haridāse dekhite āilā śīghra kariyā

SYNONYMS

prātaḥ-kāle—in the morning; *īśvara dekhi'*—after visiting Lord Jagannātha; *saba bhakta*—all the devotees; *lañā*—accompanied by; *haridāse*—Haridāsa; *dekhite*—to see; *āilā*—came; *śīghra kariyā*—hastily.

TRANSLATION

The next morning, after visiting the Jagannātha temple, Śrī Caitanya Mahāprabhu, accompanied by all His other devotees, came hastily to see Haridāsa Ṭhākura.

TEXT 46

হরিদাসের আগে আসি' দিলা দরশন ।
হরিদাস বন্দিলা প্রভুর আর বৈষ্ণব-চরণ ॥ ৪৬ ॥

haridāsera āge āsi' dilā daraśana
haridāsa vandilā prabhura āra vaiṣṇava-caraṇa

SYNONYMS

haridāsera—of Haridāsa Ṭhākura; *āge*—in front; *āsi'*—coming; *dilā daraśana*—gave His audience; *haridāsa*—Haridāsa Ṭhākura; *vandilā*—offered respect; *prabhura*—of Śrī Caitanya Mahāprabhu; *āra*—and; *vaiṣṇava*—of the Vaiṣṇavas; *caraṇa*—unto the lotus feet.

TRANSLATION

Śrī Caitanya Mahāprabhu and the other devotees came before Haridāsa Ṭhākura, who offered his respects to the lotus feet of Śrī Caitanya Mahāprabhu and all the Vaiṣṇavas.

TEXT 47

প্রভু কহে,—'হরিদাস, কহ সমাচার' ।
হরিদাস কহে,—'প্রভু, যে কৃপা তোমার' ॥ ৪৭ ॥

prabhu kahe,——'haridāsa, kaha samācāra'
haridāsa kahe,——'prabhu, ye kṛpā tomāra'

SYNONYMS

prabhu kahe—Śrī Caitanya Mahāprabhu said; *haridāsa*—My dear Haridāsa; *kaha samācāra*—what is the news; *haridāsa kahe*—Haridāsa replied; *prabhu*—my Lord; *ye*—whatever; *kṛpā*—mercy; *tomāra*—Your.

TRANSLATION

Lord Śrī Caitanya Mahāprabhu inquired, "My dear Haridāsa, what is the news?" Haridāsa Ṭhākura replied, "My Lord, whatever mercy You can bestow upon me."

TEXT 48

অঙ্গনে আরম্ভিলা প্রভু মহাসঙ্কীর্তন।
বক্রেশ্বর-পণ্ডিত তাহাঁ করেন নর্তন ॥ ৪৮ ॥

aṅgane ārambhilā prabhu mahā-saṅkīrtana
vakreśvara-paṇḍita tāhāṅ karena nartana

SYNONYMS

aṅgane—in the courtyard; *ārambhilā*—began; *prabhu*—Śrī Caitanya Mahāprabhu; *mahā-saṅkīrtana*—great congregational chanting; *vakreśvara-paṇḍita*—Vakreśvara Paṇḍita; *tāhāṅ*—there; *karena nartana*—danced.

TRANSLATION

Upon hearing this, Śrī Caitanya Mahāprabhu immediately began great congregational chanting in the courtyard. Vakreśvara Paṇḍita was the chief dancer.

TEXT 49

স্বরূপ-গোসাঞি আদি যত প্রভুর গণ।
হরিদাসে বেড়ি' করে নাম-সঙ্কীর্তন ॥ ৪৯ ॥

svarūpa-gosāñi ādi yata prabhura gaṇa
haridāse beḍi' kare nāma-saṅkīrtana

SYNONYMS

svarūpa-gosāñi—Svarūpa Dāmodara Gosvāmī; *ādi*—and others; *yata*—all; *prabhura gaṇa*—the company of the Lord; *haridāse beḍi'*—surrounding Haridāsa Ṭhākura; *kare*—performed; *nāma-saṅkīrtana*—congregational chanting.

TRANSLATION

Headed by Svarūpa Dāmodara Gosvāmī, all the devotees of Śrī Caitanya Mahāprabhu surrounded Haridāsa Ṭhākura and began congregational chanting.

TEXT 50

রামানন্দ, সার্বভৌম, সবার অগ্রেতে।
হরিদাসের গুণ প্রভু লাগিলা কহিতে ॥ ৫০ ॥

rāmānanda, sārvabhauma, sabāra agrete
haridāsera guṇa prabhu lāgilā kahite

SYNONYMS

rāmānanda—Rāmānanda Rāya; *sārvabhauma*—Sārvabhauma Bhaṭṭācārya; *sabāra*—of all; *agrete*—in front; *haridāsera*—of Haridāsa Ṭhākura; *guṇa*—attributes; *prabhu*—Śrī Caitanya Mahāprabhu; *lāgilā kahite*—began to describe.

TRANSLATION

In front of all the great devotees like Rāmānanda Rāya and Sārvabhauma Bhaṭṭācārya, Śrī Caitanya Mahāprabhu began to describe the holy attributes of Haridāsa Ṭhākura.

TEXT 51

হরিদাসের গুণ কহিতে প্রভু হইলা পঞ্চমুখ ।
কহিতে কহিতে প্রভুর বাড়ে মহাসুখ ॥ ৫১ ॥

haridāsera guṇa kahite prabhu ha-ilā pañca-mukha
kahite kahite prabhura bāḍe mahā-sukha

SYNONYMS

haridāsera—of Haridāsa Ṭhākura; *guṇa*—attributes; *kahite*—speaking; *prabhu*—Śrī Caitanya Mahāprabhu; *ha-ilā*—became; *pañca-mukha*—as if possessing five mouths; *kahite kahite*—while He was speaking; *prabhura*—of Śrī Caitanya Mahāprabhu; *bāḍe*—increased; *mahā-sukha*—great happiness.

TRANSLATION

As He described the transcendental attributes of Haridāsa Ṭhākura, Śrī Caitanya Mahāprabhu seemed to possess five mouths. The more He described, the more His great happiness increased.

TEXT 52

হরিদাসের গুণে সবার বিস্মিত হয় মন ।
সর্বভক্ত বন্দে হরিদাসের চরণ ॥ ৫২ ॥

haridāsera guṇe sabāra vismita haya mana
sarva-bhakta vande haridāsera caraṇa

SYNONYMS

haridāsera—of Haridāsa Ṭhākura; *guṇe*—by the attributes; *sabāra*—of all of them; *vismita*—struck with wonder; *haya*—become; *mana*—minds; *sarva-bhakta*—all the devotees; *vande*—worship; *haridāsera caraṇa*—the lotus feet of Haridāsa Ṭhākura.

TRANSLATION

After hearing of the transcendental qualities of Haridāsa Ṭhākura, all the devotees present were struck with wonder. They all offered their respectful obeisances to the lotus feet of Haridāsa Ṭhākura.

TEXT 53

হরিদাস নিজাগ্রেতে প্রভুরে বসাইলা ।
নিজ-নেত্র- দুই ভৃঙ্গ—মুখপদ্মে দিলা ॥ ৫৩ ॥

haridāsa nijāgrete prabhure vasāilā
nija-netra——dui bhṛṅga——mukha-padme dilā

SYNONYMS

haridāsa—Ṭhākura Haridāsa; *nija-agrete*—in front of himself; *prabhure vasāilā*—made the Lord sit down; *nija-netra*—his eyes; *dui bhṛṅga*—as if two bumblebees; *mukha-padme*—on the lotus face; *dilā*—he fixed.

TRANSLATION

Haridāsa Ṭhākura made Śrī Caitanya Mahāprabhu sit down in front of him, and then he fixed his eyes, like two bumblebees, on the lotus face of the Lord.

TEXT 54

স্ব-হৃদয়ে আনি' ধরিল প্রভুর চরণ ।
সর্বভক্ত-পদরেণু মস্তক-ভূষণ ॥ ৫৪ ॥

sva-hṛdaye āni' dharila prabhura caraṇa
sarva-bhakta-pada-reṇu mastaka-bhūṣaṇa

SYNONYMS

sva-hṛdaye—upon his heart; *āni'*—bringing; *dharila*—held; *prabhura caraṇa*—the lotus feet of Śrī Caitanya Mahāprabhu; *sarva-bhakta*—of all the devotees; *pada-reṇu*—the dust of the feet; *mastaka-bhūṣaṇa*—the ornament of his head.

TRANSLATION

He held the lotus feet of Śrī Caitanya Mahāprabhu on his heart and then took the dust of the feet of all the devotees present and put it on his head.

TEXT 55

'শ্রীকৃষ্ণচৈতন্য' শব্দ বলেন বার বার ।
প্রভুমুখ-মাধুরী পিয়ে, নেত্রে জলধার ॥ ৫৫ ॥

'śrī-kṛṣṇa-caitanya' śabda balena bāra bāra
prabhu-mukha-mādhurī piye, netre jala-dhāra

SYNONYMS

śrī-kṛṣṇa-caitanya—Lord Śrī Kṛṣṇa Caitanya; *śabda*—vibration; *balena*—speaks; *bāra bāra*—again and again; *prabhu-mukha-mādhurī*—the sweetness of the face of Śrī Caitanya Mahāprabhu; *piye*—he drinks; *netre*—through the eyes; *jala-dhāra*—a continuous flow of water.

TRANSLATION

He began to chant the holy name of Śrī Kṛṣṇa Caitanya again and again. As he drank the sweetness of the face of the Lord, tears constantly glided down from his eyes.

TEXT 56

'শ্রীকৃষ্ণচৈতন্য'-শব্দ করিতে উচ্চারণ ।
নামের সহিত প্রাণ কৈল উৎক্রামণ ॥ ৫৬ ॥

'śrī-kṛṣṇa-caitanya' śabda karite uccāraṇa
nāmera sahita prāṇa kaila utkrāmaṇa

SYNONYMS

śrī-kṛṣṇa-caitanya—Śrī Kṛṣṇa Caitanya; *śabda*—the sound vibration; *karite uccāraṇa*—chanting; *nāmera sahita*—with the name; *prāṇa*—life; *kaila utkrāmaṇa*—went away.

TRANSLATION

While chanting the holy name of Śrī Kṛṣṇa Caitanya, he gave up his air of life and left his body.

TEXT 57

মহাযোগেশ্বর-প্রায় দেখি' স্বচ্ছন্দে মরণ ।
'ভীষ্মের নির্যাণ' সবার হইল স্মরণ ॥ ৫৭ ॥

mahā-yogeśvara-prāya dekhi' svacchande maraṇa
'bhīṣmera niryāṇa' sabāra ha-ila smaraṇa

SYNONYMS

mahā-yogeśvara-prāya—just like a great mystic *yogī; dekhi'*—seeing; *svacchande*—at his will; *maraṇa*—dying; *bhīṣmera niryāṇa*—the passing of Bhīṣma; *sabāra ha-ila smaraṇa*—everyone remembered.

TRANSLATION

Seeing the wonderful death of Haridāsa Ṭhākura by his own will, which was just like a great mystic yogī's, everyone remembered the passing away of Bhīṣma.

TEXT 58

'হরি' 'কৃষ্ণ'-শব্দে সবে করে কোলাহল ।
প্রেমানন্দে মহাপ্রভু হইলা বিহ্বল ॥ ৫৮ ॥

'hari' 'kṛṣṇa'-śabde sabe kare kolāhala
premānande mahāprabhu ha-ilā vihvala

SYNONYMS

hari—the holy name of Hari; *kṛṣṇa*—the holy name of Kṛṣṇa; *śabde*—with the sound vibration; *sabe*—all of them; *kare*—make; *kolāhala*—great noise; *prema-ānande*—in ecstatic love; *mahāprabhu*—Śrī Caitanya Mahāprabhu; *ha-ilā vihvala*—became overwhelmed.

TRANSLATION

There was a tumultuous noise as they all chanted the holy names "Hari" and "Kṛṣṇa." Śrī Caitanya Mahāprabhu became overwhelmed with ecstatic love.

TEXT 59

হরিদাসের তনু প্রভু কোলে নৈল উঠাঞা ।
অঙ্গনে নাচেন প্রভু প্রেমাবিষ্ট হঞা ॥ ৫৯ ॥

haridāsera tanu prabhu kole laila uṭhāñā
aṅgane nācena prabhu premāviṣṭa hañā

SYNONYMS

haridāsera—of Haridāsa Ṭhākura; *tanu*—the body; *prabhu*—Śrī Caitanya Mahāprabhu; *kole*—on the lap; *laila*—took; *uṭhāñā*—raising; *aṅgane*—in the yard; *nācena*—dances; *prabhu*—Śrī Caitanya Mahāprabhu; *premāviṣṭa hañā*—becoming overwhelmed by ecstatic love.

TRANSLATION

The Lord raised the body of Haridāsa Ṭhākura and placed it on His lap. Then He began to dance in the courtyard in great ecstatic love.

TEXT 60

প্রভুর আবেশে অবশ সর্বভক্তগণ ।
প্রেমাবেশে সবে নাচে, করেন কীর্তন ॥ ৬০ ॥

prabhura āveśe avaśa sarva-bhakta-gaṇa
premāveśe sabe nāce, karena kīrtana

SYNONYMS

prabhura āveśe—because of the ecstatic emotions of Śrī Caitanya Mahāprabhu; *avaśa*—helpless; *sarva-bhakta-gaṇa*—all the devotees; *prema-āveśe*—in great ecstatic love; *sabe*—all of them; *nāce*—dance; *karena kīrtana*—and perform congregational chanting.

TRANSLATION

Because of Śrī Caitanya Mahāprabhu's ecstatic love, all the devotees were helpless, and in ecstatic love they also began to dance and chant congregationally.

TEXT 61

এইমতে নৃত্য প্রভু কৈলা কতক্ষণ ।
স্বরূপ-গোসাঞি প্রভুরে করাইল সাবধান ॥ ৬১ ॥

ei-mate nṛtya prabhu kailā kata-kṣaṇa
svarūpa-gosāñi prabhure karāila sāvadhāna

SYNONYMS

ei-mate—in this way; *nṛtya*—dancing; *prabhu*—Śrī Caitanya Mahāprabhu; *kailā*—performed; *kata-kṣaṇa*—for some time; *svarūpa-gosāñi*—Svarūpa Dāmodara Gosvāmī; *prabhure*—unto Śrī Caitanya Mahāprabhu; *karāila*—caused to do; *sāvadhāna*—care of other rituals.

TRANSLATION

Śrī Caitanya Mahāprabhu danced for some time, and then Svarūpa Dāmodara Gosvāmī informed Him of other rituals for the body of Ṭhākura Haridāsa.

TEXT 62

হরিদাস-ঠাকুরে তবে বিমানে চড়াঞা।
সমুদ্রে লঞা গেলা তবে কীর্তন করিয়া ॥ ৬২ ॥

haridāsa-ṭhākure tabe vimāne caḍāñā
samudre lañā gelā tabe kīrtana kariyā

SYNONYMS

haridāsa-ṭhākure—Haridāsa Ṭhākura; *tabe*—then; *vimāne*—on a carrier like an airship; *caḍāñā*—raising; *samudre*—to the seashore; *lañā gelā*—took; *tabe*—then; *kīrtana kariyā*—performing congregational chanting.

TRANSLATION

The body of Haridāsa Ṭhākura was then raised onto a carrier that resembled an airship and taken to the sea, accompanied by congregational chanting.

TEXT 63

আগে মহাপ্রভু চলেন নৃত্য করিতে করিতে।
পাছে নৃত্য করে বক্রেশ্বর ভক্তগণ-সাথে ॥ ৬৩ ॥

āge mahāprabhu calena nṛtya karite karite
pāche nṛtya kare vakreśvara bhakta-gaṇa-sāthe

SYNONYMS

āge—in front; *mahāprabhu*—Śrī Caitanya Mahāprabhu; *calena*—goes; *nṛtya*—dancing; *karite karite*—performing; *pāche*—behind; *nṛtya kare*—dances; *vakreśvara*—Vakreśvara; *bhakta-gaṇa-sāthe*—with other devotees.

TRANSLATION

Śrī Caitanya Mahāprabhu danced in front of the procession, and Vakreśvara Paṇḍita, along with the other devotees, chanted and danced behind Him.

TEXT 64

হরিদাসে সমুদ্র-জলে স্নান করাইলা।
প্রভু কহে,—"সমুদ্র এই 'মহাতীর্থ' হইলা" ॥ ৬৪ ॥

haridāse samudra-jale snāna karāilā
prabhu kahe,——"samudra ei 'mahā-tīrtha' ha-ilā"

SYNONYMS

haridāse—the body of Haridāsa; *samudra-jale*—in the water of the sea; *snāna karāilā*—bathed; *prabhu kahe*—Śrī Caitanya Mahāprabhu said; *samudra*—sea; *ei*—this; *mahā-tīrtha ha-ilā*—has become a great place of pilgrimage.

TRANSLATION

Śrī Caitanya Mahāprabhu bathed the body of Haridāsa Ṭhākura in the sea and then declared, "From this day on, this sea has become a great pilgrimage site."

TEXT 65

হরিদাসের পাদোদক পিয়ে ভক্তগণ।
হরিদাসের অঙ্গে দিলা প্রসাদ-চন্দন ॥ ৬৫ ॥

haridāsera pādodaka piye bhakta-gaṇa
haridāsera aṅge dilā prasāda-candana

SYNONYMS

haridāsera—of Haridāsa Ṭhākura; *pāda-udaka*—the water that touched the lotus feet; *piye*—drink; *bhakta-gaṇa*—the devotees; *haridāsera*—of Haridāsa Ṭhākura; *aṅge*—on the body; *dilā*—smeared; *prasāda-candana*—remnants of sandalwood pulp offered to Lord Jagannātha.

TRANSLATION

Everyone drank the water that had touched the lotus feet of Haridāsa Ṭhākura, and then they smeared remnants of Lord Jagannātha's sandalwood pulp over Haridāsa Ṭhākura's body.

TEXT 66

ডোর, কড়ার, প্রসাদ, বস্ত্র অঙ্গে দিলা ।
বালুকার গর্ত করি' তাহে শোয়াইলা ॥ ৬৬ ॥

ḍora, kaḍāra, prasāda, vastra aṅge dilā
vālukāra garta kari' tāhe śoyāilā

SYNONYMS

ḍora—silken ropes; *kaḍāra*—remnants of Lord Jagannātha's sandalwood pulp; *prasāda*—remnants of Jagannātha's food; *vastra*—cloth; *aṅge*—on the body; *dilā*—gave; *vālukāra*—of sand; *garta*—a ditch; *kari'*—making; *tāhe*—within that; *śoyāilā*—put down.

TRANSLATION

After a hole was dug in the sand, the body of Haridāsa Ṭhākura was placed in it. Remnants from Lord Jagannātha, such as His silken ropes, sandalwood pulp, food and cloth, were placed on the body.

TEXT 67

চারিদিকে ভক্তগণ করেন কীর্তন ।
বক্রেশ্বর-পণ্ডিত করেন আনন্দে নর্তন ॥ ৬৭ ॥

cāri-dike bhakta-gaṇa karena kīrtana
vakreśvara-paṇḍita karena ānande nartana

SYNONYMS

cāri-dike—all around; *bhakta-gaṇa*—the devotees; *karena*—performed; *kīrtana*—congregational chanting; *vakreśvara-paṇḍita*—Vakreśvara Paṇḍita; *karena*—performed; *ānande*—in jubilation; *nartana*—dancing.

TRANSLATION

All around the body, the devotees performed congregational chanting, and Vakreśvara Paṇḍita danced in jubilation.

TEXT 68

'হরিবোল' 'হরিবোল' বলে গৌররায় ।
আপনি শ্রীহস্তে বালু দিলা তাঁর গায় ॥ ৬৮ ॥

'hari-bola' 'hari-bola' bale gaurarāya
āpani śrī-haste vālu dilā tāṅra gāya

SYNONYMS

hari-bola hari-bola—chant Hari, chant Hari; *bale*—chanted; *gaurarāya*—Śrī Caitanya Mahāprabhu; *āpani*—personally; *śrī-haste*—with His transcendental hands; *vālu dilā*—placed sand; *tāṅra gāya*—on his body.

TRANSLATION

With His transcendental hands, Śrī Caitanya Mahāprabhu personally covered the body of Haridāsa Ṭhākura with sand, chanting "Hari bol! Hari bol!"

TEXT 69

তাঁরে বালু দিয়া উপরে পিণ্ডা বাঁধাইলা ।
চৌদিকে পিণ্ডের মহা আবরণ কৈলা ॥ ৬৯ ॥

tāṅre vālu diyā upare piṇḍā bāṅdhāilā
caudike piṇḍera mahā āvaraṇa kailā

SYNONYMS

tāṅre—upon the body of Haridāsa Ṭhākura; *vālu*—sand; *diyā*—putting; *upare*—on top; *piṇḍā bāṅdhāilā*—constructed a platform; *cau-dike*—all around; *piṇḍera*—the platform; *mahā āvaraṇa kailā*—made a great protective fence.

TRANSLATION

They covered the body of Haridāsa Ṭhākura with sand and then constructed a platform upon the site. The platform was protected all around by fencing.

TEXT 70

তাহা বেড়ি' প্রভু কৈলা কীর্তন, নর্তন ।
হরিধ্বনি-কোলাহলে ভরিল ভুবন ॥ ৭০ ॥

tāhā beḍi' prabhu kailā kīrtana, nartana
hari-dhvani-kolāhale bharila bhuvana

SYNONYMS

tāhā—that; *beḍi'*—surrounding; *prabhu*—Śrī Caitanya Mahāprabhu; *kailā*—performed; *kīrtana nartana*—chanting and dancing; *hari-dhvani-kolāhale*—the tumultuous sound of the holy name of Hari; *bharila*—filled; *bhuvana*—the entire universe.

TRANSLATION

Śrī Caitanya Mahāprabhu danced and chanted all around the platform, and as the holy name of Hari roared tumultuously, the whole universe became filled with the vibration.

TEXT 71

তবে মহাপ্রভু সব ভক্তগণ-সঙ্গে ।
সমুদ্রে করিলা স্নান-জলকেলি রঙ্গে ॥ ৭১ ॥

tabe mahāprabhu saba bhakta-gaṇa-saṅge
samudre karilā snāna-jala-keli raṅge

SYNONYMS

tabe—thereupon; *mahāprabhu*—Śrī Caitanya Mahāprabhu; *saba*—all; *bhakta-gaṇa-saṅge*—with the devotees; *samudre*—in the sea; *karilā snāna*—took a bath; *jala-keli*—playing in the water; *raṅge*—in great jubilation.

TRANSLATION

After saṅkīrtana, Śrī Caitanya Mahāprabhu bathed in the sea with His devotees, swimming and playing in the water in great jubilation.

TEXT 72

হরিদাসে প্রদক্ষিণ করি' আইল সিংহদ্বারে ।
হরিকীর্তন-কোলাহল সকল নগরে ॥ ৭২ ॥

haridāse pradakṣiṇa kari' āila siṁha-dvāre
hari-kīrtana-kolāhala sakala nagare

SYNONYMS

haridāse—Haridāsa; *pradakṣiṇa kari'*—circumambulating; *āila siṁha-dvāre*—came to the gate of Jagannātha temple known as Siṁha-dvāra; *hari-kīrtana-kolāhala*—the tumultuous sound of congregational chanting; *sakala nagare*—all over the city.

TRANSLATION

After circumambulating the tomb of Haridāsa Ṭhākura, Śrī Caitanya Mahāprabhu went to the Siṁha-dvāra gate of the Jagannātha temple. The

whole city chanted in congregation, and the tumultuous sound vibrated all over the city.

TEXT 73

সিংহদ্বারে আসি' প্রভু পসারির ঠাঁই ।
আঁচল পাতিয়া প্রসাদ মাগিলা তথাই ॥ ৭৩ ॥

siṁha-dvāre āsi' prabhu pasārira ṭhāṅi
āṅcala pātiyā prasāda māgilā tathāi

SYNONYMS

siṁha-dvāre āsi'—coming in front of the Siṁha-dvāra; *prabhu*—Śrī Caitanya Mahāprabhu; *pasārira ṭhāṅi*—from all the shopkeepers; *āṅcala pātiyā*—spreading His cloth; *prasāda*—Jagannātha's *prasāda; māgilā*—begged; *tathāi*—there.

TRANSLATION

Approaching the Siṁha-dvāra gate, Śrī Caitanya Mahāprabhu spread His cloth and began to beg prasāda from all the shopkeepers there.

TEXT 74

'হরিদাস-ঠাকুরের মহোৎসবের তরে ।
প্রসাদ মাগিয়ে ভিক্ষা দেহ' ত' আমারে' ॥ ৭৪ ॥

'haridāsa-ṭhākurera mahotsavera tare
prasāda māgiye bhikṣā deha' ta' āmāre'

SYNONYMS

haridāsa-ṭhākurera—of Haridāsa Ṭhākura; *mahotsavera tare*—for holding a festival; *prasāda māgiye*—I am begging *prasāda; bhikṣā deha'*—please give alms; *ta'*—certainly; *āmāre*—unto Me.

TRANSLATION

"I am begging prasāda for a festival honoring the passing away of Haridāsa Ṭhākura," the Lord said. "Please give Me alms."

TEXT 75

শুনিয়া পসারি সব চাঙ্গড়া উঠাঞা ।
প্রসাদ দিতে আসে তারা আনন্দিত হঞা ॥ ৭৫ ॥

śuniyā pasāri saba cāṅgaḍā uṭhāñā
prasāda dite āse tārā ānandita hañā

SYNONYMS

śuniyā—hearing; *pasāri*—the shopkeepers; *saba*—all; *cāṅgaḍā uṭhāñā*—taking a big basket; *prasāda dite*—to deliver the *prasāda; āse*—come forward; *tārā*—they; *ānandita hañā*—in great jubilation.

TRANSLATION

Hearing this, all the shopkeepers immediately came forward with big baskets of prasāda, which they jubilantly delivered to Lord Caitanya.

TEXT 76

স্বরূপ-গোসাঞি পসারিকে নিষেধিল ।
চাঙ্গড়া লঞা পসারি পসারে বসিল ॥ ৭৬ ॥

svarūpa-gosāñi pasārike niṣedhila
cāṅgaḍā lañā pasāri pasāre vasila

SYNONYMS

svarūpa-gosāñi—Svarūpa Dāmodara Gosvāmī; *pasārike*—the shopkeepers; *niṣedhila*—forbade; *cāṅgaḍā lañā*—taking the baskets; *pasāri*—shopkeepers; *pasāre vasila*—sat down in their shops.

TRANSLATION

However, Svarūpa Dāmodara stopped them, and the shopkeepers returned to their shops and sat down with their baskets.

TEXT 77

স্বরূপ-গোসাঞি প্রভুরে ঘর পাঠাইলা ।
চারি বৈষ্ণব, চারি পিছাড়া সঙ্গে রাখিলা ॥ ৭৭ ॥

svarūpa-gosāñi prabhure ghara pāṭhāilā
cāri vaiṣṇava, cāri pichāḍā saṅge rākhilā

SYNONYMS

svarūpa-gosāñi—Svarūpa Dāmodara Gosvāmī; *prabhure*—Śrī Caitanya Mahāprabhu; *ghara pāṭhāilā*—sent to His residence; *cāri vaiṣṇava*—four Vaiṣṇavas; *cāri pichāḍā*—four carrier servants; *saṅge rākhilā*—he kept with him.

TRANSLATION

Svarūpa Dāmodara sent Śrī Caitanya Mahāprabhu back to His residence, and kept with him four Vaiṣṇavas and four servant carriers.

TEXT 78

স্বরূপ-গোসাঞি কহিলেন সব পসারিরে ।
এক এক দ্রব্যের এক এক পুঞ্জা দেহ' মোরে ॥ ৭৮ ॥

svarūpa-gosāñi kahilena saba pasārire
eka eka dravyera eka eka puñjā deha' more

SYNONYMS

svarūpa-gosāñi—Svarūpa Dāmodara Gosvāmī; *kahilena*—said; *saba pasārire*—to all the shopkeepers; *eka eka dravyera*—of each particular type of *prasāda; eka eka puñjā*—four palmfuls; *deha' more*—deliver to me.

TRANSLATION

Svarūpa Dāmodara said to all the shopkeepers, "Deliver to me four palmfuls of prasāda from each and every item."

TEXT 79

এইমতে নানা প্রসাদ বোঝা বান্ধাঞা ।
লঞা আইলা চারি জনের মস্তকে চড়াঞা ॥ ৭৯ ॥

ei-mate nānā prasāda bojhā bāndhāñā
lañā āilā cāri janera mastake caḍāñā

SYNONYMS

ei-mate—in this way; *nānā*—various; *prasāda*—*prasāda; bojhā*—load; *bāndhāñā*—packing; *lañā āilā*—brought; *cāri janera*—of the four persons; *mastake*—on the heads; *caḍāñā*—mounting.

TRANSLATION

In this way varieties of prasāda were collected, then packed up in different loads and carried on the heads of the four servants.

TEXT 80

বাণীনাথ পট্টনায়ক প্রসাদ আনিলা ।
কাশীমিশ্র অনেক প্রসাদ পাঠাইলা ॥ ৮০ ॥

vāṇīnātha paṭṭanāyaka prasāda ānilā
kāśī-miśra aneka prasāda pāṭhāilā

SYNONYMS

vāṇīnātha paṭṭanāyaka—Vāṇīnātha Paṭṭanāyaka; *prasāda*—*prasāda; ānilā*—brought in; *kāśī-miśra*—Kāśī Miśra; *aneka prasāda*—varieties of *prasāda; pāṭhāilā*—sent.

TRANSLATION

Not only did Svarūpa Dāmodara Gosvāmī bring prasāda, but Vāṇīnātha Paṭṭanāyaka, as well as Kāśī Miśra, sent large quantities.

TEXT 81

সব বৈষ্ণবে প্রভু বসাইলা সারি সারি।
আপনে পরিবেশে প্রভু লঞা জনা চারি ॥ ৮১ ॥

saba vaiṣṇave prabhu vasāilā sāri sāri
āpane pariveśe prabhu lañā janā cāri

SYNONYMS

saba vaiṣṇave—all the Vaiṣṇavas; *prabhu*—Śrī Caitanya Mahāprabhu; *vasāilā*—made to sit down; *sāri sāri*—in lines; *āpane*—personally; *pariveśe*—distributes; *prabhu*—Śrī Caitanya Mahāprabhu; *lañā*—taking; *janā cāri*—four men.

TRANSLATION

Śrī Caitanya Mahāprabhu made all the devotees sit in rows and personally began to distribute the prasāda, assisted by four other men.

TEXT 82

মহাপ্রভুর শ্রীহস্তে অল্প না আইসে।
একএক পাতে পঞ্চজনার ভক্ষ্য পরিবেশে ॥ ৮২ ॥

mahāprabhura śrī-haste alpa nā āise
eka eka pāte pañca-janāra bhakṣya pariveśe

SYNONYMS

mahāprabhura—of Śrī Caitanya Mahāprabhu; *śrī-haste*—in the transcendental hands; *alpa*—a small quantity; *nā āise*—did not come; *eka eka pāte*—on each and every plate; *pañca-janāra*—of five men; *bhakṣya*—eatables; *pariveśe*—He administered.

TRANSLATION

Śrī Caitanya Mahāprabhu was not accustomed to taking prasāda in small quantities. He therefore put on each plate what at least five men could eat.

TEXT 83

স্বরূপ কহে,—"প্রভু, বসি' করহ দর্শন।
আমি ইঁহা-সবা লঞা করি পরিবেশন ॥ ৮৩ ॥

svarūpa kahe,——"prabhu, vasi' karaha darśana
āmi iṅhā-sabā lañā kari pariveśana

SYNONYMS

svarūpa kahe—Svarūpa Dāmodara said; *prabhu*—my Lord; *vasi'*—sitting down; *karaha darśana*—watch; *āmi*—I; *iṅhā-sabā lañā*—with all these persons; *kari pariveśana*—shall administer.

TRANSLATION

Svarūpa Dāmodara Gosvāmī requested Śrī Caitanya Mahāprabhu, "Please sit down and watch. With these men to help me, I shall distribute the prasāda."

TEXT 84

স্বরূপ, জগদানন্দ, কাশীশ্বর, শঙ্কর।
চারিজন পরিবেশন করে নিরন্তর ॥ ৮৪ ॥

svarūpa, jagadānanda, kāśīśvara, śaṅkara
cāri-jana pariveśana kare nirantara

SYNONYMS

svarūpa—Svarūpa Dāmodara Gosvāmī; *jagadānanda*—Jagadānanda Paṇḍita; *kāśīśvara*—Kāśīśvara; *śaṅkara*—Śaṅkara; *cāri-jana*—four men; *pariveśana kare*—administer; *nirantara*—continuously.

TRANSLATION

The four men—Svarūpa, Jagadānanda, Kāśīśvara and Śaṅkara—distributed the prasāda continuously.

TEXT 85

প্রভু না খাইলে কেহ না করে ভোজন।
প্রভুরে সে দিনে কাশীমিশ্রের নিমন্ত্রণ ॥ ৮৫ ॥

prabhu nā khāile keha nā kare bhojana
prabhure se dine kāśī-miśrera nimantraṇa

SYNONYMS

prabhu nā khāile—as long as the Lord does not eat; *keha nā kare bhojana*—no one would eat; *prabhure*—unto Śrī Caitanya Mahāprabhu; *se dine*—on that day; *kāśī-miśrera*—of Kāśī Miśra; *nimantraṇa*—the invitation.

TRANSLATION

All the devotees who sat down would not accept the prasāda as long as the Lord had not eaten. On that day, however, Kāśī Miśra had extended an invitation to the Lord.

TEXT 86

আপনে কাশীমিশ্র আইলা প্রসাদ লঞা।
প্রভুরে ভিক্ষা করাইলা আগ্রহ করিয়া ॥ ৮৬ ॥

āpane kāśī-miśra āilā prasāda lañā
prabhure bhikṣā karāilā āgraha kariyā

SYNONYMS

āpane—personally; *kāśī-miśra*—Kāśī Miśra; *āilā*—came; *prasāda lañā*—taking *prasāda; prabhure*—to Śrī Caitanya Mahāprabhu; *bhikṣā karāilā*—delivered *prasāda* to eat; *āgraha kariyā*—with great attention.

TRANSLATION

Therefore Kāśī Miśra personally went there and delivered prasāda to Śrī Caitanya Mahāprabhu with great attention and made Him eat.

TEXT 87

পুরী-ভারতীর সঙ্গে প্রভু ভিক্ষা কৈলা।
সকল বৈষ্ণব তবে ভোজন করিলা ॥ ৮৭ ॥

purī-bhāratīra saṅge prabhu bhikṣā kailā
sakala vaiṣṇava tabe bhojana karilā

SYNONYMS

purī-bhāratīra saṅge—with Paramānanda Purī and Brahmānanda Bhāratī; *prabhu*—Śrī Caitanya Mahāprabhu; *bhikṣā kailā*—honored the *prasāda; sakala vaiṣṇava*—all the Vaiṣṇavas; *tabe*—then; *bhojana karilā*—began to eat.

TRANSLATION

With Paramānanda Purī and Brahmānanda Bhāratī, Śrī Caitanya Mahāprabhu sat down and accepted the prasāda. When He began to eat, so did all the Vaiṣṇavas.

TEXT 88

আকণ্ঠ পূরাঞা সবায় করাইলা ভোজন।
'দেহ' 'দেহ' বলি' প্রভু বলেন বচন ॥ ৮৮ ॥

ākaṇṭha pūrāñā sabāya karāilā bhojana
deha' deha' bali' prabhu balena vacana

SYNONYMS

ākaṇṭha pūrāñā—filling to the neck; *sabāya*—everyone; *karāilā bhojana*—He made to eat; *deha' deha'*—give them more, give them more; *bali'*—saying; *prabhu*—Śrī Caitanya Mahāprabhu; *balena vacana*—talked.

TRANSLATION

Everyone was filled up to the neck because Śrī Caitanya Mahāprabhu kept telling the distributors, "Give them more! Give them more!"

TEXT 89

ভোজন করিয়া সবে কৈলা আচমন।
সবারে পরাইলা প্রভু মাল্য-চন্দন ॥ ৮৯ ॥

bhojana kariyā sabe kailā ācamana
sabāre parāilā prabhu mālya-candana

SYNONYMS

bhojana kariyā—after eating; *sabe*—all the devotees; *kailā*—performed; *ācamana*—washing of the mouth and hands; *sabāre*—all of them; *parāilā*—put on; *prabhu*—Śrī Caitanya Mahāprabhu; *mālya*—flower garland; *candana*—sandalwood pulp.

TRANSLATION

After all the devotees finished accepting prasāda and had washed their hands and mouths, Śrī Caitanya Mahāprabhu decorated each of them with a flower garland and sandalwood pulp.

TEXT 90

প্রেমাবিষ্ট হঞা প্রভু করেন বর-দান ।
শুনি' ভক্তগণের জুড়ায় মনস্কাম ॥ ৯০ ॥

premāviṣṭa hañā prabhu karena vara-dāna
śuni' bhakta-gaṇera juḍāya manaskāma

SYNONYMS

prema-āviṣṭa hañā—being overwhelmed by ecstatic love; *prabhu*—Śrī Caitanya Mahāprabhu; *karena vara-dāna*—offered a benediction; *śuni'*—hearing; *bhakta-gaṇera*—of the devotees; *juḍāya*—became fulfilled; *manaḥ-kāma*—the desires of the mind.

TRANSLATION

Overwhelmed with ecstatic love, Śrī Caitanya Mahāprabhu offered a benediction to all the devotees, which all the devotees heard with great satisfaction.

TEXTS 91-93

"হরিদাসের বিজয়োৎসব যে কৈল দর্শন ।
যে ইহাঁ নৃত্য কৈল, যে কৈল কীর্তন ॥ ৯১ ॥
যে তাঁরে বালুকা দিতে করিল গমন ।
তার মধ্যে মহোৎসবে যে কৈল ভোজন ॥ ৯২ ॥
অচিরে হইবে তা-সবার 'কৃষ্ণপ্রাপ্তি' ।
হরিদাস-দরশনে হয় ঐছে 'শক্তি' ॥ ৯৩ ॥

"haridāsera vijayotsava ye kaila darśana
ye ihāṅ nṛtya kaila, ye kaila kīrtana

ye tāṅre vālukā dite karila gamana
tāra madhye mahotsave ye kaila bhojana

acire ha-ibe tā-sabāra 'kṛṣṇa-prāpti'
haridāsa-daraśane haya aiche 'śakti'

SYNONYMS

haridāsera—of Haridāsa Ṭhākura; *vijaya-utsava*—the festival of the passing away; *ye*—anyone who; *kaila darśana*—has seen; *ye*—anyone who; *ihāṅ*—here; *nṛtya kaila*—danced; *ye*—anyone who; *kaila kīrtana*—chanted; *ye*—anyone who; *tāṅre*—upon him; *vālukā dite*—to offer sand; *karila gamana*—came forward; *tāra madhye*—in that connection; *mahotsave*—in the festival; *ye*—anyone who; *kaila bhojana*—took *prasāda; acire*—very soon; *ha-ibe*—there will be; *tā-sabāra*—of all of them; *kṛṣṇa-prāpti*—attainment of Kṛṣṇa; *haridāsa-darasane*—by seeing Haridāsa Ṭhākura; *haya*—there is; *aiche*—such; *śakti*—power.

TRANSLATION

Śrī Caitanya Mahāprabhu gave this benediction: "Anyone who has seen the festival of Śrī Haridāsa Ṭhākura's passing away, anyone who has chanted and danced here, anyone who has offered sand on the body of Haridāsa Ṭhākura and anyone who has joined this festival to partake of the prasāda will achieve the favor of Kṛṣṇa very soon. There is such wonderful power in seeing Haridāsa Ṭhākura.

TEXT 94

কৃপা করি' কৃষ্ণ মোরে দিয়াছিলা সঙ্গ ।
স্বতন্ত্র কৃষ্ণের ইচ্ছা,—কৈলা সঙ্গ-ভঙ্গ ॥ ৯৪ ॥

kṛpā kari' kṛṣṇa more diyāchilā saṅga
svatantra kṛṣṇera icchā,——kailā saṅga-bhaṅga

SYNONYMS

kṛpā kari'—being merciful; *kṛṣṇa*—Lord Kṛṣṇa; *more*—unto Me; *diyāchilā saṅga*—gave the association; *svatantra*—independent; *kṛṣṇera*—of Lord Kṛṣṇa; *icchā*—desire; *kailā saṅga-bhaṅga*—He has broken My association.

TRANSLATION

"Being merciful upon Me, Kṛṣṇa gave Me the association of Haridāsa Ṭhākura. Being independent in His desires, He has now broken that association.

TEXT 95

হরিদাসের ইচ্ছা যবে হইল চলিতে ।
আমার শকতি তাঁরে নারিল রাখিতে ॥ ৯৫ ॥

haridāsera icchā yabe ha-ila calite
āmāra śakati tāṅre nārila rākhite

SYNONYMS

haridāsera—of Haridāsa Ṭhākura; *icchā*—the desire; *yabe*—when; *ha-ila*—was; *calite*—to go away; *āmāra śakati*—My strength; *tāṅre*—him; *nārila rākhite*—could not keep.

TRANSLATION

"When Haridāsa Ṭhākura wanted to leave this material world, it was not within My power to detain him.

TEXT 96

ইচ্ছামাত্রে কৈলা নিজপ্রাণ নিষ্ক্রামণ ।
পূর্বে যেন শুনিয়াছি ভীষ্মের মরণ ॥ ৯৬ ॥

icchā-mātre kailā nija-prāṇa niṣkrāmaṇa
pūrve yena śuniyāchi bhīṣmera maraṇa

SYNONYMS

icchā-mātre—just by desire; *kailā*—performed; *nija-prāṇa*—of his life; *niṣkrāmaṇa*—going away; *pūrve*—formerly; *yena*—as; *śuniyāchi*—we have heard; *bhīṣmera maraṇa*—the death of Bhīṣmadeva.

TRANSLATION

"Simply by his will, Haridāsa Ṭhākura could give up his life and go away, exactly like Bhīṣma, who previously died simply by his own desire, as we have heard from śāstra.

TEXT 97

হরিদাস আছিল পৃথিবীর 'শিরোমণি' ।
তাহা বিনা রত্ন-শূন্যা হইল মেদিনী ॥ ৯৭ ॥

haridāsa āchila pṛthivīra 'śiromaṇi'
tāhā vinā ratna-śūnyā ha-ila medinī

SYNONYMS

haridāsa—Ṭhākura Haridāsa; *āchila*—was; *pṛthivīra*—of this world; *śiromaṇi*—the crown jewel; *tāhā vinā*—without him; *ratna-śūnyā*—without the valuable jewel; *ha-ila*—becomes; *medinī*—this world.

TRANSLATION

"Haridāsa Ṭhākura was the crown jewel on the head of this world; without him, this world is now bereft of its valuable jewel."

TEXT 98

'জয় জয় হরিদাস' বলি' কর হরিধ্বনি" ।
এত বলি' মহাপ্রভু নাচেন আপনি ॥ ৯৮ ॥

'jaya jaya haridāsa' bali' kara hari-dhvani"
eta bali' mahāprabhu nācena āpani

SYNONYMS

jaya jaya—all glories; *haridāsa*—to Haridāsa Ṭhākura; *bali'*—saying; *kara hari-dhvani*—chant the holy name of the Lord; *eta bali'*—saying this; *mahāprabhu*—Śrī Caitanya Mahāprabhu; *nācena*—dances; *āpani*—personally.

TRANSLATION

Śrī Caitanya Mahāprabhu then told everyone, "Say 'All glories to Haridāsa Ṭhākura!' and chant the holy name of Hari." Saying this, He personally began to dance.

TEXT 99

সবে গায়,—"জয় জয় জয় হরিদাস ।
নামের মহিমা যেঁহ করিলা প্রকাশ ॥" ৯৯ ॥

sabe gāya,——"jaya jaya jaya haridāsa
nāmera mahimā yeṅha karilā prakāśa"

SYNONYMS

sabe gāya—everyone chanted; *jaya jaya jaya*—all glories; *haridāsa*—to Haridāsa Ṭhākura; *nāmera mahimā*—the glories of chanting the holy name; *yeṅha*—who; *karilā prakāśa*—revealed.

TRANSLATION

Everyone began to chant, "All glories to Haridāsa Ṭhākura, who revealed the importance of chanting the holy name of the Lord!"

TEXT 100

তবে মহাপ্রভু সব ভক্তে বিদায় দিলা ।
হর্ষ-বিষাদে প্রভু বিশ্রাম করিলা ॥ ১০০ ॥

tabe mahāprabhu saba bhakte vidāya dilā
harṣa-viṣāde prabhu viśrāma karilā

SYNONYMS

tabe—thereafter; *mahāprabhu*—Śrī Caitanya Mahāprabhu; *saba bhakte*—to all the devotees; *vidāya dilā*—bade farewell; *harṣa-viṣāde*—in mixed happiness and distress; *prabhu*—Śrī Caitanya Mahāprabhu; *viśrāma karilā*—took His rest.

TRANSLATION

Thereafter, Śrī Caitanya Mahāprabhu bid farewell to all the devotees, and He Himself, with mixed feelings of happiness and distress, took rest.

TEXT 101

এই ত' কহিলুঁ হরিদাসের বিজয় ।
যাহার শ্রবণে কৃষ্ণে দৃঢ়ভক্তি হয় ॥ ১০১ ॥

ei ta' kahiluṅ haridāsera vijaya
yāhāra śravaṇe kṛṣṇe dṛḍha-bhakti haya

SYNONYMS

ei ta'—thus; *kahiluṅ*—I have spoken; *haridāsera*—of Haridāsa Ṭhākura; *vijaya*—victory; *yāhāra śravaṇe*—by hearing which; *kṛṣṇe*—unto Lord Kṛṣṇa; *dṛḍha-bhakti*—firm devotional service; *haya*—becomes.

TRANSLATION

Thus I have spoken about the victorious passing away of Haridāsa Ṭhākura. Anyone who hears this narration will certainly fix his mind firmly in devotional service to Kṛṣṇa.

PURPORT

At Puruṣottama-kṣetra, or Jagannātha Purī, there is a temple of Ṭoṭā-gopīnātha. If one goes from there to the sea, he can discover the tomb of Haridāsa Ṭhākura still existing. Every year on the date of Ananta-caturdaśī there is a festival to commemorate the passing away of Haridāsa Ṭhākura. At the same place, three Deities of Nityānanda, Kṛṣṇa Caitanya and Advaita Prabhu were established about one hundred years ago. A gentleman named Bhramaravara from Kendrāpāḍā in the province of Orissa contributed funds to establish these Deities in the temple. The management of the temple was under the Ṭoṭā-gopīnātha *gosvāmīs.*

This temple was later sold to someone else, and this party is now maintaining the *sevā-pūjā* of the temple. Near this temple and the tomb of Haridāsa Ṭhākura, Śrīla Bhaktivinoda Ṭhākura constructed a small house, called Bhakti-kuṭī. In the Bengali year 1329, Puruṣottama-maṭha, a branch of the Gauḍīya Maṭha, was established there. In the *Bhakti-ratnākara* it is stated:

śrīnivāsa śīghra samudrera kūle gelā
haridāsa-ṭhākurera samādhi dekhilā

bhūmite paḍiyā kailā praṇati vistara
bhāgavata-gaṇa śrī-samādhi-sannidhāne
śrīnivāse sthira kailā sasneha-vacane

punaḥ śrīnivāsa śrī-samādhi praṇamiyā
ye vilāpa kailā, tā śunile drave hiyā

"Śrīnivāsa Ṭhākura quickly ran to the seashore. When he saw the tomb of Haridāsa Ṭhākura, he immediately fell down offering prayers and almost fainted. The devotees present there pacified him with very sweet and affectionate words, and Śrīnivāsa again offered his obeisances to the tomb. Hearing of the separation that Śrīnivāsa expressed in his lamentation at the tomb of Haridāsa Ṭhākura makes one's heart melt."

TEXT 102

চৈতন্যের ভক্তবাৎসল্য ইহাতেই জানি ।
ভক্তবাঞ্ছা পূর্ণ কৈলা ন্যাসি-শিরোমণি ॥ ১০২ ॥

caitanyera bhakta-vātsalya ihātei jāni
bhakta-vāñchā pūrṇa kailā nyāsi-śiromaṇi

SYNONYMS

caitanyera—of Śrī Caitanya Mahāprabhu; *bhakta-vātsalya*—affection for His devotees; *ihātei*—from this; *jāni*—one can understand; *bhakta-vāñchā*—the desire of the devotee; *pūrṇa kailā*—fully satisfied; *nyāsi-śiromaṇi*—the crown jewel of the *sannyāsīs,* Śrī Caitanya Mahāprabhu.

TRANSLATION

From the incident of Haridāsa Ṭhākura's passing away and the great care Śrī Caitanya Mahāprabhu took in commemorating it, one can understand just how affectionate He is toward His devotees. Although He is the topmost of all sannyāsīs, He fully satisfied the desire of Haridāsa Ṭhākura.

TEXT 103

শেষকালে দিলা তাঁরে দর্শন-স্পর্শন ।
তাঁরে কোলে করি' কৈলা আপনে নর্তন ॥ ১০৩ ॥

śeṣa-kāle dilā tāṅre darśana-sparśana
tāṅre kole kari' kailā āpane nartana

SYNONYMS

śeṣa-kāle—at the last stage of his life; *dilā*—gave; *tāṅre*—to Haridāsa Ṭhākura; *darśana-sparśana*—interview and touching; *tāṅre*—him; *kole kari'*—taking on the lap; *kailā*—performed; *āpane*—personally; *nartana*—dancing.

TRANSLATION

At the last stage of Haridāsa Ṭhākura's life, Śrī Caitanya Mahāprabhu gave him His company and allowed him to touch Him. Thereafter, He took the body of Ṭhākura Haridāsa on His lap and personally danced with it.

TEXT 104

আপনে শ্রীহস্তে কৃপায় তাঁরে বালু দিলা ।
আপনে প্রসাদ মাগি' মহোৎসব কৈলা ॥ ১০৪ ॥

āpane śrī-haste kṛpāya tāṅre vālu dilā
āpane prasāda māgi' mahotsava kailā

SYNONYMS

āpane—personally; *śrī-haste*—with His transcendental hands; *kṛpāya*—out of His causeless mercy; *tāṅre*—him; *vālu dilā*—covered with sand; *āpane*—personally; *prasāda māgi'*—begging *prasāda; mahotsava kailā*—performed a great festival.

TRANSLATION

Out of His causeless mercy He personally covered the body of Haridāsa Ṭhākura with sand and personally begged alms from the shopkeepers. Then

He conducted a great festival to celebrate the passing away of Haridāsa Ṭhākura.

TEXT 105

মহাভাগবত হরিদাস—পরম-বিদ্বান্ ।
এ সৌভাগ্য লাগি' আগে করিলা প্রয়াণ ॥ ১০৫ ॥

mahā-bhāgavata haridāsa——parama-vidvān
e saubhāgya lāgi' āge karilā prayāṇa

SYNONYMS

mahā-bhāgavata—great devotee; *haridāsa*—Haridāsa Ṭhākura; *parama-vidvān*—the most learned; *e saubhāgya lāgi'*—because of his great fortune; *āge*—first; *karilā prayāṇa*—he passed away.

TRANSLATION

Haridāsa Ṭhākura was not only the topmost devotee of the Lord, but also a great and learned scholar. It was his great fortune that he passed away before Śrī Caitanya Mahāprabhu.

PURPORT

Haridāsa Ṭhākura is mentioned here as the most learned scholar, *parama-vidvān.* Actually, the most important science to know is the science of getting out of the clutches of material existence. Anyone who knows this science must be considered the greatest learned person. Anyone who knows the temporary situation of this material world and is expert in achieving a permanent situation in the spiritual world, who knows that the Supreme Personality of Godhead is beyond the jurisdiction of our experimental knowledge, is understood to be the most learned scholar. Haridāsa Ṭhākura knew this science perfectly. Therefore, he is described in this connection as *parama-vidvān.* He personally preached the importance of chanting the Hare Kṛṣṇa *mahā-mantra,* which is approved by the revealed scriptures. As stated in the *Śrīmad-Bhāgavatam* (7.5.24):

iti puṁsārpitā viṣṇau
bhaktiś cen nava-lakṣaṇā
kriyeta bhagavaty addhā
tan manye 'dhītam uttamam

There are nine different processes of devotional service to Kṛṣṇa, the most important being *śravaṇaṁ kīrtanam*—hearing and chanting. Haridāsa Ṭhākura knew this science very well, and he can therefore be called, technically, *sarva-śāstrādhītī.* Anyone who has learned the essence of all the Vedic scripture is to be known as a first-class educated person, with full knowledge of all *śāstra.*

TEXT 106

চৈতন্যচরিত্র এই অমৃতের সিন্ধু ।
কর্ণ-মন তৃপ্ত করে যার এক বিন্দু ॥ ১০৬ ॥

caitanya-caritra ei amṛtera sindhu
karṇa-mana tṛpta kare yāra eka bindu

SYNONYMS

caitanya-caritra—the life and characteristics of Śrī Caitanya Mahāprabhu; *ei*—this; *amṛtera sindhu*—the ocean of nectar; *karṇa*—ear; *mana*—mind; *tṛpta kare*—pleases; *yāra*—of which; *eka*—one; *bindu*—drop.

TRANSLATION

The life and characteristics of Śrī Caitanya Mahāprabhu are exactly like an ocean of nectar, one drop of which can please the mind and ear.

TEXT 107

ভবসিন্ধু তরিবারে আছে যার চিত্ত ।
শ্রদ্ধা করি' শুন সেই চৈতন্যচরিত্র ॥ ১০৭ ॥

bhava-sindhu taribāre āche yāra citta
śraddhā kari' śuna sei caitanya-caritra

SYNONYMS

bhava-sindhu—the ocean of material existence; *taribāre*—to cross over; *āche*—is; *yāra*—whose; *citta*—desire; *śraddhā kari'*—with faith and love; *śuna*—hear; *sei*—that; *caitanya-caritra*—life and characteristics of Śrī Caitanya Mahāprabhu.

TRANSLATION

Anyone who desires to cross over the ocean of nescience, please hear with great faith the life and characteristics of Śrī Caitanya Mahāprabhu.

TEXT 108

শ্রীরূপ-রঘুনাথ-পদে যার আশ।
চৈতন্যচরিতামৃত কহে কৃষ্ণদাস॥ ১০৮॥

śrī-rūpa-raghunātha-pade yāra āśa
caitanya-caritāmṛta kahe kṛṣṇadāsa

SYNONYMS

śrī-rūpa—Śrīla Rūpa Gosvāmī; *raghunātha*—Śrīla Raghunātha dāsa Gosvāmī; *pade*—at the lotus feet; *yāra*—whose; *āśa*—expectation; *caitanya-caritāmṛta*—the book named *Caitanya-caritāmṛta; kahe*—describes; *kṛṣṇadāsa*—Śrīla Kṛṣṇadāsa Kavirāja Gosvāmī.

TRANSLATION

Praying at the lotus feet of Śrī Rūpa and Śrī Raghunātha, always desiring their mercy, I, Kṛṣṇdāsa, narrate Śrī Caitanya-caritāmṛta, following in their footsteps.

Thus end the Bhaktivedanta purports to the Śrī Caitanya-caritāmṛta, Antya-līlā, *Eleventh Chapter, describing the passing of Haridāsa Ṭhākura.*

CHAPTER 12

The Loving Dealings Between Lord Śrī Caitanya Mahāprabhu and Jagadānanda Paṇḍita

A summary of the Twelfth Chapter is given by Śrīla Bhaktivinoda Ṭhākura in his *Amṛta-pravāha-bhāṣya* as follows. This chapter discusses the transformations of ecstatic love that Śrī Caitanya Mahāprabhu exhibited day and night. The devotees from Bengal again journeyed to Jagannātha Purī to see Śrī Caitanya Mahāprabhu. As usual, the leader was Śivānanda Sena, who traveled with his wife and children. Because arrangements were delayed en route and Lord Nityānanda did not have a suitable place to reside, He became somewhat disturbed. Thus He became very angry with Śivānanda Sena, who was in charge of the affairs of the party, and kicked him in loving anger. Śivānanda Sena felt highly favored to have been kicked by Nityānanda Prabhu, but his nephew Śrīkānta Sena became upset and therefore left their company. He met Śrī Caitanya Mahāprabhu at Jagannātha Purī before the rest of the party arrived.

That year a devotee named Parameśvara dāsa Modaka also went with his family to see Śrī Caitanya Mahāprabhu at Jagannātha Purī. The devotees often invited Śrī Caitanya Mahāprabhu to eat with them. When the Lord bade them all farewell, He talked very pleasingly with them. The year before, Jagadānanda Paṇḍita had been sent to Śacīmātā with *prasāda* and cloth. This year he returned to Purī with a big pot of floral-scented oil to massage the Lord's head. The Lord, however, would not accept the oil, and because of His refusal, Jagadānanda Paṇḍita broke the pot in front of Him and began to fast. The Lord tried to pacify him and asked Jagadānanda Paṇḍita to cook for Him. Jagadānanda Paṇḍita became so pleased when Śrī Caitanya Mahāprabhu accepted his cooking that he broke his fast.

TEXT 1

শ্রূয়তাং শ্রূয়তাং নিত্যং গীয়তাং গীয়তাং মুদা।
চিন্ত্যতাং চিন্ত্যতাং ভক্তাশ্চৈতন্যচরিতামৃতম্ ॥ ১ ॥

śrūyatāṁ śrūyatāṁ nityaṁ
gīyatāṁ gīyatāṁ mudā

cintyatāṁ cintyatāṁ bhaktāś
caitanya-caritāmṛtam

SYNONYMS

śrūyatām—let it be heard; *śrūyatām*—let it be heard; *nityam*—always; *gīyatām*—let it be chanted; *gīyatām*—let it be chanted; *mudā*—with great happiness; *cintyatām*—let it be meditated upon; *cintyatām*—let it be meditated upon; *bhaktāḥ*—O devotees; *caitanya-caritāmṛtam*—the transcendental life and characteristics of Śrī Caitanya Mahāprabhu.

TRANSLATION

O devotees, may the transcendental life and characteristics of Śrī Caitanya Mahāprabhu be always heard, chanted and meditated upon with great happiness.

TEXT 2

জয় জয় শ্রীচৈতন্য জয় দয়াময় ।
জয় জয় নিত্যানন্দ কৃপাসিন্ধু জয় ॥ ২ ॥

jaya jaya śrī-caitanya jaya dayāmaya
jaya jaya nityānanda kṛpā-sindhu jaya

SYNONYMS

jaya jaya—all glories; *śrī-caitanya*—to Lord Śrī Caitanya Mahāprabhu; *jaya*—all glories; *dayā-maya*—all-merciful; *jaya jaya*—all glories; *nityānanda*—to Nityānanda Prabhu; *kṛpā-sindhu*—the ocean of mercy; *jaya*—all glories.

TRANSLATION

All glories to Śrī Caitanya Mahāprabhu, who is all-merciful! All glories to Nityānanda Prabhu, who is an ocean of mercy!

TEXT 3

জয়াদ্বৈতচন্দ্র জয় করুণা-সাগর ।
জয় গৌরভক্তগণ কৃপা-পূর্ণান্তর ॥ ৩ ॥

jayādvaita-candra jaya karuṇā-sāgara
jaya gaura-bhakta-gaṇa kṛpā-pūrṇāntara

SYNONYMS

jaya—all glories; *advaita-candra*—to Advaita Ācārya; *jaya*—all glories; *karuṇā-sāgara*—the ocean of mercy; *jaya*—all glories; *gaura-bhakta-gaṇa*—to the devotees of Śrī Caitanya Mahāprabhu; *kṛpā-pūrṇa-antara*—whose hearts are always filled with mercy.

TRANSLATION

All glories to Advaita Ācārya, who is also an ocean of mercy! All glories to all the devotees of Śrī Caitanya Mahāprabhu, whose hearts are always filled with mercy!

TEXT 4

অতঃপর মহাপ্রভুর বিষণ্ণ-অন্তর ।
কৃষ্ণের বিয়োগ-দশা স্ফুরে নিরন্তর ॥ ৪ ॥

ataḥpara mahāprabhura viṣaṇṇa-antara
kṛṣṇera viyoga-daśā sphure nirantara

SYNONYMS

ataḥpara—thereafter; *mahāprabhura*—of Śrī Caitanya Mahāprabhu; *viṣaṇṇa-antara*—morose mind; *kṛṣṇera*—of Kṛṣṇa; *viyoga-daśā*—feeling of separation; *sphure*—manifests; *nirantara*—continuously.

TRANSLATION

The mind of Śrī Caitanya Mahāprabhu was always morose because of a continuously manifested feeling of separation from Kṛṣṇa.

TEXT 5

'হাহা কৃষ্ণ প্রাণনাথ ব্রজেন্দ্রনন্দন !
কাহাঁ যাঙ কাহাঁ পাঙ, মুরলীবদন !' ৫ ॥

'hāhā kṛṣṇa prāṇa-nātha vrajendra-nandana!
kāhāṅ yāṅa kāhāṅ pāṅa, muralī-vadana!'

SYNONYMS

hāhā—O; *kṛṣṇa*—My dear Kṛṣṇa; *prāṇa-nātha*—My life and soul; *vrajendra-nandana*—the son of Mahārāja Nanda; *kāhāṅ yāṅa*—where shall I go; *kāhāṅ pāṅa*—where shall I get; *muralī*—flute; *vadana*—mouth.

TRANSLATION

The Lord would cry, "O My Lord Kṛṣṇa, My life and soul! O son of Mahārāja Nanda, where shall I go? Where shall I attain You? O Supreme Personality who plays with Your flute to Your mouth!"

TEXT 6

রাত্রি-দিন এই দশা স্বস্তি নাহি মনে ।
কষ্টে রাত্রি গোঙায় স্বরূপ-রামানন্দ-সনে ॥ ৬ ॥

rātri-dina ei daśā svasti nāhi mane
kaṣṭe rātri goṅāya svarūpa-rāmānanda-sane

SYNONYMS

rātri-dina—day and night; *ei daśā*—this situation; *svasti nāhi mane*—no peace of mind; *kaṣṭe*—with great difficulty; *rātri goṅāya*—passes the night; *svarūpa-rāmānanda-sane*—in the company of Svarūpa Dāmodara Gosvāmī and Rāmānanda Rāya.

TRANSLATION

This was His situation day and night. Unable to find peace of mind, He passed His nights with great difficulty in the company of Svarūpa Dāmodara and Rāmānanda Rāya.

TEXT 7

এথা গৌড়দেশে প্রভুর যত ভক্তগণ ।
প্রভু দেখিবারে সবে করিলা গমন ॥ ৭ ॥

ethā gauḍa-deśe prabhura yata bhakta-gaṇa
prabhu dekhibāre sabe karilā gamana

SYNONYMS

ethā—on the other hand; *gauḍa-deśe*—in Bengal; *prabhura*—of Śrī Caitanya Mahāprabhu; *yata*—all; *bhakta-gaṇa*—devotees; *prabhu dekhibāre*—to see Śrī Caitanya Mahāprabhu; *sabe*—all; *karilā gamana*—went.

TRANSLATION

Meanwhile, all the devotees journeyed from their homes in Bengal to see Śrī Caitanya Mahāprabhu.

TEXT 8

শিবানন্দ-সেন আর আচার্য-গোসাঞি ।
নবদ্বীপে সব ভক্ত হৈলা এক ঠাঞি ॥ ৮ ॥

śivānanda-sena āra ācārya-gosāñi
navadvīpe saba bhakta hailā eka ṭhāñi

SYNONYMS

śivānanda-sena—Śivānanda Sena; *āra*—and; *ācārya-gosāñi*—Advaita Ācārya; *navadvīpe*—at Navadvīpa; *saba bhakta*—all devotees; *hailā*—became; *eka ṭhāñi*—assembled in one place.

TRANSLATION

Headed by Śivānanda Sena, Advaita Ācārya and others, all the devotees assembled in Navadvīpa.

TEXT 9

কুলীনগ্রামবাসী আর যত খণ্ডবাসী ।
একত্র মিলিলা সব নবদ্বীপে আসি' ॥ ৯ ॥

kulīna-grāma-vāsī āra yata khaṇḍa-vāsī
ekatra mililā saba navadvīpe āsi'

SYNONYMS

kulīna-grāma-vāsī—the inhabitants of Kulīna-grāma; *āra*—as well as; *yata*—all; *khaṇḍa-vāsī*—the inhabitants of Khaṇḍa; *ekatra*—at one place; *mililā*—met; *saba*—all of them; *navadvīpe āsi'*—coming to Navadvīpa.

TRANSLATION

The inhabitants of Kulīna-grāma and Khaṇḍa village also assembled at Navadvīpa.

TEXT 10

নিত্যানন্দ-প্রভুরে যদ্যপি আজ্ঞা নাই ।
তথাপি দেখিতে চলেন চৈতন্য-গোসাঞি ॥ ১০ ॥

nityānanda-prabhure yadyapi ājñā nāi
tathāpi dekhite calena caitanya-gosāñi

SYNONYMS

nityānanda-prabhure—unto Lord Nityānanda; *yadyapi*—although; *ājñā nāi*—there was no order; *tathāpi*—still; *dekhite*—to see; *calena*—He went; *caitanya-gosāñi*—Lord Caitanya.

TRANSLATION

Because Nityānanda Prabhu was preaching in Bengal, Śrī Caitanya Mahāprabhu had ordered Him not to come to Jagannātha Purī. That year, however, He went with the rest of the party to see the Lord.

TEXT 11

শ্রীবাসাদি চারি ভাই, সঙ্গেতে মালিনী।
আচার্যরত্নের সঙ্গে তাঁহার গৃহিণী ॥ ১১ ॥

śrīvāsādi cāri bhāi, saṅgete mālinī
ācāryaratnera saṅge tāṅhāra gṛhiṇī

SYNONYMS

śrīvāsa-ādi—headed by Śrīvāsa Ṭhākura; *cāri bhāi*—four brothers; *saṅgete mālinī*—accompanied by his wife, Mālinī; *ācāryaratnera saṅge*—and with Ācāryaratna; *tāṅhāra gṛhiṇī*—his wife.

TRANSLATION

Śrīvāsa Ṭhākura was also there with his three brothers and his wife, Mālinī. Ācāryaratna was similarly accompanied by his wife.

TEXT 12

শিবানন্দ-পত্নী চলে তিন-পুত্র লঞা।
রাঘব-পণ্ডিত চলে ঝালি সাজাঞা ॥ ১২ ॥

śivānanda-patnī cale tina-putra lañā
rāghava-paṇḍita cale jhāli sājāñā

SYNONYMS

śivānanda-patnī—the wife of Śivānanda; *cale*—was going; *tina-putra lañā*—accompanied by her three sons; *rāghava-paṇḍita cale*—Rāghava Paṇḍita was going; *jhāli sājāñā*—carrying his bags.

TRANSLATION

The wife of Śivānanda Sena also came, along with their three sons. Rāghava Paṇḍita joined them, carrying his famous bags of food.

TEXT 13

দত্ত, গুপ্ত, বিদ্যানিধি, আর যত জন।
দুই-তিন শত ভক্ত করিলা গমন ॥ ১৩ ॥

datta, gupta, vidyānidhi, āra yata jana
dui-tina śata bhakta karilā gamana

SYNONYMS

datta—Vāsudeva Datta; *gupta*—Murāri Gupta; *vidyānidhi*—Vidyānidhi; *āra*—and; *yata jana*—all persons; *dui-tina śata*—two hundred to three hundred; *bhakta*—devotees; *karilā gamana*—went.

TRANSLATION

Vāsudeva Datta, Murāri Gupta, Vidyānidhi and many other devotees went to see Śrī Caitanya Mahāprabhu. All together, they numbered two or three hundred.

TEXT 14

শচীমাতা দেখি' সবে তাঁর আজ্ঞা লঞা।
আনন্দে চলিলা কৃষ্ণকীর্তন করিয়া ॥ ১৪ ॥

śacīmātā dekhi' sabe tāṅra ājñā lañā
ānande calilā kṛṣṇa-kīrtana kariyā

SYNONYMS

śacī-mātā dekhi'—seeing Śacīmātā; *sabe*—all of them; *tāṅra ājñā lañā*—taking her permission; *ānande*—with great jubilation; *calilā*—they proceeded; *kṛṣṇa-kīrtana kariyā*—performing congregational chanting.

TRANSLATION

The devotees first saw Śacīmātā and took her permission. Then, in great happiness, they started for Jagannātha Purī, congregationally chanting the holy name of the Lord.

TEXT 15

শিবানন্দ-সেন করে ঘাটী-সমাধান।
সবারে পালন করি' সুখে লঞা যান ॥ ১৫ ॥

śivānanda-sena kare ghāṭī-samādhāna
sabāre pālana kari' sukhe lañā yāna

SYNONYMS

śivānanda-sena—Śivānanda Sena; *kare*—does; *ghāṭī-samādhāna*—management of payment of tolls; *sabāre pālana kari'*—maintaining everyone; *sukhe*—in happiness; *lañā*—taking; *yāna*—goes.

TRANSLATION

Śivānanda Sena managed the payment of tolls at different places. Maintaining everyone, he guided all the devotees in great happiness.

PURPORT

Ghāṭī refers to the different toll booths used by the Zamindars to collect taxes in each state. Generally, this tax was collected to maintain the roads governed by the various Zamindars. Since the devotees from Bengal were going to Jagannātha Purī, they had to pass through many such toll booths. Śivānanda Sena was in charge of paying the tolls.

TEXT 16

সবার সব কার্য করেন, দেন বাসস্থান ।
শিবানন্দ জানে উড়িয়া-পথের সন্ধান ॥ ১৬ ॥

sabāra saba kārya karena, dena vāsa-sthāna
śivānanda jāne uḍiyā-pathera sandhāna

SYNONYMS

sabāra—of everyone; *saba*—all; *kārya*—business; *karena*—performs; *dena*—gives; *vāsa-sthāna*—place of residence; *śivānanda*—Śivānanda Sena; *jāne*—knows; *uḍiyā-pathera*—of the path going to Orissa; *sandhāna*—junctions.

TRANSLATION

Śivānanda Sena took care of everyone and gave each devotee places to stay. He knew all the paths leading to Orissa.

TEXT 17

একদিন সব লোক ঘাটিয়ালে রাখিলা ।
সবা ছাড়াঞা শিবানন্দ একেলা রহিলা ॥ ১৭ ॥

eka-dina saba loka ghāṭiyāle rākhilā
sabā chāḍāñā śivānanda ekalā rahilā

SYNONYMS

eka-dina—one day; *saba loka*—all the members of the party; *ghāṭiyāle rākhilā*—were checked by the toll collector; *sabā*—all of them; *chāḍāñā*—causing to be let go; *śivānanda*—Śivānanda Sena; *ekalā rahilā*—remained alone.

TRANSLATION

One day when the party was being checked by a toll collector, the devotees were allowed to pass, and Śivānanda Sena remained behind alone to pay the taxes.

TEXT 18

সবে গিয়া রহিলা গ্রাম-ভিতর বৃক্ষতলে ।
শিবানন্দ বিনা বাসস্থান নাহি মিলে ॥ ১৮ ॥

sabe giyā rahilā grāma-bhitara vṛkṣa-tale
śivānanda vinā vāsa-sthāna nāhi mile

SYNONYMS

sabe—all of them; *giyā*—going; *rahilā*—remained; *grāma-bhitara*—inside a village; *vṛkṣa-tale*—under a tree; *śivānanda vinā*—without Śivānanda Sena; *vāsa-sthāna*—residential quarters; *nāhi mile*—no one could get.

TRANSLATION

The party went into a village and waited beneath a tree because no one but Śivānanda Sena could arrange for their residential quarters.

TEXT 19

নিত্যানন্দপ্রভু ভোখে ব্যাকুল হঞা ।
শিবানন্দে গালি পাড়ে বাসা না পাঞা ॥ ১৯ ॥

nityānanda-prabhu bhokhe vyākula hañā
śivānanda gāli pāḍe vāsā nā pāñā

SYNONYMS

nityānanda-prabhu—Lord Nityānanda Prabhu; *bhokhe*—became very hungry; *vyākula hañā*—being disturbed; *śivānanda gāli pāḍe*—was calling Śivānanda ill names; *vāsā nā pāñā*—not getting residential quarters.

TRANSLATION

Nityānanda Prabhu meanwhile became very hungry and upset. Because He had not yet obtained a suitable residence, He began calling Śivānanda Sena ill names.

TEXT 20

'তিন পুত্র মরুক শিবার, এখন না আইল ।
ভোখে মরি' গেনু, মোরে বাসা না দেওয়াইল' ॥২০॥

'tina putra maruka śivāra, ekhana nā āila
bhokhe mari' genu, more vāsā nā deoyāila'

SYNONYMS

tina putra—three sons; *maruka*—let them die; *śivāra*—of Śivānanda Sena; *ekhana*—here; *nā āila*—he does not come; *bhokhe mari' genu*—I am dying from hunger; *more*—for Me; *vāsā*—residential place; *nā deoyāila*—he did not arrange.

TRANSLATION

"Śivānanda Sena has not arranged for My residence," He complained, "and I am so hungry I could die. Because he has not come, I curse his three sons to die."

TEXT 21

শুনি' শিবানন্দের পত্নী কান্দিতে লাগিলা ।
হেনকালে শিবানন্দ ঘাটী হৈতে আইলা ॥ ২১ ॥

śuni' śivānandera patnī kāndite lāgilā
hena-kāle śivānanda ghāṭī haite āilā

SYNONYMS

śuni'—hearing; *śivānandera*—of Śivānanda Sena; *patnī*—the wife; *kāndite lāgilā*—began to cry; *hena-kāle*—at this time; *śivānanda*—Śivānanda Sena; *ghāṭī haite*—from the toll station; *āilā*—came.

TRANSLATION

Hearing this curse, Śivānanda Sena's wife began to cry. Just then, Śivānanda returned from the toll station.

TEXT 22

শিবানন্দের পত্নী তাঁরে কহেন কান্দিয়া ।
'পুত্রে শাপ দিছেন গোসাঞি বাসা না পাঞা' ॥২২॥

śivānandera patnī tāṅre kahena kāndiyā
'putre śāpa dichena gosāñi vāsā nā pāñā'

SYNONYMS

śivānandera—of Śivānanda Sena; *patnī*—the wife; *tāṅre*—unto him; *kahena*—says; *kāndiyā*—crying; *putre*—on our sons; *śāpa*—curse; *dichena*—awarded; *gosāñi*—Nityānanda Prabhu; *vāsā nā pāñā*—not getting His residential quarters.

TRANSLATION

Crying, his wife informed him, "Lord Nityānanda has cursed our sons to die because His quarters have not been provided."

TEXT 23

তেঁহো কহে,—"বাউলি, কেনে মরিস্ কান্দিয়া ?
মরুক আমার তিন পুত্র তাঁর বালাই লঞা ।" ২৩ ॥

teṅho kahe,——"bāuli, kene maris kāndiyā?
maruka āmāra tina putra tāṅra bālāi lañā"

SYNONYMS

teṅho kahe—he said; *bāuli*—crazy woman; *kene*—why; *maris*—are you dying; *kāndiyā*—crying; *maruka*—let die; *āmāra*—my; *tina*—three; *putra*—sons; *tāṅra*—His; *bālāi*—inconveniences; *lañā*—taking.

TRANSLATION

Śivānanda Sena replied, "You crazy woman! Why are you needlessly crying? Let my three sons die for all the inconvenience we have caused Nityānanda Prabhu."

TEXT 24

এত বলি' প্রভু-পাশে গেলা শিবানন্দ ।
উঠি' তাঁরে লাথি মাইলা প্রভু নিত্যানন্দ ॥ ২৪ ॥

eta bali' prabhu-pāśe gelā śivānanda
uṭhi' tāṅre lāthi māilā prabhu nityānanda

SYNONYMS

eta bali'—saying this; *prabhu-pāśe*—to Nityānanda Prabhu; *gelā*—went; *śivā-nanda*—Śivānanda Sena; *uṭhi'*—standing up; *tāṅre*—him; *lāthi māilā*—kicked; *prabhu*—the Lord; *nityānanda*—Nityānanda.

TRANSLATION

After saying this, Śivānanda Sena went to Nityānanda Prabhu, who then stood up and kicked him.

TEXT 25

আনন্দিত হৈলা শিবাই পাদপ্রহার পাঞা ।
শীঘ্র বাসা-ঘর কৈলা গৌড়-ঘরে গিয়া ॥ ২৫ ॥

ānandita hailā śivāi pāda-prahāra pāñā
śīghra vāsā-ghara kailā gauḍa-ghare giyā

SYNONYMS

ānandita hailā—became very pleased; *śivāi*—Śivānanda Sena; *pāda-prahāra pāñā*—being kicked; *śīghra*—very soon; *vāsā-ghara*—residential place; *kailā*—arranged; *gauḍa-ghare*—to a milkman's house; *giyā*—going.

TRANSLATION

Very pleased at being kicked, Śivānanda Sena quickly arranged for a milkman's house to be the Lord's residence.

TEXT 26

চরণে ধরিয়া প্রভুরে বাসায় লঞা গেলা ।
বাসা দিয়া হৃষ্ট হঞা কহিতে লাগিলা ॥ ২৬ ॥

caraṇe dhariyā prabhure vāsāya lañā gelā
vāsā diyā hṛṣṭa hañā kahite lāgilā

SYNONYMS

caraṇe—the feet; *dhariyā*—catching; *prabhure*—Lord Nityānanda Prabhu; *vāsāya*—to His residence; *lañā*—taking; *gelā*—went; *vāsā diyā*—after giving His residential quarters; *hṛṣṭa hañā*—being very pleased; *kahite lāgilā*—began to speak.

TRANSLATION

Śivānanda Sena touched the lotus feet of Nityānanda Prabhu and led Him to His residence. After giving the Lord His quarters, Śivānanda Sena, being very pleased, spoke as follows.

TEXT 27

"আজি মোরে ভৃত্য করি' অঙ্গীকার কৈলা।
যেমন অপরাধ ভৃত্যের, যোগ্য ফল দিলা ॥ ২৭ ॥

"āji more bhṛtya kari' aṅgīkāra kailā
yemana aparādha bhṛtyera, yogya phala dilā

SYNONYMS

āji—today; *more*—me; *bhṛtya*—servant; *kari'*—as; *aṅgīkāra*—acceptance; *kailā*—You have done; *yemana*—as; *aparādha*—offense; *bhṛtyera*—of the servant; *yogya*—proper; *phala*—result; *dilā*—You have given.

TRANSLATION

"Today You have accepted me as Your servant and have properly punished me for my offense.

TEXT 28

'শাস্তি'-ছলে কৃপা কর,—এ তোমার 'করুণা'।
ত্রিজগতে তোমার চরিত্র বুঝে কোন্ জনা? ২৮ ॥

'śāsti'-chale kṛpā kara,——e tomāra 'karuṇā'
trijagate tomāra caritra bujhe kon janā?

SYNONYMS

śāsti-chale—on the pretext of chastisement; *kṛpā kara*—You bestow mercy; *e*—this; *tomāra karuṇā*—Your causeless mercy; *tri-jagate*—within the three worlds; *tomāra*—Your; *caritra*—character; *bujhe*—understands; *kon janā*—what person.

TRANSLATION

"My dear Lord, Your chastising me is Your causeless mercy. Who within the three worlds can understand Your real character?

TEXT 29

ব্রহ্মার দুর্লভ তোমার শ্রীচরণ-রেণু ।
হেন চরণ-স্পর্শ পাইল মোর অধম তনু ॥ ২৯ ॥

brahmāra durlabha tomāra śrī-caraṇa-reṇu
hena caraṇa-sparśa pāila mora adhama tanu

SYNONYMS

brahmāra—by Lord Brahmā; *durlabha*—almost unattainable; *tomāra*—Your; *śrī-caraṇa-reṇu*—dust of the lotus feet; *hena*—such; *caraṇa-sparśa*—touch of the lotus feet; *pāila*—got; *mora*—my; *adhama*—most fallen; *tanu*—body.

TRANSLATION

"The dust of Your lotus feet is not attainable even by Lord Brahmā, yet Your lotus feet have touched my wretched body.

TEXT 30

আজি মোর সফল হৈল জন্ম, কুল, কর্ম ।
আজি পাইনু কৃষ্ণভক্তি, অর্থ, কাম, ধর্ম ॥" ৩০ ॥

āji mora saphala haila janma, kula, karma
āji pāinu kṛṣṇa-bhakti, artha, kāma, dharma"

SYNONYMS

āji—today; *mora*—my; *sa-phala*—successful; *haila*—became; *janma*—birth; *kula*—family; *karma*—activities; *āji*—today; *pāinu*—I have gotten; *kṛṣṇa-bhakti*—devotional service to Lord Kṛṣṇa; *artha*—economic development; *kāma*—satisfaction of the senses; *dharma*—religion.

TRANSLATION

"Today my birth, my family and my activities have all become successful. Today I have achieved the fulfillment of religious principles, economic development, satisfaction of the senses and ultimately devotional service to Lord Kṛṣṇa."

TEXT 31

শুনি' নিত্যানন্দপ্রভুর আনন্দিত মন ।
উঠি' শিবানন্দে কৈলা প্রেম-আলিঙ্গন ॥ ৩১ ॥

śuni' nityānanda-prabhura ānandita mana
uṭhi' śivānande kailā prema-āliṅgana

SYNONYMS

śuni'—hearing; *nityānanda-prabhura*—of Lord Nityānanda; *ānandita*—very pleased; *mana*—mind; *uṭhi'*—standing up; *śivānande*—unto Śivānanda Sena; *kailā*—performed; *prema*—in love; *āliṅgana*—embracing.

TRANSLATION

When Lord Nityānanda heard this, He was very happy. He rose and embraced Śivānanda Sena in great love.

TEXT 32

আনন্দিত শিবানন্দ করে সমাধান ।
আচার্যাদি-বৈষ্ণবেরে দিলা বাসাস্থান ॥ ৩২ ॥

ānandita śivānanda kare samādhāna
ācāryādi-vaiṣṇavere dilā vāsā-sthāna

SYNONYMS

ānandita—pleased; *śivānanda*—Śivānanda Sena; *kare samādhāna*—began to arrange things; *ācārya-ādi-vaiṣṇavere*—unto all the Vaiṣṇavas, headed by Advaita Ācārya; *dilā*—gave; *vāsā-sthāna*—residential places.

TRANSLATION

Being very pleased by Nityānanda Prabhu's behavior, Śivānanda Sena began to arrange residential quarters for all the Vaiṣṇavas, headed by Advaita Ācārya.

TEXT 33

নিত্যানন্দপ্রভুর সব চরিত্র—'বিপরীত' ।
ক্রুদ্ধ হঞা লাথি মারি' করে তার হিত ॥ ৩৩ ॥

nityānanda-prabhura saba caritra——'viparīta'
kruddha hañā lāthi māri' kare tāra hita

SYNONYMS

nityānanda-prabhura—of Lord Śrī Nityānanda Prabhu; *saba caritra*—all characteristics; *viparīta*—contradictory; *kruddha hañā*—becoming angry; *lāthi māri'*—kicking; *kare*—performs; *tāra hita*—his benefit.

TRANSLATION

One of Śrī Nityānanda Prabhu's characteristics is His contradictory nature. When He becomes angry and kicks someone, it is actually to his benefit.

TEXT 34

শিবানন্দের ভাগিনা,—শ্রীকান্ত-সেন নাম ।
মামার অগোচরে কহে করি' অভিমান ॥ ৩৪ ॥

śivānandera bhāginā,——śrīkānta-sena nāma
māmāra agocare kahe kari' abhimāna

SYNONYMS

śivānandera—of Śivānanda Sena; *bhāginā*—the sister's son; *śrīkānta-sena nāma*—named Śrīkānta Sena; *māmāra*—of his maternal uncle; *agocare*—in the absence of; *kahe*—said; *kari' abhimāna*—with an offended state of mind.

TRANSLATION

Śivānanda Sena's nephew, Śrīkānta, the son of his sister, felt offended, and he commented on the matter when his uncle was absent.

TEXT 35

"চৈতন্যের পারিষদ মোর মাতুলের খ্যাতি ।
'ঠাকুরালী' করেন গোসাঞি, তাঁরে মারে লাথি" ॥

"caitanyera pāriṣada mora mātulera khyāti
'ṭhākurālī' karena gosāñi, tāṅre māre lāthi"

SYNONYMS

caitanyera pāriṣada—associate of Śrī Caitanya Mahāprabhu; *mora*—my; *mātulera*—of the maternal uncle; *khyāti*—reputation; *ṭhākurālī*—superiority; *karena*—exhibits; *gosāñi*—Nityānanda Prabhu; *tāṅre*—him; *māre lāthi*—kicks.

TRANSLATION

"My uncle is well known as one of the associates of Śrī Caitanya Mahāprabhu, but Lord Nityānanda Prabhu asserts His superiority by kicking him."

TEXT 36

এত বলি শ্রীকান্ত, বালক আগে চলি' যান ।
সঙ্গ ছাড়ি' আগে গেলা মহাপ্রভুর স্থান ॥ ৩৬ ॥

eta bali' śrīkānta, bālaka āge cali' yāna
saṅga chāḍi' āge gelā mahāprabhura sthāna

SYNONYMS

eta bali'—saying this; *śrīkānta*—the nephew of Śivānanda Sena; *bālaka*—a boy; *āge cali' yāna*—went forward; *saṅga chāḍi'*—giving up their association; *āge*—forward; *gelā*—went; *mahāprabhura sthāna*—to the place of Śrī Caitanya Mahāprabhu.

TRANSLATION

After saying this, Śrīkānta, who was only a boy, left the group and traveled on alone to the residence of Śrī Caitanya Mahāprabhu.

TEXT 37

পেটাঙ্গি-গায় করে দণ্ডবৎ-নমস্কার ।
গোবিন্দ কহে,—'শ্রীকান্ত, আগে পেটাঙ্গি উতার' ॥

peṭāṅgi-gāya kare daṇḍavat-namaskāra
govinda kahe,——'śrīkānta, āge peṭāṅgi utāra'

SYNONYMS

peṭāṅgi—shirt and coat; *gāya*—on the body; *kare*—performs; *daṇḍavat-namaskāra*—offering of obeisances; *govinda kahe*—Govinda said; *śrīkānta*—my dear Śrīkānta; *āge*—first; *peṭāṅgi utāra*—take off your shirt and coat.

TRANSLATION

When Śrīkānta offered obeisances to the Lord, he was still wearing his shirt and coat. Therefore Govinda told him, "My dear Śrīkānta, first take off these garments."

PURPORT

One is forbidden to enter the Deity room or offer anything to the Deity while wearing a shirt or coat. In the *tantras* it is said:

vastreṇāvṛta-dehas tu
yo naraḥ praṇamed dharim
śvitrī bhavati mūḍhātmā
sapta janmāni bhāvini

"Anyone who offers respects and obeisances to the Deity while wearing garments on the upper portion of his body is condemned to be a leper for seven births."

TEXT 38

প্রভু কহে,—"শ্রীকান্ত আসিয়াছে পাঞা মনোদুঃখ।
কিছু না বলিহ, করুক, যাতে ইহার সুখ ॥" ৩৮ ॥

prabhu kahe,——"śrīkānta āsiyāche pāñā mano-duḥkha
kichu nā baliha, karuka, yāte ihāra sukha"

SYNONYMS

prabhu kahe—Śrī Caitanya Mahāprabhu said; *śrīkānta*—Śrīkānta; *āsiyāche*—has come; *pāñā*—getting; *manaḥ-duḥkha*—distress in the mind; *kichu*—anything; *nā baliha*—do not say; *karuka*—let him do; *yāte*—by which; *ihāra*—his; *sukha*—happiness.

TRANSLATION

As Govinda was warning Śrīkānta, Śrī Caitanya Mahāprabhu said, "Don't bother him. Let Śrīkānta do whatever he likes, for he has come here in a distressed state of mind."

TEXT 39

বৈষ্ণবের সমাচার গোসাঞি পুছিলা।
একে একে সবার নাম শ্রীকান্ত জানাইলা ॥ ৩৯ ॥

vaiṣṇavera samācāra gosāñi puchilā
eke eke sabāra nāma śrīkānta jānāilā

SYNONYMS

vaiṣṇavera—of all the Vaiṣṇavas; *samācāra*—news; *gosāñi*—Śrī Caitanya Mahāprabhu; *puchilā*—inquired; *eke eke*—one after another; *sabāra*—of all of them; *nāma*—names; *śrīkānta*—the nephew of Śivānanda Sena; *jānāilā*—informed.

TRANSLATION

Śrī Caitanya Mahāprabhu inquired from Śrīkānta about all the Vaiṣṇavas, and the boy informed the Lord about them, naming them one after another.

TEXT 40

'দুঃখ পাঞা আসিয়াছে'—এই প্রভুর বাক্য শুনি' ।
জানিলা 'সর্বজ্ঞ প্রভু'—এত অনুমানি' ॥ ৪০ ॥

'duḥkha pāñā āsiyāche'——ei prabhura vākya śuni'
jānilā 'sarvajña prabhu'——eta anumāni'

SYNONYMS

duḥkha—unhappiness; *pāñā*—getting; *āsiyāche*—he has come; *ei*—this; *prabhura*—of Śrī Caitanya Mahāprabhu; *vākya*—statement; *śuni'*—hearing; *jānilā*—could understand; *sarvajña prabhu*—the Lord is omniscient; *eta*—this; *anumāni'*—guessing.

TRANSLATION

When Śrīkānta Sena heard the Lord say, "He is distressed," he could understand that the Lord is omniscient.

TEXT 41

শিবানন্দে লাথি মারিলা,—ইহা না কহিলা ।
এথা সব বৈষ্ণবগণ আসিয়া মিলিলা ॥ ৪১ ॥

śivānande lāthi mārilā,——ihā nā kahilā
ethā saba vaiṣṇava-gaṇa āsiyā mililā

SYNONYMS

śivānande—Śivānanda Sena; *lāthi mārilā*—(Lord Nityānanda) has kicked; *ihā*—this; *nā kahilā*—he did not say; *ethā*—here; *saba*—all; *vaiṣṇava-gaṇa*—devotees; *āsiyā*—coming; *mililā*—met.

TRANSLATION

As he described the Vaiṣṇavas, therefore, he did not mention Lord Nityānanda's kicking Śivānanda Sena. Meanwhile, all the devotees arrived and went to meet the Lord.

TEXT 42

পূর্ব্ববৎ প্রভু কৈলা সবার মিলন ।
স্ত্রী-সব দূর হইতে কৈলা প্রভুর দরশন ॥ ৪২ ॥

pūrvavat prabhu kailā sabāra milana
strī-saba dūra ha-ite kailā prabhura daraśana

SYNONYMS

pūrva-vat—as previously; *prabhu*—Śrī Caitanya Mahāprabhu; *kailā*—performed; *sabāra milana*—meeting everyone; *strī*—women; *saba*—all; *dūra ha-ite*—from a distance; *kailā*—performed; *prabhura daraśana*—seeing the Lord.

TRANSLATION

Śrī Caitanya Mahāprabhu received them all, just as He had in previous years. The women, however, saw the Lord from a distance.

TEXT 43

বাসাঘর পূর্ব্ববৎ সবারে দেওয়াইলা ।
মহাপ্রসাদ-ভোজনে সবারে বোলাইলা ॥ ৪৩ ॥

vāsā-ghara pūrvavat sabāre deoyāilā
mahāprasāda-bhojane sabāre bolāilā

SYNONYMS

vāsā-ghara—residential quarters; *pūrva-vat*—as previously; *sabāre*—unto all of them; *deoyāilā*—caused to be given; *mahā-prasāda*—the remnants of food from Jagannātha; *bhojane*—to eat; *sabāre*—unto everyone; *bolāilā*—He called.

TRANSLATION

The Lord again arranged for the residential quarters of all the devotees and thereafter called them to partake of the remnants of food offered to Lord Jagannātha.

TEXT 44

শিবানন্দ তিনপুত্রে গোসাঞিরে মিলাইলা ।
শিবানন্দ-সম্বন্ধে সবায় বহুকৃপা কৈলা ॥ ৪৪ ॥

śivānanda tina-putre gosāñire milāilā
śivānanda-sambandhe sabāya bahu-kṛpā kailā

SYNONYMS

śivānanda—Śivānanda Sena; *tina-putre*—three sons; *gosāñire*—unto Śrī Caitanya Mahāprabhu; *milāilā*—introduced; *śivānanda-sambandhe*—because they were sons of Śivānanda Sena; *sabāya*—unto all of them; *bahu-kṛpā kailā*—showed much mercy.

TRANSLATION

Śivānanda Sena introduced his three sons to Śrī Caitanya Mahāprabhu. Because they were his sons, the Lord showed the boys great mercy.

TEXT 45

ছোটপুত্রে দেখি' প্রভু নাম পুছিলা ।
'পরমানন্দদাস'-নাম সেন জানাইলা ॥ ৪৫ ॥

choṭa-putre dekhi' prabhu nāma puchilā
'paramānanda-dāsa'-nāma sena jānāilā

SYNONYMS

choṭa-putre—the youngest son; *dekhi'*—seeing; *prabhu*—Śrī Caitanya Mahāprabhu; *nāma puchilā*—inquired about his name; *paramānanda-dāsa*—Paramānanda dāsa; *nāma*—name; *sena*—Śivānanda Sena; *jānāilā*—informed.

TRANSLATION

Lord Caitanya asked the youngest son's name, and Śivānanda Sena informed the Lord that his name was Paramānanda dāsa.

TEXTS 46-47

পূর্বে যবে শিবানন্দ প্রভুস্থানে আইলা ।
তবে মহাপ্রভু তাঁরে কহিতে লাগিলা ॥ ৪৬ ॥
"এবার তোমার যেই হইবে কুমার ।
'পুরীদাস' বলি' নাম ধরিহ তাহার ॥ ৪৭ ॥

pūrve yabe śivānanda prabhu-sthāne āilā
tabe mahāprabhu tāṅre kahite lāgilā

"e-bāra tomāra yei ha-ibe kumāra
'purī-dāsa' bali' nāma dhariha tāhāra

SYNONYMS

pūrve—formerly; *yabe*—when; *śivānanda*—Śivānanda Sena; *prabhu-sthāne*—to the place of Lord Caitanya Mahāprabhu; *āilā*—came; *tabe*—at that time; *mahāprabhu*—Śrī Caitanya Mahāprabhu; *tāṅre*—unto him; *kahite lāgilā*—began to speak; *e-bāra*—this time; *tomāra*—your; *yei*—that; *ha-ibe*—will be; *kumāra*—son; *purī-dāsa*—Purī dāsa; *bali'*—as; *nāma*—name; *dhariha*—gave; *tāhāra*—his.

TRANSLATION

Once before when Śivānanda Sena had visited Śrī Caitanya Mahāprabhu at His residence, the Lord had told him, "When this son is born, give him the name Purī dāsa."

TEXT 48

তবে মায়ের গর্ভে হয় সেই ত' কুমার ।
শিবানন্দ ঘরে গেলে, জন্ম হৈল তার ॥ ৪৮ ॥

tabe māyera garbhe haya sei ta' kumāra
śivānanda ghare gele, janma haila tāra

SYNONYMS

tabe—at that time; *māyera garbhe*—the womb of the mother; *haya*—was; *sei ta' kumāra*—that son; *śivānanda ghare gele*—when Śivānanda Sena returned home; *janma haila tāra*—he was born.

TRANSLATION

The son was in the womb of his wife, and when he returned home the son was born.

TEXT 49

প্রভু-আজ্ঞায় ধরিলা নাম—'পরমানন্দ-দাস' ।
'পুরীদাস' করি' প্রভু করেন উপহাস ॥ ৪৯ ॥

prabhu-ājñāya dharilā nāma——'paramānanda-dāsa'
'purī-dāsa' kari' prabhu karena upahāsa

SYNONYMS

prabhu-ājñāya—under the order of Śrī Caitanya Mahāprabhu; *dharilā nāma*—held the name; *paramānanda-dāsa*—Paramānanda dāsa; *purī-dāsa*—Purī dāsa; *kari'*—as; *prabhu*—Śrī Caitanya Mahāprabhu; *karena upahāsa*—began to joke.

TRANSLATION

The child was named Paramānanda dāsa in accordance with the Lord's order, and the Lord jokingly called him Purī dāsa.

TEXT 50

শিবানন্দ যবে সেই বালকে মিলাইলা।
মহাপ্রভু পাদাঙ্গুষ্ঠ তার মুখে দিলা ॥ ৫০ ॥

śivānanda yabe sei bālake milāilā
mahāprabhu pādāṅguṣṭha tāra mukhe dilā

SYNONYMS

śivānanda—Śivānanda Sena; *yabe*—when; *sei*—that; *bālake*—child; *milāilā*—introduced; *mahāprabhu*—Mahāprabhu; *pāda-aṅguṣṭha*—His toe; *tāra*—his; *mukhe*—within the mouth; *dilā*—pushed.

TRANSLATION

When Śivānanda Sena introduced the child to Śrī Caitanya Mahāprabhu, the Lord put His toe in the child's mouth.

PURPORT

In this connection one may refer to *Antya-līlā,* Chapter Sixteen, verses 65-75, for information about the later manifestations of the Lord's mercy.

TEXT 51

শিবানন্দের ভাগ্যসিন্ধু কে পাইবে পার ?
যাঁর সব গোষ্ঠীকে প্রভু কহে 'আপনার' ॥ ৫১ ॥

śivānandera bhāgya-sindhu ke pāibe pāra?
yāṅra saba goṣṭhīke prabhu kahe 'āpanāra'

SYNONYMS

śivānandera—of Śivānanda Sena; *bhāgya-sindhu*—the ocean of fortune; *ke*—who; *pāibe pāra*—can cross over; *yāṅra*—whose; *saba goṣṭhīke*—whole family; *prabhu*—Śrī Caitanya Mahāprabhu; *kahe*—says; *āpanāra*—His own.

TRANSLATION

No one can cross over the ocean of Śivānanda Sena's good fortune, for the Lord considered Śivānanda's whole family His own.

TEXT 52

তবে সব ভক্ত লঞা করিলা ভোজন।
গোবিন্দেরে আজ্ঞা দিলা করি' আচমন ॥ ৫২ ॥

tabe saba bhakta lañā karilā bhojana
govindere ājñā dilā kari' ācamana

SYNONYMS

tabe—then; *saba bhakta lañā*—with all the devotees; *karilā bhojana*—took lunch; *govindere*—unto Govinda; *ājñā dilā*—gave the order; *kari' ācamana*—after washing His hands and mouth.

TRANSLATION

The Lord ate lunch in the company of all the other devotees, and after washing His hands and mouth He gave an order to Govinda.

TEXT 53

"শিবানন্দের 'প্রকৃতি', পুত্র—যাবৎ এথায়।
আমার অবশেষ-পাত্র তারা যেন পায় ॥"৫৩ ॥

"śivānandera 'prakṛti', putra——yāvat ethāya
āmāra avaśeṣa-pātra tārā yena pāya"

SYNONYMS

śivānandera—of Śivānanda Sena; *prakṛti*—wife; *putra*—sons; *yāvat*—as long as; *ethāya*—here; *āmāra*—My; *avaśeṣa-pātra*—plate of the remnants of food; *tārā*—all of them; *yena*—must; *pāya*—get.

TRANSLATION

"As long as Śivānanda Sena's wife and children stay in Jagannātha Purī," He said, "they must be given the remnants of My food."

TEXT 54

নদীয়া-বাসী মোদক, তার নাম—'পরমেশ্বর'।
মোদক বেচে, প্রভুর বাটীর নিকট তার ঘর ॥ ৫৪ ॥

nadīyā-vāsī modaka, tāra nāma——'parameśvara'
modaka vece, prabhura vāṭīra nikaṭa tāra ghara

SYNONYMS

nadīyā-vāsī—inhabitant of the district of Nadia; *modaka*—one confectioner; *tāra nāma*—his name; *parameśvara*—Parameśvara; *modaka vece*—does the business of a confectioner; *prabhura*—of Śrī Caitanya Mahāprabhu; *vāṭīra nikaṭa*—near the house; *tāra ghara*—his house.

TRANSLATION

There was a resident of Nadia named Parameśvara, who was a confectioner living near the home of Śrī Caitanya Mahāprabhu.

TEXT 55

বালক-কালে প্রভু তার ঘরে বারবার যা'ন ।
দুগ্ধ, খণ্ড মোদক দেয়, প্রভু তাহা খা'ন ॥ ৫৫ ॥

bālaka-kāle prabhu tāra ghare bāra bāra yā'na
dugdha, khaṇḍa modaka deya, prabhu tāhā khā'na

SYNONYMS

bālaka-kāle—when He was a boy; *prabhu*—Śrī Caitanya Mahāprabhu; *tāra ghare*—at his house; *bāra bāra*—again and again; *yā'na*—used to go; *dugdha*—milk; *khaṇḍa*—sweetmeats; *modaka deya*—the confectioner used to give; *prabhu*—Lord Śrī Caitanya Mahāprabhu; *tāhā*—that; *khā'na*—used to eat.

TRANSLATION

When the Lord was a boy, He would visit the house of Parameśvara Modaka again and again. The confectioner would supply the Lord milk and sweetmeats, and the Lord would eat them.

TEXT 56

প্রভু-বিষয়ে স্নেহ তার বালক-কাল হৈতে ।
সে বৎসর সেহ আইল প্রভুরে দেখিতে ॥ ৫৬ ॥

prabhu-viṣaye sneha tāra bālaka-kāla haite
se vatsara seha āila prabhure dekhite

SYNONYMS

prabhu-viṣaye—in regard to Śrī Caitanya Mahāprabhu; *sneha*—affection; *tāra*—of Parameśvara Modaka; *bālaka-kāla haite*—since He was a boy; *se vatsara*—that year; *seha*—he also; *āila*—came; *prabhure dekhite*—to see the Lord.

TRANSLATION

Parameśvara Modaka had been affectionate toward the Lord since His childhood, and he was one of those who came that year to see the Lord at Jagannātha Purī.

TEXT 57

'পরমেশ্বরা মুঞি' বলি' দণ্ডবৎ কৈল ।
তারে দেখি' প্রভু প্রীতে তাহারে পুছিল ॥ ৫৭ ॥

'parameśvarā muñi' bali' daṇḍavat kaila
tāre dekhi' prabhu prīte tāhāre puchila

SYNONYMS

parameśvara—O Parameśvara; *kuśala hao*—be blessed; *bhāla haila*—it is very good; *āilā*—you have come; *mukundāra mātā*—the mother of Mukunda; *āsiyāche*—has come; *seha*—he; *prabhure kahilā*—informed the Lord.

TRANSLATION

When he offered his obeisances to the Lord, he said, "I am the same Parameśvara." Upon seeing him, the Lord asked him questions with great affection.

TEXT 58

'পরমেশ্বর কুশল হও, ভাল হৈল, আইলা' ।
'মুকুন্দার মাতা আসিয়াছে', সেহ প্রভুরে কহিলা ॥৫৮॥

'parameśvara kuśala hao, bhāla haila, āilā'
'mukundāra mātā āsiyāche', seha prabhure kahilā

SYNONYMS

parameśvara—O Parameśvara; *kuśula hao*—be blessed; *bhāla haila*—it is very good; *āilā*—you have come; *mukundāra mātā*—the mother of Mukunda; *āsiyāche*—has come; *seha*—he; *prabhure kahilā*—informed the Lord.

TRANSLATION

Śrī Caitanya Mahāprabhu said, "Parameśvara, may you be blessed. It is very good that you have come here." Parameśvara then informed the Lord, "Mukundāra Mātā has also come."

TEXT 59

মুকুন্দার মাতার নাম শুনি' প্রভু সঙ্কোচ হৈলা ।
তথাপি তাহার প্রীতে কিছু না বলিলা ॥ ৫৯ ॥

mukundāra mātāra nāma śuni' prabhu saṅkoca hailā
tathāpi tāhāra prīte kichu nā balilā

SYNONYMS

mukundāra mātāra—of the mother of Mukunda; *nāma*—name; *śuni'*—hearing; *prabhu*—Śrī Caitanya Mahāprabhu; *saṅkoca hailā*—felt some hesitation; *tathāpi*—still; *tāhāra*—of Parameśvara; *prīte*—out of affection; *kichu*—anything; *nā balilā*—did not say.

TRANSLATION

Hearing the name of Mukundāra Mātā, Lord Caitanya hesitated, but because of affection for Parameśvara, He did not say anything.

PURPORT

A *sannyāsī* is restricted from even hearing a woman's name, and Śrī Caitanya Mahāprabhu conducted Himself very strictly in His vow. Parameśvara informed the Lord that his wife, Mukundāra Mātā, had come with him. He should not have mentioned her, and therefore the Lord hesitated for a moment, but due to His affection for Parameśvara, He did not say anything. Śrī Caitanya Mahāprabhu had known Parameśvara Modaka since His childhood, and therefore Parameśvara did not think twice about informing the Lord of his wife's arrival.

TEXT 60

প্রশ্রয়-পাগল শুদ্ধ-বৈদগ্ধী না জানে ।
অন্তরে সুখী হৈলা প্রভু তার সেই গুণে ॥ ৬০ ॥

praśraya-pāgala śuddha-vaidagdhī nā jāne
antare sukhī hailā prabhu tāra sei guṇe

SYNONYMS

praśraya—due to indulgence; *pāgala*—foolish; *śuddha*—pure; *vaidagdhī*—etiquette; *nā jāne*—does not know; *antare*—within the heart; *sukhī hailā*—became very happy; *prabhu*—Śrī Caitanya Mahāprabhu; *tāra*—his; *sei guṇe*—by that attribute.

TRANSLATION

An intimate relationship sometimes makes a person overstep formal etiquette. Thus Parameśvara actually pleased the Lord in His heart by his simple and affectionate behavior.

PURPORT

Praśraya means affection, humility, faith, a demand for some special concession, or indulgence in such a concession. *Pāgala* means impudence, arrogance, and influence. *Vaidagdhī* means cunningness, humor, beauty, expertise, learning, tricky behavior, and indications.

TEXT 61

পূর্ব্ববৎ সবা লঞা গুণ্ডিচা-মার্জন ।
রথ-আগে পূর্ব্ববৎ করিলা নর্তন ॥ ৬১ ॥

pūrvavat sabā lañā guṇḍicā-mārjana
ratha-āge pūrvavat karilā nartana

SYNONYMS

pūrva-vat—as previously; *sabā*—all the devotees; *lañā*—taking; *guṇḍicā-mārjana*—the cleaning of the Guṇḍicā temple; *ratha-āge*—in front of the chariot; *pūrva-vat*—as previously; *karilā nartana*—danced.

TRANSLATION

All the devotees engaged in the cleansing ceremony of the Guṇḍicā temple and danced in front of the Ratha-yātrā chariot, just as they had done in the past.

TEXT 62

চাতুর্মাস্য সব যাত্রা কৈলা দরশন ।
মালিনীপ্রভৃতি প্রভুরে কৈলা নিমন্ত্রণ ॥ ৬২ ॥

cāturmāsya saba yātrā kailā daraśana
mālinī-prabhṛti prabhure kailā nimantraṇa

SYNONYMS

cāturmāsya—for four months; *saba yātrā*—all the festivals; *kailā daraśana*—saw; *mālinī-prabhṛti*—ladies like Mālinī, the wife of Śrīvāsa Ṭhākura; *prabhure*—unto Śrī Caitanya Mahāprabhu; *kailā nimantraṇa*—made invitations.

TRANSLATION

For four consecutive months, the devotees observed all the festivals. The wives, such as Mālinī, extended invitations for lunch to Śrī Caitanya Mahāprabhu.

TEXT 63

প্রভুর প্রিয় নানা দ্রব্য আনিয়াছে দেশ হৈতে ।
সেই ব্যঞ্জন করি' ভিক্ষা দেন ঘর-ভাতে ॥ ৬৩ ॥

prabhura priya nānā dravya āniyāche deśa haite
sei vyañjana kari' bhikṣā dena ghara-bhāte

SYNONYMS

prabhura—of Śrī Caitanya Mahāprabhu; *priya*—dear; *nānā dravya*—varieties of things; *āniyāche*—brought; *deśa haite*—from their country; *sei vyañjana kari'*—preparing those vegetables; *bhikṣā dena*—offer food; *ghara-bhāte*—cooking at home.

TRANSLATION

From Bengal the devotees had brought varieties of Bengali food that Śrī Caitanya Mahāprabhu liked. They also cooked various grains and vegetables in their homes and offered them to the Lord.

TEXT 64

দিনে নানা ক্রীড়া করে লঞা ভক্তগণ ।
রাত্র্যে কৃষ্ণ-বিচ্ছেদে প্রভু করেন রোদন ॥ ৬৪ ॥

dine nānā krīḍā kare lañā bhakta-gaṇa
rātrye kṛṣṇa-vicchede prabhu karena rodana

SYNONYMS

dine—during the day; *nānā*—various; *krīḍā kare*—performed pastimes; *lañā bhakta-gaṇa*—with His devotees; *rātrye*—at night; *kṛṣṇa-vicchede*—because of separation from Kṛṣṇa; *prabhu*—Śrī Caitanya Mahāprabhu; *karena rodana*—cries.

TRANSLATION

During the day, Śrī Caitanya Mahāprabhu engaged in various activities with His devotees, but at night He felt great separation from Kṛṣṇa and used to cry.

TEXT 65

এইমত নানা-লীলায় চাতুর্মাস্য গেল ।
গৌড়দেশে যাইতে তবে ভক্তে আজ্ঞা দিল ॥ ৬৫ ॥

ei-mata nānā-līlāya cāturmāsya gela
gauḍa-deśe yāite tabe bhakte ājñā dila

SYNONYMS

ei-mata—in this way; *nānā-līlāya*—in various pastimes; *cāturmāsya gela*—the four months of the rainy season passed; *gauḍa-deśe yāite*—to return to Bengal; *tabe*—at that time; *bhakte*—all the devotees; *ājñā dila*—Śrī Caitanya Mahāprabhu ordered.

TRANSLATION

In this way the Lord spent the four months of the rainy season in various pastimes, and then He ordered the Bengali devotees to return to their homes.

TEXT 66

সব ভক্ত করেন মহাপ্রভুর নিমন্ত্রণ ।
সর্বভক্তে কহেন প্রভু মধুর বচন ॥ ৬৬ ॥

saba bhakta karena mahāprabhura nimantraṇa
sarva-bhakte kahena prabhu madhura vacana

SYNONYMS

saba bhakta—all the devotees; *karena mahāprabhura nimantraṇa*—invite Śrī Caitanya Mahāprabhu to lunch; *sarva-bhakte*—to all the devotees; *kahena*—speaks; *prabhu*—Śrī Caitanya Mahāprabhu; *madhura vacana*—sweet words.

TRANSLATION

All the devotees from Bengal would regularly invite Śrī Caitanya Mahāprabhu for lunch, and the Lord would speak to them in very sweet words.

TEXT 67

"প্রতিবর্ষে আইস সবে আমারে দেখিতে ।
আসিতে যাইতে দুঃখ পাও বহুমতে ॥ ৬৭ ॥

"prati-varṣe āisa sabe āmāre dekhite
āsite yāite duḥkha pāo bahu-mate

SYNONYMS

prati-varṣe—every year; *āisa*—come; *sabe*—all of you; *āmāre dekhite*—to see Me; *āsite*—to come; *yāite*—to return; *duḥkha pāo*—you get much trouble; *bahu-mate*—in various ways.

TRANSLATION

"All of you come to see Me every year," the Lord said. "To come here and then return must certainly give you great trouble.

TEXT 68

তোমা-সবার দুঃখ জানি' চাহি নিষেধিতে ।
তোমা-সবার সঙ্গসুখে লোভ বাড়ে চিত্তে ॥ ৬৮ ॥

tomā-sabāra duḥkha jāni' cāhi niṣedhite
tomā-sabāra saṅga-sukhe lobha bāḍe citte

SYNONYMS

tomā-sabāra—of all of you; *duḥkha*—trouble; *jāni'*—understanding; *cāhi niṣedhite*—I want to stop this; *tomā-sabāra*—of all of you; *saṅga-sukhe*—for the happiness of association; *lobha*—desire; *bāḍe*—increases; *citte*—in My mind.

TRANSLATION

"I would like to forbid you to do this, but I enjoy your company so much that My desire for your association only increases.

TEXT 69

নিত্যানন্দে আজ্ঞা দিলুঁ গৌড়েতে রহিতে ।
আজ্ঞা লঙ্ঘি' আইলা, কি পারি বলিতে ? ৬৯ ॥

nityānande ājñā diluṅ gauḍete rahite
ājñā laṅghi' āilā, ki pāri balite?

SYNONYMS

nityānande—unto Śrī Nityānanda Prabhu; *ājñā diluṅ*—I ordered; *gauḍete rahite*—to stay in Bengal; *ājñā laṅghi'*—transgressing My order; *āilā*—He has come; *ki*—what; *pāri balite*—can I say.

TRANSLATION

"I ordered Śrī Nityānanda Prabhu not to leave Bengal, but He has transgressed My order and come to see Me. What can I say?

TEXT 70

আইলেন আচার্য-গোসাঞি মোরে কৃপা করি'।
প্রেম-ঋণে বদ্ধ আমি, শুধিতে না পারি ॥ ৭০ ॥

āilena ācārya-gosāñi more kṛpā kari'
prema-ṛṇe baddha āmi, śudhite nā pāri

SYNONYMS

āilena—has come; *ācārya-gosāñi*—Advaita Ācārya; *more*—to Me; *kṛpā kari'*—giving mercy; *prema*—of love; *ṛṇe*—by the debt; *baddha āmi*—I am bound; *śudhite*—to pay back; *nā pāri*—I am unable.

TRANSLATION

"Out of His causeless mercy upon Me, Advaita Ācārya has also come here. I am indebted to Him for His affectionate behavior. This debt is impossible for Me to liquidate.

TEXT 71

মোর লাগি' স্ত্রী-পুত্র-গৃহাদি ছাড়িয়া।
নানা দুর্গম পথ লঙ্ঘি' আইসেন ধাঞা ॥ ৭১ ॥

mora lāgi' strī-putra-gṛhādi chāḍiyā
nānā durgama patha laṅghi' āisena dhāñā

SYNONYMS

mora lāgi'—for Me; *strī*—wife; *putra*—sons; *gṛha-ādi*—home and so on; *chāḍiyā*—leaving aside; *nānā*—various; *durgama*—difficult; *patha*—paths; *laṅghi'*—crossing; *āisena dhāñā*—come here with great haste.

TRANSLATION

"All My devotees come here just for Me. Leaving aside their homes and families, they travel by very difficult paths to come here in great haste.

TEXT 72

আমি এই নীলাচলে রহি যে বসিয়া।
পরিশ্রম নাহি মোর তোমা সবার লাগিয়া ॥ ৭২ ॥

āmi ei nīlācale rahi ye vasiyā
pariśrama nāhi mora tomā sabāra lāgiyā

SYNONYMS

āmi—I; *ei*—this; *nīlācale*—at Jagannātha Purī; *rahi*—remain; *ye vasiyā*—sitting; *pariśrama nāhi mora*—I have no fatigue; *tomā sabāra lāgiyā*—due to all of you.

TRANSLATION

"There is no fatigue or trouble for Me, for I stay here at Nīlācala, Jagannātha Purī, and do not move at all. This is the favor of all of you.

TEXT 73

সন্ন্যাসী মানুষ মোর, নাহি কোন ধন ।
কি দিয়া তোমার ঋণ করিমু শোধন ? ৭৩ ॥

sannyāsī mānuṣa mora, nāhi kona dhana
ki diyā tomāra ṛṇa karimu śodhana?

SYNONYMS

sannyāsī mānuṣa—in the renounced order of life; *mora*—My; *nāhi*—there is not; *kona*—any; *dhana*—money; *ki*—what; *diyā*—giving; *tomāra ṛṇa*—the debt to you; *karimu śodhana*—shall I repay.

TRANSLATION

"I am a mendicant and have no money. How can I clear My debt for the favor you have shown Me?

TEXT 74

দেহমাত্র ধন তোমায় কৈলুঁ সমর্পণ ।
তাহাঁ বিকাই, যাহাঁ বেচিতে তোমার মন ॥" ৭৪ ॥

deha-mātra dhana tomāya kailuṅ samarpaṇa
tāhāṅ vikāi, yāhāṅ vecite tomāra mana"

SYNONYMS

deha—body; *mātra*—only; *dhana*—asset; *tomāya*—unto you; *kailuṅ samarpaṇa*—I have dedicated; *tāhāṅ*—there; *vikāi*—I sell; *yāhāṅ*—where; *vecite*—to sell; *tomāra mana*—your mind.

TRANSLATION

"I have only this body, and therefore I surrender it unto you. Now, if you wish, you may sell it anywhere you like. It is your property."

TEXT 75

প্রভুর বচনে সবার দ্রবীভূত মন ।
অঝোর-নয়নে সবে করেন ক্রন্দন ॥ ৭৫ ॥

prabhura vacane sabāra dravī-bhūta mana
ajhora-nayane sabe karena krandana

SYNONYMS

prabhura—of Śrī Caitanya Mahāprabhu; *vacane*—by the words; *sabāra*—of everyone; *dravī-bhūta*—melted; *mana*—hearts; *ajhora*—incessantly pouring tears; *nayane*—eyes; *sabe*—all; *karena krandana*—were crying.

TRANSLATION

When all the devotees heard these sweet words of Lord Śrī Caitanya Mahāprabhu, their hearts melted, and they began to shed incessant tears.

TEXT 76

প্রভু সবার গলা ধরি' করেন রোদন ।
কান্দিতে কান্দিতে সবায় কৈলা আলিঙ্গন ॥ ৭৬ ॥

prabhu sabāra galā dhari' karena rodana
kāndite kāndite sabāya kailā āliṅgana

SYNONYMS

prabhu—Śrī Caitanya Mahāprabhu; *sabāra*—of all of them; *galā*—necks; *dhari'*—catching; *karena rodana*—began to cry; *kāndite kāndite*—crying and crying; *sabāya*—all of them; *kailā āliṅgana*—He embraced.

TRANSLATION

Catching hold of His devotees, the Lord embraced them all and began to cry and cry.

TEXT 77

সবাই রহিল, কেহ চলিতে নারিল ।
আর দিন পাঁচ-সাত এইমতে গেল ॥ ৭৭ ॥

sabāi rahila, keha calite nārila
āra dina pāṅca-sāta ei-mate gela

SYNONYMS

sabāi rahila—all of them stayed; *keha calite nārila*—no one could move; *āra*—further; *dina pāṅca-sāta*—five to seven days; *ei-mate*—in this way; *gela*—passed.

TRANSLATION

Unable to leave, everyone remained there, and five to seven more days thus passed by.

TEXT 78

অদ্বৈত অবধূত কিছু কহে প্রভু-পায় ।
"সহজে তোমার গুণে জগৎ বিকায় ॥ ৭৮ ॥

advaita avadhūta kichu kahe prabhu-pāya
"sahaje tomāra guṇe jagat vikāya

SYNONYMS

advaita—Advaita Prahbu; *avadhūta*—Nityānanda Prabhu; *kichu*—something; *kahe*—said; *prabhu-pāya*—at the lotus feet of Śrī Caitanya Mahāprabhu; *sahaje*—naturally; *tomāra*—Your; *guṇe*—because of transcendental attributes; *jagat vikāya*—the whole world is obligated to You.

TRANSLATION

Advaita Prabhu and Lord Nityānanda Prabhu submitted these words at the lotus feet of the Lord: "The entire world is naturally obligated to You for Your transcendental attributes.

TEXT 79

আবার তাতে বান্ধ'—ঐছে কৃপা-বাক্য-ডোরে ।
তোমা ছাড়ি' কেবা কাহাঁ যাইবারে পারে ?" ৭৯ ॥

ābāra tāte bāndha'——aiche kṛpā-vākya-ḍore
tomā chāḍi' kebā kāhāṅ yāibāre pāre?"

SYNONYMS

ābāra—again; *tāte*—by that; *bāndha'*—You bind; *aiche*—such; *kṛpā*—merciful; *vākya*—of words; *ḍore*—by the rope; *tomā chāḍi'*—leaving You; *kebā*—who; *kāhāṅ*—anywhere; *yāibāre pāre*—can go.

TRANSLATION

"Yet You bind Your devotees again with Your sweet words. Under these circumstances, who can go anywhere?"

TEXT 80

তবে প্রভু সবাকারে প্রবোধ করিয়া।
সবারে বিদায় দিলা সুস্থির হঞা॥ ৮০ ॥

tabe prabhu sabākāre prabodha kariyā
sabāre vidāya dilā susthira hañā

SYNONYMS

tabe—thereafter; *prabhu*—Śrī Caitanya Mahāprabhu; *sabākāre*—all of them; *prabodha kariyā*—pacifying; *sabāre*—to every one of them; *vidāya dilā*—bade farewell; *su-sthira hañā*—being in a peaceful condition.

TRANSLATION

Then Śrī Caitanya Mahāprabhu peacefully calmed them all and bade each of them farewell.

TEXT 81

নিত্যানন্দে কহিলা—"তুমি না আসিহ বারবার।
তথাই আমার সঙ্গ হইবে তোমার॥" ৮১ ॥

nityānande kahilā——"tumi nā āsiha bāra-bāra
tathāi āmāra saṅga ha-ibe tomāra"

SYNONYMS

nityānande—unto Nityānanda Prabhu; *kahilā*—said; *tumi*—You; *nā āsiha*—do not come; *bāra-bāra*—again and again; *tathāi*—there (in Bengal); *āmāra*—My; *saṅga*—association; *ha-ibe*—there will be; *tomāra*—Your.

TRANSLATION

The Lord specifically advised Nityānanda Prabhu, "You should not come here again and again. You will have My association in Bengal."

TEXT 82

চলে সব ভক্তগণ রোদন করিয়া।
মহাপ্রভু রহিলা ঘরে বিষণ্ণ হঞা॥ ৮২ ॥

cale saba bhakta-gaṇa rodana kariyā
mahāprabhu rahilā ghare viṣaṇṇa hañā

SYNONYMS

cale—proceed; *saba*—all; *bhakta-gaṇa*—the devotees; *rodana kariyā*—crying; *mahāprabhu*—Śrī Caitanya Mahāprabhu; *rahilā*—remained; *ghare*—at His place; *viṣaṇṇa hañā*—being very morose.

TRANSLATION

The devotees of Śrī Caitanya Mahāprabhu began their journey crying, while the Lord remained morosely at His residence.

TEXT 83

নিজ-কৃপাগুণে প্রভু বান্ধিলা সবারে ।
মহাপ্রভুর কৃপা-ঋণ কে শোধিতে পারে ? ৮৩ ॥

nija-kṛpā-guṇe prabhu bāndhilā sabāre
mahāprabhura kṛpā-ṛṇa ke śodhite pāre?

SYNONYMS

nija—own; *kṛpā-guṇe*—by the attribute of mercy; *prabhu*—Śrī Caitanya Mahāprabhu; *bāndhilā*—bound; *sabāre*—everyone; *mahāprabhura*—of Śrī Caitanya Mahāprabhu; *kṛpā-ṛṇa*—debt for the mercy; *ke*—who; *śodhite pāre*—can repay.

TRANSLATION

The Lord bound everyone by His transcendental mercy. Who can repay his debt for the mercy of Śrī Caitanya Mahāprabhu?

TEXT 84

যারে যৈছে নাচায় প্রভু স্বতন্ত্র ঈশ্বর ।
তাতে তাঁরে ছাড়ি' লোক যায় দেশান্তর ॥ ৮৪ ॥

yāre yaiche nācāya prabhu svatantra īśvara
tāte tāṅre chāḍi' loka yāya deśāntara

SYNONYMS

yāre—whomever; *yaiche*—as; *nācāya*—causes to dance; *prabhu*—Śrī Caitanya Mahāprabhu; *svatantra īśvara*—the fully independent Personality of Godhead;

tāte—therefore; *tāṅre*—Him; *chāḍi'*—leaving; *loka*—people; *yāya*—go; *deśa-antara*—to different parts of the country.

TRANSLATION

Śrī Caitanya Mahāprabhu is the fully independent Personality of Godhead and makes everyone dance as He likes. Leaving His company, therefore, all the devotees returned to their homes in different parts of the country.

TEXT 85

কাষ্ঠের পুতলী যেন কুহকে নাচায় ।
ঈশ্বর-চরিত্র কিছু বুঝন না যায় ॥ ৮৫ ॥

kāṣṭhera putalī yena kuhake nācāya
īśvara-caritra kichu bujhana nā yāya

SYNONYMS

kāṣṭhera—made of wood; *putalī*—doll; *yena*—as; *kuhake*—a magician; *nācāya*—causes to dance; *īśvara-caritra*—the characteristic of the Supreme Personality of Godhead; *kichu bujhana nā yāya*—no one can understand.

TRANSLATION

As a wooden doll dances to the will of a puppeteer, everything is accomplished by the will of the Lord. Who can understand the characteristics of the Supreme Personality of Godhead?

TEXT 86

পূর্ববর্ষে জগদানন্দ 'আই' দেখিবারে ।
প্রভু-আজ্ঞা লঞা আইলা নদীয়া-নগরে ॥ ৮৬ ॥

pūrva-varṣe jagadānanda 'āi' dekhibāre
prabhu-ājñā lañā āilā nadīyā-nagare

SYNONYMS

pūrva-varṣe—in the previous year; *jagadānanda*—Jagadānanda Paṇḍita; *āi*—Śacīmātā; *dekhibāre*—to see; *prabhu-ājñā lañā*—taking the permission of Śrī Caitanya Mahāprabhu; *āilā*—came; *nadīyā-nagare*—to the city of Nadia.

TRANSLATION

The previous year, Jagadānanda Paṇḍita, following the Lord's order, had returned to the city of Nadia to see Śacīmātā.

TEXT 87

আইর চরণ যাই' করিলা বন্দন।
জগন্নাথের বস্ত্র-প্রসাদ কৈলা নিবেদন ॥ ৮৭ ॥

āira caraṇa yāi' karilā vandana
jagannāthera vastra-prasāda kailā nivedana

SYNONYMS

āira—of Śacīmātā; *caraṇa*—to the lotus feet; *yāi'*—going; *karilā vandana*—offered prayers; *jagannāthera*—of Lord Jagannātha; *vastra-prasāda*—cloth and *prasāda; kailā nivedana*—offered.

TRANSLATION

When he arrived, he offered prayers at her lotus feet and then offered her the cloth and prasāda of Lord Jagannātha.

TEXT 88

প্রভুর নামে মাতারে দণ্ডবৎ কৈলা।
প্রভুর বিনতি-স্তুতি মাতারে কহিলা ॥ ৮৮ ॥

prabhura nāme mātāre daṇḍavat kailā
prabhura vinati-stuti mātāre kahilā

SYNONYMS

prabhura nāme—in the name of Śrī Caitanya Mahāprabhu; *mātāre*—to His mother; *daṇḍavat kailā*—he offered obeisances; *prabhura*—of Śrī Caitanya Mahāprabhu; *vinati-stuti*—very submissive prayers; *mātāre*—to His mother; *kahilā*—he informed.

TRANSLATION

He offered obeisances to Śacīmātā in the name of Lord Caitanya Mahāprabhu and informed her of all the Lord's submissive prayers to her.

TEXT 89

জগদানন্দে পাঞা মাতা আনন্দিত মনে।
তেঁহো প্রভুর কথা কহে, শুনে রাত্রি-দিনে ॥ ৮৯ ॥

jagadānande pāñā mātā ānandita mane
teṅho prabhura kathā kahe, śune rātri-dine

SYNONYMS

jagadānande—Jagadānanda; *pāñā*—getting; *mātā*—Śacīmātā; *ānandita mane*—in great satisfaction; *teṅho*—he; *prabhura kathā*—the pastimes of Śrī Caitanya Mahāprabhu; *kahe*—speaks; *śune*—listens; *rātri-dine*—day and night.

TRANSLATION

Jagadānanda's coming pleased mother Śacī very much. As he talked of Lord Caitanya Mahāprabhu, she listened day and night.

TEXT 90

জগদানন্দ কহে,—"মাতা, কোন কোন দিনে ।
তোমার এথা আসি' প্রভু করেন ভোজনে ॥ ৯০ ॥

jagadānanda kahe,——"mātā, kona kona dine
tomāra ethā āsi' prabhu karena bhojane

SYNONYMS

jagadānanda kahe—Jagadānanda said; *mātā*—mother; *kona kona dine*—sometimes; *tomāra ethā āsi'*—coming here to your place; *prabhu*—the Lord; *karena bhojane*—accepts food.

TRANSLATION

Jagadānanda Paṇḍita said, "My dear mother, sometimes the Lord comes here and eats all the food you have offered.

TEXT 91

ভোজন করিয়া কহে আনন্দিত হঞা ।
মাতা আজি খাওয়াইলা আকণ্ঠ পূরিয়া ॥ ৯১ ॥

bhojana kariyā kahe ānandita hañā
mātā āji khāoyāilā ākaṇṭha pūriyā

SYNONYMS

bhojana kariyā—after eating; *kahe*—says; *ānandita hañā*—being very pleased; *mātā*—mother; *āji*—today; *khāoyāilā*—fed; *ākaṇṭha*—up to the neck; *pūriyā*—filling.

TRANSLATION

"After eating the food, the Lord says, 'Today, mother has fed Me up to My neck.

TEXT 92

আমি যাই' ভোজন করি—মাতা নাহি জানে।
সাক্ষাতে খাই আমি' তেঁহো 'স্বপ্ন' হেন মানে ॥"৯২॥

āmi yāi' bhojana kari——mātā nāhi jāne
sākṣāte khāi āmi' teṅho 'svapna' hena māne"

SYNONYMS

āmi—I; *yāi'*—going; *bhojana kari*—eat; *mātā*—mother; *nāhi jāne*—cannot understand; *sākṣāte*—directly; *khāi āmi'*—I eat; *teṅho*—she; *svapna*—a dream; *hena*—as; *māne*—thinks.

TRANSLATION

" 'I go there and eat the food My mother offers, but she cannot understand that I am eating it directly. She thinks that this is a dream.' "

TEXT 93

মাতা কহে,—"কত রান্ধি উত্তম ব্যঞ্জন।
নিমাঞি ইহাঁ খায়,—ইচ্ছা হয় মোর মন ॥ ৯৩ ॥

mātā kahe,——"kata rāndhi uttama vyañjana
nimāñi ihāṅ khāya,——icchā haya mora mana

SYNONYMS

mātā kahe—mother said; *kata*—how many; *rāndhi*—I cook; *uttama vyañjana*—first-class vegetables; *nimāñi*—Nimāi; *ihāṅ*—here; *khāya*—may eat; *icchā*—desire; *haya*—is; *mora mana*—my mind.

TRANSLATION

Śacīmātā said, "I wish Nimāi would eat all the nice vegetables I cook. That is my desire.

TEXT 94

নিমাঞি খাঞাছে,—ঐছে হয় মোর মন।
পাছে জ্ঞান হয়,—মুঞি দেখিনু 'স্বপন' ॥" ৯৪ ॥

nimāñi khāñāche,——aiche haya mora mana
pāche jñāna haya,——muñi dekhinu 'svapana' "

SYNONYMS

nimāñi khāñāche—Nimāi has eaten; *aiche*—such; *haya*—is; *mora*—my; *mana*—mind; *pāche*—afterwards; *jñāna haya*—I think; *muñi*—I; *dekhinu svapana*—saw a dream.

TRANSLATION

"Sometimes I think that Nimāi has eaten them, but afterwards I think that I was only dreaming."

TEXT 95

এইমত জগদানন্দ শচীমাতা-সনে ।
চৈতন্যের সুখ-কথা কহে রাত্রি-দিনে ॥ ৯৫ ॥

ei-mata jagadānanda śacīmātā-sane
caitanyera sukha-kathā kahe rātri-dine

SYNONYMS

ei-mata—in this way; *jagadānanda*—Jagadānanda Paṇḍita; *śacīmātā-sane*—with mother Śacī; *caitanyera*—of Śrī Caitanya Mahāprabhu; *sukha-kathā*—words of happiness; *kahe*—says; *rātri-dine*—day and night.

TRANSLATION

In this way, Jagadānanda Paṇḍita and mother Śacī talked day and night about the happiness of Śrī Caitanya Mahāprabhu.

TEXT 96

নদীয়ার ভক্তগণে সবারে মিলিলা ।
জগদানন্দে পাঞা সবে আনন্দিত হৈলা ॥ ৯৬ ॥

nadīyāra bhakta-gaṇe sabāre mililā
jagadānande pāñā sabe ānandita hailā

SYNONYMS

nadīyāra—of Nadia, or Navadvīpa; *bhakta-gaṇe*—the devotees; *sabāre*—all; *mililā*—met; *jagadānande*—Jagadānanda; *pāñā*—getting; *sabe*—everyone; *ānandita hailā*—became very happy.

TRANSLATION

Jagadānanda Paṇḍita met all the other devotees in Nadia. They were all very happy to have him present.

TEXT 97

আচার্য মিলিতে তবে গেলা জগদানন্দ ।
জগদানন্দে পাঞা হৈল আচার্য আনন্দ ॥ ৯৭ ॥

ācārya milite tabe gelā jagadānanda
jagadānande pāñā haila ācārya ānanda

SYNONYMS

ācārya milite—to meet Advaita Ācārya; *tabe*—thereafter; *gelā*—went; *jagadānanda*—Jagadānanda; *jagadānande pāñā*—getting Jagadānanda; *haila*—became; *ācārya*—Advaita Ācārya; *ānanda*—very happy.

TRANSLATION

Jagadānanda Paṇḍita thereafter went to meet Advaita Ācārya, who also was very happy to have him.

TEXT 98

বাসুদেব, মুরারি-গুপ্ত জগদানন্দে পাঞা ।
আনন্দে রাখিলা ঘরে, না দেন ছাড়িয়া ॥ ৯৮ ॥

vāsudeva, murāri-gupta jagadānande pāñā
ānande rākhilā ghare, nā dena chāḍiyā

SYNONYMS

vāsudeva—Vāsudeva; *murāri-gupta*—Murāri Gupta; *jagadānande pāñā*—getting Jagadānanda; *ānande*—in great happiness; *rākhilā*—kept; *ghare*—at home; *nā dena chāḍiyā*—did not allow to go out.

TRANSLATION

Vāsudeva Datta and Murāri Gupta were so pleased to see Jagadānanda Paṇḍita that they kept him at their homes and would not allow him to leave.

TEXT 99

চৈতন্যের মর্মকথা শুনে তাঁর মুখে ।
আপনা পাসরে সবে চৈতন্য-কথা-সুখে ॥ ৯৯ ॥

caitanyera marma-kathā śune tāṅra mukhe
āpanā pāsare sabe caitanya-kathā-sukhe

SYNONYMS

caitanyera—of Lord Caitanya Mahāprabhu; *marma-kathā*—confidential talks; *śune*—they hear; *tāṅra mukhe*—through his mouth; *āpanā pāsare*—forget themselves; *sabe*—all of them; *caitanya-kathā-sukhe*—in the happiness of talks of Lord Caitanya.

TRANSLATION

They heard confidential narrations about Śrī Caitanya Mahāprabhu from the mouth of Jagadānanda Paṇḍita and forgot themselves in the great happiness of hearing about the Lord.

TEXT 100

জগদানন্দ মিলিতে যায় যেই ভক্ত-ঘরে ।
সেই সেই ভক্ত সুখে আপনা পাসরে ॥ ১০০ ॥

jagadānanda milite yāya yei bhakta-ghare
sei sei bhakta sukhe āpanā pāsare

SYNONYMS

jagadānanda—Jagadānanda Paṇḍita; *milite*—to meet; *yāya*—goes; *yei*—which; *bhakta-ghare*—to a devotee's house; *sei sei*—that; *bhakta*—devotee; *sukhe*—in happiness; *āpanā pāsare*—forgets himself.

TRANSLATION

Whenever Jagadānanda Paṇḍita went to visit a devotee's house, that devotee immediately forgot himself in great happiness.

TEXT 101

চৈতন্যের প্রেমপাত্র জগদানন্দ ধন্য ।
যারে মিলে সেই মানে,—'পাইলুঁ চৈতন্য' ॥ ১০১ ॥

caitanyera prema-pātra jagadānanda dhanya
yāre mile sei māne,——'pāiluṅ caitanya'

SYNONYMS

caitanyera—of Śrī Caitanya Mahāprabhu; *prema-pātra*—recipient of affection; *jagadānanda*—Jagadānanda Paṇḍita; *dhanya*—glorious; *yāre mile*—whomever he meets; *sei māne*—he understands; *pāiluṅ caitanya*—I have gotten Lord Caitanya.

TRANSLATION

All glories to Jagadānanda Paṇḍita! He is so favored by Śrī Caitanya Mahāprabhu that anyone who meets him thinks, "Now I have gotten the association of Śrī Caitanya Mahāprabhu directly."

TEXT 102

শিবানন্দসেন-গৃহে যাঞা রহিলা ।
'চন্দনাদি' তৈল তাহাঁ একমাত্রা কৈলা ॥ ১০২ ॥

śivānanda-sena-gṛhe yāñā rahilā
'candanādi' taila tāhāṅ eka-mātrā kailā

SYNONYMS

śivānanda-sena-gṛhe—to the house of Śivānanda Sena; *yāñā*—going; *rahilā*—remained; *candana-ādi taila*—oil distilled from sandalwood and other substances; *tāhāṅ*—there; *eka-mātrā*—one *mātrā* (sixteen seers, or *seras*); *kailā*—prepared.

TRANSLATION

Jagadānanda Paṇḍita stayed at Śivānanda Sena's house for some time, and they prepared about sixteen seers of scented sandalwood oil.

TEXT 103

সুগন্ধি করিয়া তৈল গাগরী ভরিয়া ।
নীলাচলে লঞা আইলা যতন করিয়া ॥ ১০৩ ॥

sugandhi kariyā taila gāgarī bhariyā
nīlācale lañā āilā yatana kariyā

SYNONYMS

su-gandhi kariyā—making aromatic; *taila*—oil; *gāgarī*—a big pot; *bhariyā*—filling; *nīlācale*—to Jagannātha Purī; *lañā*—taking; *āilā*—came; *yatana kariyā*—with great care.

TRANSLATION

They filled a large earthen pot with the aromatic oil, and with great care Jagadānanda Paṇḍita brought it to Nīlācala, Jagannātha Purī.

TEXT 104

গোবিন্দের ঠাঞি তৈল ধরিয়া রাখিলা ।
"প্রভু-অঙ্গে দিহ' তৈল" গোবিন্দে কহিলা ॥ ১০৪ ॥

govindera ṭhāñi taila dhariyā rākhilā
"prabhu-aṅge diha' taila" govinde kahilā

SYNONYMS

govindera ṭhāñi—in the care of Govinda; *taila*—the oil; *dhariyā rākhilā*—was kept; *prabhu-aṅge*—over the body of Śrī Caitanya Mahāprabhu; *diha'*—put; *taila*—oil; *govinde kahilā*—he advised Govinda.

TRANSLATION

This oil was placed in the care of Govinda, and Jagadānanda requested him, "Please rub this oil on the body of the Lord."

TEXT 105

তবে প্রভু-ঠাঞি গোবিন্দ কৈল নিবেদন ।
"জগদানন্দ চন্দনাদি-তৈল আনিয়াছেন ॥ ১০৫ ॥

tabe prabhu-ṭhāñi govinda kaila nivedana
"jagadānanda candanādi-taila āniyāchena

SYNONYMS

tabe—thereafter; *prabhu-ṭhāñi*—before Lord Śrī Caitanya Mahāprabhu; *govinda*—Govinda; *kaila nivedana*—submitted; *jagadānanda*—Jagadānanda Paṇḍita; *candana-ādi-taila*—scented sandalwood oil; *āniyāchena*-has brought.

TRANSLATION

Govinda therefore told Śrī Caitanya Mahāprabhu, "Jagadānanda Paṇḍita has brought some scented sandalwood oil.

TEXT 106

তাঁর ইচ্ছা,—প্রভু অল্প মস্তকে লাগায় ।
পিত্ত-বায়ু-ব্যাধি-প্রকোপ শান্ত হঞা যায় ॥ ১০৬ ॥

tāṅra icchā,——prabhu alpa mastake lāgāya
pitta-vāyu-vyādhi-prakopa śānta hañā yāya

SYNONYMS

tāṅra icchā—his desire; *prabhu*—Śrī Caitanya Mahāprabhu; *alpa*—very little; *mastake lāgāya*—smears over the head; *pitta-vāyu-vyādhi*—of blood pressure due to bile and air; *prakopa*—severity; *śānta hañā yāya*—will be decreased.

TRANSLATION

"It is his desire that Your Lordship apply a little of this oil on Your head so that blood pressure due to bile and air will be considerably diminished.

TEXT 107

এক-কলস সুগন্ধি তৈল গৌড়েতে করিয়া ।
ইহাঁ আনিয়াছে বহু যতন করিয়া ॥" ১০৭ ॥

eka-kalasa sugandhi taila gauḍete kariyā
ihāṅ āniyāche bahu yatana kariyā"

SYNONYMS

eka-kalasa—one big full jug; *su-gandhi taila*—scented oil; *gauḍete kariyā*—manufacturing in Bengal; *ihāṅ*—here; *āniyāche*—has brought; *bahu yatana kariyā*—with great care.

TRANSLATION

"He prepared a large jug of it in Bengal, and with great care he has brought it here."

TEXT 108

প্রভু কহে,—"সন্ন্যাসীর নাহি তৈলে অধিকার ।
তাহাতে সুগন্ধি তৈল,—পরম ধিক্কার ! ১০৮ ॥

prabhu kahe,—"sannyāsīra nāhi taile adhikāra
tāhāte sugandhi taila,—parama dhikkāra!

SYNONYMS

prabhu kahe—Śrī Caitanya Mahāprabhu replied; *sannyāsīra*—for a *sannyāsī; nāhi*—there is not; *taile*—with oil; *adhikāra*—use; *tāhāte*—over and above this; *su-gandhi taila*—perfumed oil; *parama dhik-kāra*—immediately to be rejected.

TRANSLATION

The Lord replied, "A sannyāsī has no use for oil, especially perfumed oil such as this. Take it out immediately."

PURPORT

According to Raghunandana Bhaṭṭācārya, the spokesman for the *smārta* regulative principles:

prātaḥ-snāne vrate śrāddhe
dvādaśyāṁ grahaṇe tathā
madya-lepa-samaṁ tailaṁ
tasmāt tailaṁ vivarjayet

"If one who has taken a vow smears oil on his body while bathing in the morning, while observing a ritualistic ceremony like the *śrāddha* ceremony, or on *dvādaśī* day, he may as well pour wine over his body. Therefore, oil should be rejected." This word *vrata* (vow) is sometimes understood to refer to the *sannyāsa-vrata*. Raghunandana Bhaṭṭācārya has also said in his book *Tithi-tattva:*

ghṛtaṁ ca sārṣapaṁ tailaṁ
yat tailaṁ puṣpa-vāsitam
aduṣṭaṁ pakva-tailaṁ ca
tailābhyaṅge ca nityaśaḥ

This means that clarified butter (ghee), mustard oil, floral oil and boiled oil may be used only by *gṛhasthas,* householders.

TEXT 109

জগন্নাথে দেহ' তৈল,—দীপ যেন জ্বলে ।
তার পরিশ্রম হৈব পরম-সফলে ॥" ১০৯ ॥

jagannāthe deha' taila,——dīpa yena jvale
tāra pariśrama haiba parama-saphale"

SYNONYMS

jagannāthe—unto Lord Jagannātha; *deha'*—deliver ; *taila*—oil; *dīpa*—lamps; *yena*—so; *jvale*—burn; *tāra pariśrama*—his labor; *haiba*—will become; *parama-saphale*—completely successful.

TRANSLATION

"Deliver this oil to the temple of Jagannātha, where it may be burned in the lamps. In this way, Jagadānanda's labor to manufacture the oil will be perfectly successful."

TEXT 110

এই কথা গোবিন্দ জগদানন্দেরে কহিল।
মৌন করি' রহিল পণ্ডিত, কিছু না কহিল ॥ ১১০ ॥

ei kathā govinda jagadānandere kahila
mauna kari' rahila paṇḍita, kichu nā kahila

SYNONYMS

ei kathā—this message; *govinda*—Govinda; *jagadānandere kahila*—informed Jagadānanda; *mauna kari'*—keeping silent; *rahila*—remained; *paṇḍita*—Jagadānanda Paṇḍita; *kichu*—anything; *nā kahila*—did not reply.

TRANSLATION

When Govinda informed Jagadānanda Paṇḍita of this message, Jagadānanda remained silent, not saying even a word.

TEXT 111

দিন দশ গেলে গোবিন্দ জানাইল আরবার।
পণ্ডিতের ইচ্ছা,—'তৈল প্রভু করে অঙ্গীকার' ॥১১১॥

dina daśa gele govinda jānāila āra-bāra
paṇḍitera icchā,——'taila prabhu kare aṅgīkāra'

SYNONYMS

dina daśa gele—when ten days passed; *govinda*—Govinda; *jānāila*—informed; *āra-bāra*—again; *paṇḍitera icchā*—the desire of Jagadānanda Paṇḍita; *taila*—oil; *prabhu*—Śrī Caitanya Mahāprabhu; *kare aṅgīkāra*—accepts.

TRANSLATION

When ten days had passed, Govinda again told Śrī Caitanya Mahāprabhu, "It is the desire of Jagadānanda Paṇḍita that Your Lordship accept the oil."

TEXT 112

শুনি' প্রভু কহে কিছু সক্রোধ বচন।
মর্দনিয়া এক রাখ করিতে মর্দন ! ১১২ ॥

śuni' prabhu kahe kichu sakrodha vacana
mardaniyā eka rākha karite mardana!

SYNONYMS

śuni'—hearing; *prabhu*—Śrī Caitanya Mahāprabhu; *kahe*—says; *kichu*—some; *sa-krodha vacana*—angry words; *mardaniyā*—masseur; *eka*—one; *rākha*—keep; *karite mardana*—to give massages.

TRANSLATION

When the Lord heard this, He angrily said, "Why not keep a masseur to massage Me?

TEXT 113

এই সুখ লাগি' আমি করিলুঁ সন্ন্যাস !
আমার 'সর্বনাশ'—তোমা-সবার 'পরিহাস' ॥ ১১৩ ॥

ei sukha lāgi' āmi kariluṅ sannyāsa!
āmāra 'sarva-nāśa'——tomā-sabāra 'parihāsa'

SYNONYMS

ei—this; *sukha*—happiness; *lāgi'*—for; *āmi*—I; *kariluṅ sannyāsa*—have taken to the renounced order; *āmāra sarva-nāśa*—My ruination; *tomā-sabāra*—of all of you; *parihāsa*—joking.

TRANSLATION

"Have I taken sannyāsa for such happiness? Accepting this oil would bring My ruination, and all of you would laugh.

PURPORT

Śrī Caitanya Mahāprabhu declared Himself a strict *sannyāsī*. A *sannyāsī* is not supposed to take help from anyone. Retaining a masseur to give Him massages would indicate His dependence on others. Śrī Caitanya Mahāprabhu wanted to follow very strictly the principle of not accepting anyone's help for His bodily comfort.

TEXT 114

পথে যাইতে তৈলগন্ধ মোর যেই পাবে ।
'দারী সন্ন্যাসী' করি' আমারে কহিবে ॥ ১১৪ ॥

pathe yāite taila-gandha mora yei pābe
'dārī sannyāsī' kari' āmāre kahibe

SYNONYMS

pathe yāite—while passing on the road; *taila-gandha*—the scent of the oil; *mora*—My; *yei pābe*—anyone who smells; *dārī sannyāsī*—a tantric *sannyāsī* who keeps women for sense gratification; *kari'*—as; *āmāre kahibe*—they will speak of Me.

TRANSLATION

"If someone passing on the road smelled this oil on My head, he would think Me a dārī sannyāsī, a tantric sannyāsī who keeps women."

TEXT 115

শুনি প্রভুর বাক্য গোবিন্দ মৌন করিলা।
প্রাতঃকালে জগদানন্দ প্রভু-স্থানে আইলা ॥ ১১৫ ॥

śuni prabhura vākya govinda mauna karilā
prātaḥ-kāle jagadānanda prabhu-sthāne āilā

SYNONYMS

śuni—hearing; *prabhura vākya*—the statement of Śrī Caitanya Mahāprabhu; *govinda*—Govinda; *mauna karilā*—remained silent; *prātaḥ-kāle*—in the morning; *jagadānanda*—Jagadānanda Paṇḍita; *prabhu-sthāne*—to Śrī Caitanya Mahāprabhu; *āilā*—came.

TRANSLATION

Hearing these words of Śrī Caitanya Mahāprabhu, Govinda remained silent. The next morning, Jagadānanda went to see the Lord.

TEXT 116

প্রভু কহে,—"পণ্ডিত, তৈল আনিলা গৌড় হইতে।
আমি ত' সন্ন্যাসী,—তৈল না পারি লইতে ॥১১৬॥

prabhu kahe,——"paṇḍita, taila ānilā gauḍa ha-ite
āmi ta' sannyāsī,——taila nā pāri la-ite

SYNONYMS

prabhu kahe—Śrī Caitanya Mahāprabhu said; *paṇḍita*—My dear Paṇḍita; *taila*—oil; *ānilā*—you have brought; *gauḍa ha-ite*—from Bengal; *āmi*—I; *ta'*—but; *sannyāsī*—a *sannyāsī*; *taila*—oil; *nā pāri la-ite*—I cannot accept.

TRANSLATION

Śrī Caitanya Mahāprabhu said to Jagadānanda Paṇḍita, "My dear Paṇḍita, you have brought Me some oil from Bengal, but since I am in the renounced order, I cannot accept it.

TEXT 117

জগন্নাথে দেহ' লঞা দীপ যেন জ্বলে ।
তোমার সকল শ্রম হইবে সফলে ॥" ১১৭ ॥

jagannāthe deha' lañā dīpa yena jvale
tomāra sakala śrama ha-ibe saphale"

SYNONYMS

jagannāthe—unto Lord Jagannātha; *deha'*—deliver; *lañā*—taking; *dīpa*—lamps; *yena*—so that; *jvale*—burn; *tomāra*—your; *sakala*—all; *śrama*—labor; *ha-ibe sa-phale*—will be fruitful.

TRANSLATION

"Deliver the oil to the temple of Jagannātha so that it may be burned in the lamps. Thus your labor in preparing the oil will be fruitful."

TEXT 118

পণ্ডিত কহে,—'কে তোমারে কহে মিথ্যা বাণী ।
আমি গৌড় হৈতে তৈল কভু নাহি আনি ॥' ১১৮ ॥

paṇḍita kahe,——'ke tomāre kahe mithyā vāṇī
āmi gauḍa haite taila kabhu nāhi āni'

SYNONYMS

paṇḍita kahe—Jagadānanda Paṇḍita said; *ke*—who; *tomāre*—unto You; *kahe*—says; *mithyā vāṇī*—false stories; *āmi*—I; *gauḍa haite*—from Bengal; *taila*—oil; *kabhu nāhi āni'*—never brought.

TRANSLATION

Jagadānanda Paṇḍita replied, "Who tells You all these false stories? I never brought any oil from Bengal."

TEXT 119

এত বলি' ঘর হৈতে তৈল-কলস লঞা।
প্রভুর আগে আঙ্গিনাতে ফেলিলা ভাঙ্গিয়া॥ ১১৯॥

eta bali' ghara haite taila-kalasa lañā
prabhura āge āṅgināte phelilā bhāṅgiyā

SYNONYMS

eta bali'—saying this; *ghara haite*—from the room; *taila-kalasa*—the jugful of oil; *lañā*—taking; *prabhura āge*—in front of Śrī Caitanya Mahāprabhu; *āṅgināte*—in the courtyard; *phelilā*—threw; *bhāṅgiyā*—breaking.

TRANSLATION

After saying this, Jagadānanda Paṇḍita took the jug of oil from the room and threw it down before Śrī Caitanya Mahāprabhu in the courtyard and broke it.

TEXT 120

তৈল ভাঙ্গি' সেই পথে নিজ-ঘর গিয়া।
শুইয়া রহিলা ঘরে কপাট খিলিয়া॥ ১২০॥

taila bhāṅgi' sei pathe nija-ghara giyā
śuiyā rahilā ghare kapāṭa khiliyā

SYNONYMS

taila bhāṅgi'—breaking the pot of oil; *sei*—he; *pathe*—by the path; *nija-ghara*—to his room; *giyā*—going; *śuiyā rahilā*—lay down; *ghare*—in the room; *kapāṭa*—the door; *khiliyā*—bolting closed.

TRANSLATION

After breaking the jug, Jagadānanda Paṇḍita returned to his residence, bolted the door and lay down.

TEXT 121

তৃতীয় দিবসে প্রভু তাঁর দ্বারে যাঞা।
'উঠহ' পণ্ডিত'— করি' কহেন ডাকিয়া॥ ১২১॥

tṛtīya divase prabhu tāṅra dvāre yāñā
'uṭhaha' paṇḍita'——kari' kahena ḍākiyā

SYNONYMS

tṛtīya divase—on the third day; *prabhu*—Śrī Caitanya Mahāprabhu; *tāṅra*—of Jagadānanda Paṇḍita; *dvāre*—to the door; *yāñā*—going; *uṭhaha'*—please get up; *paṇḍita*—My dear Jagadānanda Paṇḍita; *kari'*—saying; *kahena*—said; *ḍākiyā*—calling.

TRANSLATION

Three days later, Śrī Caitanya Mahāprabhu went to the door of his room and said, "My dear Jagadānanda Paṇḍita, please get up.

TEXT 122

'আজি ভিক্ষা দিবা আমায় করিয়া রন্ধনে ।
মধ্যাহ্নে আসিব, এবে যাই দরশনে ॥' ১২২ ॥

'āji bhikṣā dibā āmāya kariyā randhane
madhyāhne āsiba, ebe yāi daraśane'

SYNONYMS

āji—today; *bhikṣā dibā*—give lunch; *āmāya*—unto Me; *kariyā randhane*—cooking; *madhyāhne āsiba*—I shall come at noon; *ebe*—now; *yāi daraśane*—I am going to see Lord Jagannātha.

TRANSLATION

"I want you personally to cook My lunch today. I am going now to see the Lord in the temple. I shall return at noon."

TEXT 123

এত বলি' প্রভু গেলা, পণ্ডিত উঠিলা ।
স্নান করি' নানা ব্যঞ্জন রন্ধন করিলা ॥ ১২৩ ॥

eta bali' prabhu gelā, paṇḍita uṭhilā
snāna kari' nānā vyañjana randhana karilā

SYNONYMS

eta bali'—saying this; *prabhu gelā*—Śrī Caitanya Mahāprabhu left; *paṇḍita uṭhilā*—Jagadānanda Paṇḍita got up; *snāna kari'*—taking his bath; *nānā*—various; *vyañjana*—vegetables; *randhana karilā*—cooked.

TRANSLATION

After Śrī Caitanya Mahāprabhu said this and left, Jagadānanda Paṇḍita got up from his bed, bathed, and began to cook varieties of vegetables.

TEXT 124

মধ্যাহ্ন করিয়া প্রভু আইলা ভোজনে।
পাদ প্রক্ষালন করি' দিলেন আসনে ॥ ১২৪ ॥

madhyāhna kariyā prabhu āilā bhojane
pāda prakṣālana kari' dilena āsane

SYNONYMS

madhyāhna kariyā—after finishing his noon ritualistic ceremonies; *prabhu*—Śrī Caitanya Mahāprabhu; *āilā*—came; *bhojane*—to take lunch; *pāda prakṣālana kari'*—after washing His feet; *dilena āsane*—offered a sitting place.

TRANSLATION

After finishing His noontime ritualistic duties, the Lord arrived for lunch. Jagadānanda Paṇḍita washed the Lord's feet and gave the Lord a sitting place.

TEXT 125

সঘৃত শাল্যন্ন কলাপাতে স্তূপ কৈলা।
কলার ডোঙ্গা ভরি' ব্যঞ্জন চৌদিকে ধরিলা ॥ ১২৫ ॥

saghṛta śālyanna kalā-pāte stūpa kailā
kalāra ḍoṅgā bhari' vyañjana caudike dharilā

SYNONYMS

sa-ghṛta—mixed with ghee; *śāli-anna*—very fine rice; *kalā-pāte*—on a banana leaf; *stūpa kailā*—stacked; *kalāra ḍoṅgā*—pots made of the bark of a banana tree; *bhari'*—filling; *vyañjana*—vegetables; *cau-dike*—all around; *dharilā*—placed.

TRANSLATION

He had cooked fine rice, mixed it with ghee and piled it high on a banana leaf. There were also varieties of vegetables, placed all around in pots made of banana tree bark.

TEXT 126

অন্ন-ব্যঞ্জনোপরি তুলসী-মঞ্জরী।
জগন্নাথের পিঠা-পানা আগে আনে ধরি' ॥ ১২৬ ॥

anna-vyañjanopari tulasī-mañjarī
jagannāthera piṭhā-pānā āge āne dhari'

SYNONYMS

anna—rice; *vyañjana*—vegetables; *upari*—on; *tulasī-mañjarī*—flowers of *tulasī; jagannāthera*—of Lord Jagannātha; *piṭhā-pānā*—cakes and sweet rice; *āge*—in front; *āne dhari'*—brings.

TRANSLATION

On the rice and vegetables were tulasī flowers, and in front of the Lord were cakes, sweet rice and other prasāda of Jagannātha.

TEXT 127

প্রভু কহে,—"দ্বিতীয়-পাতে বাড়' অন্ন-ব্যঞ্জন।
তোমায় আমায় আজি একত্র করিব ভোজন ॥১২৭॥

prabhu kahe,—"dvitīya-pāte bāḍa' anna-vyañjana
tomāya āmāya āji ekatra kariba bhojana

SYNONYMS

prabhu kahe—Śrī Caitanya Mahāprabhu said; *dvitīya-pāte*—on a second leaf; *bāḍa'*—deliver; *anna-vyañjana*—cooked rice and vegetables; *tomāya āmāya*—both you and I; *āji*—today; *ekatra*—together; *kariba bhojana*—will take lunch.

TRANSLATION

The Lord said, "Spread another leaf with a helping of rice and vegetables so that today you and I may take lunch together."

TEXT 128

হস্ত তুলি' রহেন প্রভু, না করেন ভোজন।
তবে পণ্ডিত কহেন কিছু সপ্রেম বচন ॥ ১২৮ ॥

hasta tuli' rahena prabhu, nā karena bhojana
tabe paṇḍita kahena kichu saprema vacana

SYNONYMS

hasta tuli'—raising His hands; *rahena prabhu*—Śrī Caitanya Mahāprabhu remained; *nā karena bhojana*—did not eat; *tabe*—at that time; *paṇḍita kahena*—Jagadānanda said; *kichu*—some; *sa-prema vacana*—words with great affection and love.

TRANSLATION

Śrī Caitanya Mahāprabhu kept His hands raised and would not accept the prasāda until Jagadānanda Paṇḍita, with great affection and love, spoke the following words.

TEXT 129

"আপনে প্রসাদ লহ, পাছে মুঞি লইমু ।
তোমার আগ্রহ আমি কেমনে খণ্ডিমু ?" ১২৯ ॥

"āpane prasāda laha, pāche muñi la-imu
tomāra āgraha āmi kemane khaṇḍimu?"

SYNONYMS

āpane—Yourself; *prasāda laha*—take *prasāda; pāche*—afterwards; *muñi la-imu*—I shall take; *tomāra*—Your; *āgraha*—insistence; *āmi*—I; *kemane*—how; *khaṇḍimu*—shall disobey.

TRANSLATION

"Please first take prasāda Yourself, and I shall eat later. I shall not refuse Your request."

TEXT 130

তবে মহাপ্রভু সুখে ভোজনে বসিলা ।
ব্যঞ্জনের স্বাদ পাঞা কহিতে লাগিলা ॥ ১৩০ ॥

tabe mahāprabhu sukhe bhojane vasilā
vyañjanera svāda pāñā kahite lāgilā

SYNONYMS

tabe—thereafter; *mahāprabhu*—Śrī Caitanya Mahāprabhu; *sukhe*—in happiness; *bhojane vasilā*—sat to take His food; *vyañjanera svāda*—the taste of the vegetables; *pāñā*—getting; *kahite lāgilā*—began to say.

TRANSLATION

In great happiness, Śrī Caitanya Mahāprabhu then accepted the lunch. When He had tasted the vegetables, He again began to speak.

TEXT 131

"ক্রোধাবেশের পাকের হয় ঐছে স্বাদ !
এই ত' জানিয়ে তোমায় কৃষ্ণের 'প্রসাদ' ॥ ১৩১ ॥

"krodhāveśera pākera haya aiche svāda!
ei ta' jāniye tomāya kṛṣṇera 'prasāda'

SYNONYMS

krodha-āveśera—in an angry mood; *pākera*—of cooking; *haya*—is; *aiche*—such; *svāda*—taste; *ei ta'*—for this reason; *jāniye*—I can understand; *tomāya*—unto you; *kṛṣṇera prasāda*—the mercy of Kṛṣṇa.

TRANSLATION

"Even when you cook in an angry mood," He said, "the food is very tasteful. This shows how pleased Kṛṣṇa is with you.

TEXT 132

আপনে খাইবে কৃষ্ণ, তাহার লাগিয়া।
তোমার হস্তে পাক করায় উত্তম করিয়া ॥ ১৩২ ॥

āpane khāibe kṛṣṇa, tāhāra lāgiyā
tomāra haste pāka karāya uttama kariyā

SYNONYMS

āpane—personally; *khāibe*—will eat; *kṛṣṇa*—Lord Kṛṣṇa; *tāhāra lāgiyā*—for that reason; *tomāra haste*—by your hands; *pāka karāya*—causes to cook; *uttama kariyā*—so nicely.

TRANSLATION

"Because He will personally eat the food, Kṛṣṇa makes you cook so nicely.

TEXT 133

ঐছে অমৃত-অন্ন কৃষ্ণে কর সমর্পণ।
তোমার ভাগ্যের সীমা কে করে বর্ণন ?" ১৩৩ ॥

aiche amṛta-anna kṛṣṇe kara samarpaṇa
tomāra bhāgyera sīmā ke kare varṇana?"

SYNONYMS

aiche—such; *amṛta-anna*—nectarean rice; *kṛṣṇe*—unto Lord Kṛṣṇa; *kara samarpaṇa*—you offer; *tomāra*—your; *bhāgyera*—of fortune; *sīmā*—limit; *ke*—who; *kare varṇana*—can describe.

TRANSLATION

"You offer such nectarean rice to Kṛṣṇa. Who can estimate the limit of your fortune?"

TEXT 134

পণ্ডিত কহে,—"যে খাইবে, সেই পাককর্তা ।
আমি-সব—কেবলমাত্র সামগ্রী-আহর্তা ॥" ১৩৪ ॥

paṇḍita kahe,——"ye khāibe, sei pāka-kartā
āmi-saba——kevala-mātra sāmagrī-āhartā"

SYNONYMS

paṇḍita kahe—the Paṇḍita said; *ye khāibe*—He who will eat; *sei*—He; *pāka-kartā*—the cook; *āmi-saba*—as far as I am concerned; *kevala-mātra*—only; *sāmagrī*—of ingredients; *āhartā*—collector.

TRANSLATION

Jagadānanda Paṇḍita replied, "He who will eat has cooked this. As far as I am concerned, I simply collect the ingredients."

TEXT 135

পুনঃ পুনঃ পণ্ডিত নানা ব্যঞ্জন পরিবেশে ।
ভয়ে কিছু না বলেন প্রভু, খায়েন হরিষে ॥ ১৩৫ ॥

punaḥ punaḥ paṇḍita nānā vyañjana pariveśe
bhaye kichu nā balena prabhu, khāyena hariṣe

SYNONYMS

punaḥ punaḥ—again and again; *paṇḍita*—Jagadānanda Paṇḍita; *nānā vyañjana*—various vegetables; *pariveśe*—administered; *bhaye*—out of fear; *kichu*—anything; *nā balena*—does not speak; *prabhu*—Śrī Caitanya Mahāprabhu; *khāyena*—eats; *hariṣe*—very happily.

TRANSLATION

Jagadānanda Paṇḍita continued to offer the Lord varieties of vegetables. Out of fear, the Lord said nothing, but continued eating happily.

TEXT 136

আগ্রহ করিয়া পণ্ডিত করাইলা ভোজন।
আর দিন হৈতে ভোজন হৈল দশগুণ ॥ ১৩৬ ॥

āgraha kariyā paṇḍita karāilā bhojana
āra dina haite bhojana haila daśa-guṇa

SYNONYMS

āgraha kariyā—with great eagerness; *paṇḍita*—Jagadānanda Paṇḍita; *karāilā bhojana*—fed; *āra dina*—other days; *haite*—than; *bhojana*—the eating; *haila*—was; *daśa-guṇa*—ten times greater.

TRANSLATION

Jagadānanda Paṇḍita eagerly forced the Lord to eat so much that He ate ten times more than on other days.

TEXT 137

বারবার প্রভু উঠিতে করেন মন।
সেইকালে পণ্ডিত পরিবেশে ব্যঞ্জন ॥ ১৩৭ ॥

bāra-bāra prabhu uṭhite karena mana
sei-kāle paṇḍita pariveśe vyañjana

SYNONYMS

bāra-bāra—again and again; *prabhu*—Śrī Caitanya Mahāprabhu; *uṭhite*—to get up; *karena mana*—desires; *sei-kāle*—at that time; *paṇḍita*—Jagadānanda Paṇḍita; *pariveśe*—gives; *vyañjana*—vegetables.

TRANSLATION

Again and again when the Lord wished to get up, Jagadānanda Paṇḍita would feed Him more vegetables.

TEXT 138

কিছু বলিতে নারেন প্রভু, খায়েন তরাসে।
না খাইলে জগদানন্দ করিবে উপবাসে ॥ ১৩৮ ॥

kichu balite nārena prabhu, khāyena tarāse
nā khāile jagadānanda karibe upavāse

SYNONYMS

kichu—anything; *balite nārena*—could not say; *prabhu*—Śrī Caitanya Mahāprabhu; *khāyena*—eats; *tarāse*—out of fear; *nā khāile*—if He did not eat; *jagadānanda*—Jagadānanda Paṇḍita; *karibe upavāse*—would fast.

TRANSLATION

Śrī Caitanya Mahāprabhu dared not forbid him to feed Him more. He just continued eating, fearful that Jagadānanda would fast if He stopped.

TEXT 139

তবে প্রভু কহেন করি' বিনয়-সম্মান ।
'দশগুণ খাওয়াইলা এবে কর সমাধান' ॥ ১৩৯ ॥

tabe prabhu kahena kari' vinaya-sammāna
'daśa-guṇa khāoyāilā ebe kara samādhāna'

SYNONYMS

tabe—at that time; *prabhu*—Śrī Caitanya Mahāprabhu; *kahena*—says; *kari'*—making; *vinaya-sammāna*—submissive respect; *daśa-guṇa*—ten times more; *khāoyāilā*—you have made to eat; *ebe*—now; *kara samādhāna*—please stop.

TRANSLATION

At last the Lord respectfully submitted, "My dear Jagadānanda, you have already made Me eat ten times more than I am used to. Now, please stop."

TEXT 140

তবে মহাপ্রভু উঠি' কৈলা আচমন ।
পণ্ডিত আনিল, মুখবাস, মাল্য, চন্দন ॥ ১৪০ ॥

tabe mahāprabhu uṭhi' kailā ācamana
paṇḍita ānila, mukhavāsa, mālya, candana

SYNONYMS

tabe—at that time; *mahāprabhu*—Śrī Caitanya Mahāprabhu; *uṭhi'*—getting up; *kailā ācamana*—performed washing of the hands and mouth; *paṇḍita*—Jagadānanda Paṇḍita; *ānila*—brought; *mukha-vāsa*—spices; *mālya*—flower garland; *candana*—sandalwood pulp.

TRANSLATION

Śrī Caitanya Mahāprabhu stood up and washed His hands and mouth, while Jagadānanda Paṇḍita brought spices, a garland, and sandalwood pulp.

TEXT 141

চন্দনাদি লঞা প্রভু বসিলা সেই স্থানে ।
'আমার আগে আজি তুমি করহ ভোজনে' ॥১৪১॥

candanādi lañā prabhu vasilā sei sthāne
'āmāra āge āji tumi karaha bhojane'

SYNONYMS

candana-ādi lañā—accepting the sandalwood pulp and other items; *prabhu*—Śrī Caitanya Mahāprabhu; *vasilā*—sat down; *sei sthāne*—at that place; *āmāra āge*— in front of Me; *āji*—now; *tumi*—you; *karaha*—perform; *bhojane*—eating.

TRANSLATION

Accepting the sandalwood pulp and garland, the Lord sat down and said, "Now, in front of Me, you must eat."

TEXT 142

পণ্ডিত কহে,—"প্রভু যাই' করুন বিশ্রাম ।
মুই, এবে লইব প্রসাদ করি' সমাধান ॥ ১৪২ ॥

paṇḍita kahe,——"prabhu yāi' karuna viśrāma
mui, ebe la-iba prasāda kari' samādhāna

SYNONYMS

paṇḍita kahe—Jagadānanda Paṇḍita said; *prabhu*—my Lord; *yāi'*—going; *karuna viśrāma*—take rest; *mui*—I; *ebe*—now; *la-iba prasāda*—shall take *prasāda; kari' samādhāna*—after arranging.

TRANSLATION

Jagadānanda replied, "My Lord, You go take rest. I shall take prasāda after I finish making some arrangements.

TEXT 143

রস্থইর কার্য কৈরাছে রামাই, রঘুনাথ ।
ইঁহা সবায় দিতে চাহি কিছু ব্যঞ্জন-ভাত ॥" ১৪৩ ॥

rasuira kārya kairāche rāmāi, raghunātha
iṅhā sabāya dite cāhi kichu vyañjana-bhāta"

SYNONYMS

rasuira—of cooking; *kārya*—the work; *kairāche*—have done; *rāmāi*—Rāmāi; *raghunātha*—Raghunātha Bhaṭṭa; *iṅhā*—to them; *sabāya*—all; *dite cāhi*—I want to give; *kichu*—some; *vyañjana-bhāta*—rice and vegetables.

TRANSLATION

"Rāmāi Paṇḍita and Raghunātha Bhaṭṭa did the cooking, and I want to give them some rice and vegetables."

TEXT 144

প্রভু কহেন,—"গোবিন্দ, তুমি ইহাঁই রহিবা ।
পণ্ডিত ভোজন কৈলে, আমারে কহিবা ॥" ১৪৪ ॥

prabhu kahena,—"govinda, tumi ihāṅi rahibā
paṇḍita bhojana kaile, āmāre kahibā"

SYNONYMS

prabhu kahena—Śrī Caitanya Mahāprabhu said; *govinda*—Govinda; *tumi*—you; *ihāṅi rahibā*—will stay here; *paṇḍita*—Jagadānanda Paṇḍita; *bhojana kaile*—after he has taken his meal; *āmāre kahibā*—you should inform Me.

TRANSLATION

Śrī Caitanya Mahāprabhu then told Govinda, "You remain here. When the Paṇḍita has taken his food, come inform Me.

TEXT 145

এত কহি' মহাপ্রভু করিলা গমন ।
গোবিন্দেরে পণ্ডিত কিছু কহেন বচন ॥ ১৪৫ ॥

eta kahi' mahāprabhu karilā gamana
govindere paṇḍita kichu kahena vacana

SYNONYMS

eta kahi'—saying this; *mahāprabhu*—Śrī Caitanya Mahāprabhu; *karilā gamana*—left; *govindere*—unto Govinda; *paṇḍita*—Jagadānanda Paṇḍita; *kichu*—some; *kahena*—said; *vacana*—words.

TRANSLATION

After Śrī Caitanya Mahāprabhu had said this and left, Jagadānanda Paṇḍita spoke to Govinda.

TEXT 146

"তুমি শীঘ্র যাহ করিতে পাদসম্বাহনে ।
কহিহ,—'পণ্ডিত এবে বসিল ভোজনে' ॥১৪৬॥

"tumi śīghra yāha karite pāda-samvāhane
kahiha,——'paṇḍita ebe vasila bhojane'

SYNONYMS

tumi—you; *śīghra*—hastily; *yāha*—go; *karite*—to perform; *pāda-samvāhane*—massaging the feet; *kahiha*—say; *paṇḍita*—Jagadānanda Paṇḍita; *ebe*—just now; *vasila bhojane*—sat down to eat.

TRANSLATION

"Go quickly and massage the Lord's feet," he said. "You may tell Him, 'The Paṇḍita has just sat down to take his meal.'

TEXT 147

তোমারে প্রভুর 'শেষ' রাখিমু ধরিয়া ।
প্রভু নিদ্রা গেলে, তুমি খাইহ আসিয়া ॥" ১৪৭ ॥

tomāre prabhura 'śeṣa' rākhimu dhariyā
prabhu nidrā gele, tumi khāiha āsiyā"

SYNONYMS

tomāre—for you; *prabhura*—of Śrī Caitanya Mahāprabhu; *śeṣa*—remnants of food; *rākhimu*—I shall keep; *dhariyā*—taking; *prabhu nidrā gele*—when Śrī Caitanya Mahāprabhu is asleep; *tumi*—you; *khāiha āsiyā*—come and eat.

TRANSLATION

"I shall keep some remnants of the Lord's food for you. When He is asleep, come and take your portion."

TEXT 148

রামাই, নন্দাই, আর গোবিন্দ, রঘুনাথ ।
সবারে বাঁটিয়া দিলা প্রভুর ব্যঞ্জন-ভাত ॥ ১৪৮ ॥

rāmāi, nandāi āra govinda, raghunātha
sabāre bāṅṭiyā dilā prabhura vyañjana-bhāta

SYNONYMS

rāmāi—Rāmāi Paṇḍita; *nandāi*—Nandāi; *āra*—and; *govinda*—Govinda; *raghunātha*—Raghunātha Bhaṭṭa; *sabāre*—for all of them; *bāṅṭiyā dilā*—distributed; *prabhura*—of Śrī Caitanya Mahāprabhu; *vyañjana-bhāta*—vegetables and rice.

TRANSLATION

Jagadānanda Paṇḍita thus distributed remnants of the Lord's food to Rāmāi, Nandāi, Govinda and Raghunātha Bhaṭṭa.

TEXT 149

আপনে প্রভুর 'শেষ' করিলা ভোজন ।
তবে গোবিন্দেরে প্রভু পাঠাইলা পুনঃ ॥ ১৪৯ ॥

āpane prabhura 'śeṣa' karilā bhojana
tabe govindere prabhu pāṭhāilā punaḥ

SYNONYMS

āpane—personally; *prabhura*—of Śrī Caitanya Mahāprabhu; *śeṣa*—remnants of food; *karilā bhojana*—ate; *tabe*—at that time; *govindere*—Govinda; *prabhu*—Śrī Caitanya Mahāprabhu; *pāṭhāilā*—sent; *punaḥ*—again.

TRANSLATION

He also personally ate the remnants of food left by Śrī Caitanya Mahāprabhu. Then the Lord again sent Govinda.

TEXT 150

"দেখ,—জগদানন্দ প্রসাদ পায় কি না পায় ।
শীঘ্র আসি' সমাচার কহিবে আমায় ॥" ১৫০ ॥

"dekha,——jagadānanda prasāda pāya ki nā pāya
śīghra āsi' samācāra kahibe āmāya"

SYNONYMS

dekha—see; *jagadānanda*—Jagadānanda Paṇḍita; *prasāda*—*prasāda; pāya*—gets; *ki*—or; *nā*—not; *pāya*—gets; *śīghra āsi'*—coming hastily; *samācāra*—the news; *kahibe*—inform; *āmāya*—to Me.

TRANSLATION

The Lord told him, "Go see whether Jagadānanda Paṇḍita is eating. Then quickly return and let Me know."

TEXT 151

গোবিন্দ আসি' দেখি' কহিল পণ্ডিতের ভোজন ।
তবে মহাপ্রভু স্বস্ত্যে করিল শয়ন ॥ ১৫১ ॥

govinda āsi' dekhi' kahila paṇḍitera bhojana
tabe mahāprabhu svastye karila śayana

SYNONYMS

govinda—Govinda; *āsi'*—coming; *dekhi'*—seeing; *kahila*—informed; *paṇḍitera bhojana*—the eating of Jagadānanda Paṇḍita; *tabe*—thereupon; *mahāprabhu*—Śrī Caitanya Mahāprabhu; *svastye*—in peace; *karila śayana*—went to sleep.

TRANSLATION

Seeing that Jagadānanda Paṇḍita was indeed eating, Govinda informed the Lord, who then became peaceful and went to sleep.

TEXT 152

জগদানন্দে-প্রভুতে প্রেম চলে এইমতে ।
সত্যভামা-কৃষ্ণে যৈছে শুনি ভাগবতে ॥ ১৫২ ॥

jagadānande-prabhute prema cale ei-mate
satyabhāmā-kṛṣṇe yaiche śuni bhāgavate

SYNONYMS

jagadānande-prabhute—between Jagadānanda Paṇḍita and the Lord; *prema*—affection; *cale*—goes on; *ei-mate*—in this way; *satyabhāmā-kṛṣṇe*—between Satyabhāmā and Kṛṣṇa; *yaiche*—as; *śuni*—we learn; *bhāgavate*—in the *Śrīmad-Bhāgavatam.*

TRANSLATION

The affectionate loving exchanges between Jagadānanda Paṇḍita and Lord Śrī Caitanya Mahāprabhu continued in this manner, exactly like the exchanges between Satyabhāmā and Lord Kṛṣṇa related in Śrīmad-Bhāgavatam.

TEXT 153

জগদানন্দের সৌভাগ্যের কে কহিবে সীমা ?
জগদানন্দের সৌভাগ্যের তেঁহ সে উপমা ॥ ১৫৩ ॥

jagadānandera saubhāgyera ke kahibe sīmā?
jagadānandera saubhāgyera teṅha se upamā

SYNONYMS

jagadānandera—of Jagadānanda Paṇḍita; *saubhāgyera*—of the fortune; *ke*—who; *kahibe*—shall speak; *sīmā*—the limit; *jagadānandera*—of Jagadānanda; *saubhāgyera*—of the fortune; *teṅha*—he; *se*—the; *upamā*—example.

TRANSLATION

Who can estimate the limit of Jagadānanda Paṇḍita's fortune? He himself is the example of his own great fortune.

TEXT 154

জগদানন্দের 'প্রেমবিবর্ত' শুনে যেই জন ।
প্রেমের 'স্বরূপ' জানে, পায় প্রেমধন ॥ ১৫৪ ॥

jagadānandera 'prema-vivarta' śune yei jana
premera 'svarūpa' jāne, pāya prema-dhana

SYNONYMS

jagadānandera—of Jagadānanda; *prema-vivarta*—loving exchange; *śune*—hears; *yei jana*—any person who; *premera*—of love; *svarūpa*—identity; *jāne*—he knows; *pāya*—gets; *prema-dhana*—the wealth of ecstatic love of Kṛṣṇa.

TRANSLATION

Anyone who hears about the loving exchanges between Jagadānanda Paṇḍita and Śrī Caitanya Mahāprabhu, or who reads Jagadānanda's book Prema-vivarta, can understand what love is. Moreover, he achieves ecstatic love of Kṛṣṇa.

PURPORT

The word *vivarta* means accepting something to be the opposite of what it appears. Here, Jagadānanda Paṇḍita appeared very angry, but this anger was a manifestation of his great love for Śrī Caitanya Mahāprabhu. *Prema-vivarta* is also the name of a book written by Jagadānanda Paṇḍita. Therefore the author of *Caitanya-caritāmṛta,* Kṛṣṇadāsa Kavirāja Gosvāmī, uses the words *prema-vivarta* to refer to one who reads the book or hears about Jagadānanda Paṇḍita's relationships with Śrī Caitanya Mahāprabhu. In either case, such a person very soon achieves love of Kṛṣṇa.

TEXT 155

শ্রীরূপ-রঘুনাথ-পদে যার আশ ।
চৈতন্যচরিতামৃত কহে কৃষ্ণদাস ॥ ১৫৫ ॥

śrī-rūpa-raghunātha-pade yāra āśa
caitanya-caritāmṛta kahe kṛṣṇadāsa

SYNONYMS

śrī-rūpa—Śrīla Rūpa Gosvāmī; *raghunātha*—Śrīla Raghunātha dāsa Gosvāmī; *pade*—at the lotus feet; *yāra*—whose; *āśa*—expectation; *caitanya-caritāmṛta*—the book named *Caitanya-caritāmṛta; kahe*—describes; *kṛṣṇadāsa*—Śrīla Kṛṣṇadāsa Kavirāja Gosvāmī.

TRANSLATION

Praying at the lotus feet of Śrī Rūpa and Śrī Raghunātha, always desiring their mercy, I, Kṛṣṇadāsa, narrate Śrī Caitanya-caritāmṛta, following in their footsteps.

Thus end the Bhaktivedanta purports to the Śrī Caitanya-caritāmṛta, Antya-līlā, *Twelfth Chapter, describing Jagadānanda Paṇḍita's loving dealings with Śrī Caitanya Mahāprabhu.*

CHAPTER 13

Pastimes with Jagadānanda Paṇḍita and Raghunātha Bhaṭṭa Gosvāmī

Śrīla Bhaktivinoda Ṭhākura gives the following summary of the Thirteenth Chapter in his *Amṛta-pravāha-bhāṣya.* Thinking Śrī Caitanya Mahaprabhu to be uncomfortable sleeping on bark of plantain trees, Jagadānanda made a pillow and quilt for Him. The Lord, however, did not accept them. Then Svarūpa Dāmodara Gosvāmī made another pillow and quilt from finely shredded plantain leaves, and after strongly objecting, the Lord accepted them. With the permission of Śrī Caitanya Mahāprabhu, Jagadānanda Paṇḍita went to Vṛndāvana, where he discussed many devotional subjects with Sanātana Gosvāmī. There was also a discussion about Mukunda Sarasvatī's garment. When Jagadānanda returned to Jagannātha Purī, he presented Śrī Caitanya Mahāprabhu some gifts from Sanātana Gosvāmī, and the incident of the *pīlu* fruit took place.

Once, Śrī Caitanya Mahāprabhu became ecstatic upon hearing the songs of a *deva-dāsī.* Unaware of who was singing, He ran toward her through thorny bushes, but when Govinda informed the Lord that it was a woman singing, He immediately stopped. By this incident, Śrī Caitanya Mahāprabhu instructed everyone that *sannyāsīs* and Vaiṣṇavas should not hear women singing.

When Raghunātha Bhaṭṭa Gosvāmī left Vārāṇasī on his way to Jagannātha Purī after completing his education, he met Rāmadāsa Viśvāsa Paṇḍita. Viśvāsa Paṇḍita was very proud of his education, and being an impersonalist, he was not well received by Śrī Caitanya Mahāprabhu. A partial study of the life of Raghunātha Bhaṭṭa Gosvāmī comprises the end of this chapter.

TEXT 1

কৃষ্ণবিচ্ছেদজাতার্ত্যা ক্ষীণে চাপি মনস্তনূ ।
দধাতে ফুল্লতাং ভাবৈর্যস্য তং গৌরমাশ্রয়ে ॥ ১ ॥

kṛṣṇa-viccheda-jātārtyā
kṣīṇe cāpi manas-tanū
dadhāte phullatāṁ bhāvair
yasya taṁ gauram āśraye

SYNONYMS

kṛṣṇa-viccheda—by separation from Kṛṣṇa; *jāta*—produced; *ārtyā*—by the pain; *kṣīṇe*—thin, exhausted; *cā*—and; *api*—although; *manaḥ*—mind; *tanū*—and body; *dadhāte*—assumes; *phullatām*—developed state; *bhāvaiḥ*—by ecstatic emotions; *yasya*—of whom; *tam*—unto Him; *gauram*—Śrī Caitanya Mahāprabhu; *āśraye*—I take shelter.

TRANSLATION

Let me take shelter at the lotus feet of Lord Gauracandra. His mind became exhausted and His body very thin from the pain of separation from Kṛṣṇa, but when He felt ecstatic love for the Lord, He again became fully developed.

TEXT 2

জয় জয় শ্রীচৈতন্য জয় নিত্যানন্দ ।
জয়াদ্বৈতচন্দ্র জয় গৌরভক্তবৃন্দ ॥ ২ ॥

jaya jaya śrī-caitanya jaya nityānanda
jayādvaita-candra jaya gaura-bhakta-vṛnda

SYNONYMS

jaya jaya—all glories; *śrī-caitanya*—to Lord Śrī Caitanya Mahāprabhu; *jaya*—all glories; *nityānanda*—to Lord Nityānanda; *jaya*—all glories; *advaita-candra*—to Advaita Ācārya; *jaya*—all glories; *gaura-bhakta-vṛnda*—to the devotees of Lord Śrī Caitanya Mahāprabhu.

TRANSLATION

All glories to Śrī Caitanya Mahāprabhu! All glories to Nityānanda Prabhu! All glories to Advaita Ācārya! And all glories to the devotees of the Lord!

TEXT 3

হেনমতে মহাপ্রভু জগদানন্দ-সঙ্গে ।
নানামতে আস্বাদয় প্রেমের তরঙ্গে ॥ ৩ ॥

hena-mate mahāprabhu jagadānanda-saṅge
nānā-mate āsvādaya premera taraṅge

SYNONYMS

hena-mate—in this way; *mahāprabhu*—Śrī Caitanya Mahāprabhu; *jagadānanda-saṅge*—in the company of Jagadānanda Paṇḍita; *nānā-mate*—in various ways; *āsvādaya*—tastes; *premera taraṅge*—the waves of spiritual loving affairs.

TRANSLATION

In the company of Jagadānanda Paṇḍita, Śrī Caitanya Mahāprabhu would taste various transcendental relationships of pure love.

TEXT 4

কৃষ্ণবিচ্ছেদে দুঃখে ক্ষীণ মন-কায় ।
ভাবাবেশে প্রভু কভু প্রফুল্লিত হয় ॥ ৪ ॥

kṛṣṇa-vicchede duḥkhe kṣīṇa mana-kāya
bhāvāveśe prabhu kabhu praphullita haya

SYNONYMS

kṛṣṇa-vicchede—because of separation from Kṛṣṇa; *duḥkhe*—in unhappiness; *kṣīṇa*—thin; *mana-kāya*—mind and body; *bhāva-āveśe*—by ecstatic love; *prabhu*—Śrī Caitanya Mahāprabhu; *kabhu*—sometimes; *praphullita haya*—becomes healthy and developed.

TRANSLATION

The unhappiness of separation from Kṛṣṇa exhausted the Lord's mind and reduced the structure of His body, but when He felt emotions of ecstatic love, He again became developed and healthy.

TEXT 5

কলার শরলাতে, শয়ন, অতি ক্ষীণ কায় ।
শরলাতে হাড় লাগে, ব্যথা হয় গায় ॥ ৫ ॥

kalāra śaralāte, śayana, ati kṣīṇa kāya
śaralāte hāḍa lāge, vyathā haya gāya

SYNONYMS

kalāra śaralāte—on the dry bark of a plantain tree; *śayana*—lying down; *ati*—very; *kṣīṇa kāya*—skinny body; *śaralāte*—on the dry bark of a plantain tree; *hāḍa lāge*—bones contact; *vyathā*—pain; *haya*—is; *gāya*—in the body.

TRANSLATION

Because He was very thin, when He lay down to rest on the dry bark of plantain trees, it caused Him pain in His bones.

TEXT 6

দেখি' সব ভক্তগণ মহাদুঃখ পায়।
সহিতে নারে জগদানন্দ, সৃজিলা উপায় ॥ ৬ ॥

dekhi' saba bhakta-gaṇa mahā-duḥkha pāya
sahite nāre jagadānanda, sṛjilā upāya

SYNONYMS

dekhi'—seeing; *saba bhakta-gaṇa*—all the devotees; *mahā-duḥkha*—great unhappiness; *pāya*—get; *sahite*—to tolerate; *nāre*—was unable; *jagadānanda*—Jagadānanda Paṇḍita; *sṛjilā upāya*—devised a means.

TRANSLATION

All the devotees felt very unhappy to see Śrī Caitanya Mahāprabhu in pain. Indeed, they could not tolerate it. Then Jagadānanda Paṇḍita devised a remedy.

TEXT 7

সূক্ষ্ম বস্ত্র আনি' গৈরিক দিয়া রাঙ্গাইলা।
শিমুলীর তুলা দিয়া তাহা পূরাইলা ॥ ৭ ॥

sūkṣma vastra āni' gaurika diyā rāṅgāilā
śimulīra tulā diyā tāhā pūrāilā

SYNONYMS

sūkṣma vastra—fine cloth; *āni'*—bringing; *gaurika*—red oxide; *diyā*—with the help of; *rāṅgāilā*—made reddish; *śimulīra*—of the *śimula* tree; *tulā*—cotton; *diyā*—with; *tāhā*—that; *pūrāilā*—filled.

TRANSLATION

He acquired some fine cloth and colored it with red oxide. Then he filled it with cotton from a śimula tree.

TEXT 8

এক তুলী-বালিস গোবিন্দের হাতে দিলা।
'প্রভুরে শোয়াইহ ইহায়'—তাহারে কহিলা ॥ ৮ ॥

eka tulī-bālisa govindera hāte dilā
'prabhure śoyāiha ihāya'——tāhāre kahilā

SYNONYMS

eka—one; *tulī-bālisa*—quilt and pillow; *govindera*—of Govinda; *hāte*—in the hand; *dilā*—delivered; *prabhure*—Śrī Caitanya Mahāprabhu; *śoyāiha*—ask to lie down; *ihāya*—on this; *tāhāre*—to him; *kahilā*—said.

TRANSLATION

In this way he made a quilt and a pillow, which he then gave to Govinda, saying, "Ask the Lord to lie on this."

TEXT 9

স্বরূপ-গোসাঞিকে কহে জগদানন্দ।
'আজি আপনে যাঞা প্রভুরে করাইহ শয়ন' ॥ ৯ ॥

svarūpa-gosāñike kahe jagadānanda
'āji āpane yāñā prabhure karāiha śayana'

SYNONYMS

svarūpa-gosāñike—to Svarūpa Dāmodara Gosvāmī; *kahe*—says; *jagadānanda*—Jagadānanda Paṇḍita; *āji*—today; *āpane*—Your Honor; *yāñā*—going; *prabhure*—Śrī Caitanya Mahāprabhu; *karāiha śayana*—cause to lie down.

TRANSLATION

Jagadānanda said to Svarūpa Dāmodara Gosvāmī, "Today please personally persuade Śrī Caitanya Mahāprabhu to lie down on the bed."

TEXT 10

শয়নের কালে স্বরূপ তাহাঁই রহিলা।
তুলী-বালিস দেখি' প্রভু ক্রোধাবিষ্ট হইলা ॥ ১০ ॥

śayanera kāle svarūpa tāhāṅi rahilā
tulī-bālisa dekhi' prabhu krodhāviṣṭa ha-ilā

SYNONYMS

śayanera kāle—at bedtime; *svarūpa*—Svarūpa Dāmodara Gosvāmī; *tāhāṅi rahilā*—remained there; *tulī*—quilt; *bālisa*—pillow; *dekhi'*—seeing; *prabhu*—Śrī Caitanya Mahāprabhu; *krodha-āviṣṭa ha-ilā*—became very angry.

TRANSLATION

When it was time for the Lord to go to bed, Svarūpa Dāmodara stayed nearby, but when Śrī Caitanya Mahāprabhu saw the quilt and pillow, He was immediately very angry.

TEXT 11

গোবিন্দেরে পুছেন, —'ইহা করাইল কোন্ জন ?'
জগদানন্দের নাম শুনি' সঙ্কোচ হৈল মন ॥ ১১ ॥

govindere puchena,——'ihā karāila kon jana?'
jagadānandera nāma śuni' saṅkoca haila mana

SYNONYMS

govindere puchena—He inquired from Govinda; *ihā*—this; *karāila*—has made; *kon jana*—what person; *jagadānandera*—of Jagadānanda Paṇḍita; *nāma*—name; *śuni'*—hearing; *saṅkoca*—afraid; *haila*—was; *mana*—mind.

TRANSLATION

The Lord inquired from Govinda, "Who has made this?" When Govinda named Jagadānanda Paṇḍita, Śrī Caitanya Mahāprabhu was somewhat fearful.

TEXT 12

গোবিন্দেরে কহি' সেই তুলি দূর কৈলা ।
কলার শরলা-উপর শয়ন করিলা ॥ ১২ ॥

govindere kahi' sei tūli dūra kailā
kalāra śaralā-upara śayana karilā

SYNONYMS

govindere kahi'—by asking Govinda; *sei tūli*—that quilt; *dūra kailā*—put aside; *kalāra*—of a plantain tree; *śaralā-upara*—on the dry bark; *śayana karilā*—He lay down.

TRANSLATION

After asking Govinda to put aside the quilt and pillow, the Lord lay down on the dry plantain bark.

TEXT 13

স্বরূপ কহে,—'তোমার ইচ্ছা, কি কহিতে পারি ?
শয্যা উপেক্ষিলে পণ্ডিত দুঃখ পাবে ভারী ॥' ১৩ ॥

svarūpa kahe,——'tomāra icchā, ki kahite pāri?
śayyā upekṣile paṇḍita duḥkha pābe bhārī'

SYNONYMS

svarūpa kahe—Svarūpa Dāmodara Gosvāmī said; *tomāra icchā*—Your will; *ki*—who; *kahite pāri*—can say; *śayyā upekṣile*—if You do not accept the bedding; *paṇḍita*—Jagadānanda Paṇḍita; *duḥkha*—unhappiness; *pābe*—will feel; *bhārī*—great.

TRANSLATION

Svarūpa Dāmodara said to the Lord, "I cannot contradict Your supreme will, my Lord, but if You do not accept the bedding, Jagadānanda Paṇḍita will feel great unhappiness."

TEXT 14

প্রভু কহেন,—"খাট এক আনহ পাড়িতে ।
জগদানন্দ চাহে আমায় বিষয় ভুঞ্জাইতে ॥ ১৪ ॥

prabhu kahena,——"khāṭa eka ānaha pāḍite
jagadānanda cāhe āmāya viṣaya bhuñjāite

SYNONYMS

prabhu kahena—Śrī Caitanya Mahāprabhu said; *khāṭa*—bedstead; *eka*—one; *ānaha*—bring; *pāḍite*—to lie down; *jagadānanda*—Jagadānanda Paṇḍita; *cāhe*—wants; *āmāya*—Me; *viṣaya bhuñjāite*—to cause to enjoy material happiness.

TRANSLATION

Śrī Caitanya Mahāprabhu replied, "You should bring a bedstead here for Me to lie on. Jagadānanda wants Me to enjoy material happiness.

TEXT 15

সন্ন্যাসী মানুষ আমার ভূমিতে শয়ন ।
আমারে খাট-তুলি-বালিস মস্তক-মুণ্ডন !" ১৫ ॥

sannyāsī mānuṣa āmāra bhūmite śayana
āmāre khāṭa-tūli-bālisa mastaka-muṇḍana

SYNONYMS

sannyāsī mānuṣa—a person in the renounced order of life; *āmāra*—My; *bhūmite śayana*—lying on the floor; *āmāre*—for Me; *khāṭa*—bedstead; *tūli*—quilt; *bālisa*—pillow; *mastaka-muṇḍana*—a great shame.

TRANSLATION

"I am in the renounced order, and therefore I must lie on the floor. For Me to use a bedstead, quilt or pillow would be very shameful."

TEXT 16

স্বরূপ-গোসাঞি আসি' পণ্ডিতে কহিলা ।
শুনি' জগদানন্দ মনে মহাদুঃখ পাইলা ॥ ১৬ ॥

svarūpa-gosāñi āsi' paṇḍite kahilā
śuni' jagadānanda mane mahā-duḥkha pāilā

SYNONYMS

svarūpa-gosāñi—Svarūpa Dāmodara Gosvāmī; *āsi'*—returning; *paṇḍite kahilā*—said to Jagadānanda Paṇḍita; *śuni'*—hearing; *jagadānanda*—Jagadānanda Paṇḍita; *mane*—within the mind; *mahā-duḥkha pāilā*—felt great unhappiness.

TRANSLATION

When Svarūpa Dāmodara returned and related all these incidents, Jagadānanda Paṇḍita felt very unhappy.

TEXT 17

স্বরূপ-গোসাঞি তবে সৃজিলা প্রকার ।
কদলীর শুষ্কপত্র আনিলা অপার ॥ ১৭ ॥

svarūpa-gosāñi tabe sṛjilā prakāra
kadalīra śuṣka-patra ānilā apāra

SYNONYMS

svarūpa-gosāñi—Svarūpa Dāmodara Gosvāmī; *tabe*—thereafter; *sṛjilā prakāra*—devised a means; *kadalīra*—of banana; *śuṣka-patra*—dry leaves; *ānilā*—brought; *apāra*—in great quantity.

TRANSLATION

Then Svarūpa Dāmodara Gosvāmī devised another method. First he secured a large quantity of dry banana leaves.

TEXT 18

নখে চিরি' চিরি' তাহা অতি সূক্ষ্ম কৈলা ।
প্রভুর বহির্বাস দুইতে সে সব ভরিলা ॥ ১৮ ॥

nakhe ciri' ciri' tāhā ati sūkṣma kailā
prabhura bahirvāsa duite se saba bharilā

SYNONYMS

nakhe—with the nails; *ciri' ciri'*—tearing and tearing; *tāhā*—them; *ati*—very; *sūkṣma*—fine; *kailā*—made; *prabhura*—of Śrī Caitanya Mahāprabhu; *bahirvāsa*—covering cloths; *duite*—in two; *se saba*—all those; *bharilā*—filled.

TRANSLATION

He then tore the leaves into very fine fibers with his nails and filled two of Śrī Caitanya Mahāprabhu's outer garments with the fibers.

TEXT 19

এইমত দুই কৈলা ওড়ন-পাড়নে ।
অঙ্গীকার কৈলা প্রভু অনেক যতনে ॥ ১৯ ॥

ei-mata dui kailā oḍana-pāḍane
aṅgīkāra kailā prabhu aneka yatane

SYNONYMS

ei-mata—in this way; *dui*—two pieces; *kailā*—made; *oḍana-pāḍane*—one for bedding, one for the pillow; *aṅgīkāra kailā*—did accept; *prabhu*—Śrī Caitanya Mahāprabhu; *aneka yatane*—after much endeavor.

TRANSLATION

In this way, Svarūpa Dāmodara made some bedding and a pillow, and after much endeavor by the devotees, Śrī Caitanya Mahāprabhu accepted them.

TEXT 20

তাতে শয়ন করেন প্রভু,—দেখি' সবে সুখী ।
জগদানন্দ—ভিতরে ক্রোধ বাহিরে মহাদুঃখী ॥ ২০ ॥

tāte śayana karena prabhu,——dekhi' sabe sukhī
jagadānanda——bhitare krodha bāhire mahā-duḥkhī

SYNONYMS

tāte—on that; *śayana karena*—lies down; *prabhu*—Śrī Caitanya Mahāprabhu; *dekhi'*—seeing; *sabe sukhī*—everyone became happy; *jagadānanda*—Jagadānanda Paṇḍita; *bhitare*—within his mind; *krodha*—angry; *bāhire*—externally; *mahā-duḥkhī*—very unhappy.

TRANSLATION

Everyone was happy to see the Lord lie down on that bed, but Jagadānanda was inwardly angry, and externally he appeared very unhappy.

TEXT 21

পূর্বে জগদানন্দের ইচ্ছা বৃন্দাবন যাইতে ।
প্রভু আজ্ঞা না দেন তাঁরে, না পারে চলিতে ॥ ২১ ॥

pūrve jagadānandera icchā vṛndāvana yāite
prabhu ājñā nā dena tāṅre, nā pāre calite

SYNONYMS

pūrve—formerly; *jagadānandera*—of Jagadānanda Paṇḍita; *icchā*—desire; *vṛndāvana yāite*—to go to Vṛndāvana; *prabhu*—Śrī Caitanya Mahāprabhu; *ājñā*—permission; *nā dena*—did not give; *tāṅre*—to him; *nā pāre calite*—he could not go.

TRANSLATION

Formerly, when Jagadānanda Paṇḍita had desired to go to Vṛndāvana, Śrī Caitanya Mahāprabhu had not given His permission, and therefore he could not go.

TEXT 22

ভিতরের ক্রোধ-দুঃখ প্রকাশ না কৈল ।
মথুরা যাইতে প্রভু-স্থানে আজ্ঞা মাগিল ॥ ২২ ॥

bhitarera krodha-duḥkha prakāśa nā kaila
mathurā yāite prabhu-sthāne ājñā māgila

SYNONYMS

bhitarera—internal; *krodha-duḥkha*—anger and unhappiness; *prakāśa nā kaila*—did not disclose; *mathurā yāite*—to go to Mathurā; *prabhu-sthāne*—from Śrī Caitanya Mahāprabhu; *ājñā māgila*—asked for permission.

TRANSLATION

Now, concealing his anger and unhappiness, Jagadānanda Paṇḍita again asked Śrī Caitanya Mahāprabhu for permission to go to Mathurā.

TEXT 23

প্রভু কহে,—"মথুরা যাইবা আমায় ক্রোধ করি'।
আমায় দোষ লাগাঞা তুমি হইবা ভিখারী ॥" ২৩ ॥

prabhu kahe,——"mathurā yāibā āmāya krodha kari'
āmāya doṣa lāgāñā tumi ha-ibā bhikhārī"

SYNONYMS

prabhu kahe—the Lord said; *mathurā yāibā*—you would go to Mathurā; *āmāya*—at Me; *krodha kari'*—being angry; *āmāya*—Me; *doṣa lāgāñā*—accusing; *tumi*—you; *ha-ibā*—will become; *bhikhārī*—a beggar.

TRANSLATION

With great affection, Śrī Caitanya Mahāprabhu said, "If you are angry with Me when you go to Mathurā, you will merely become a beggar and criticize Me."

TEXT 24

জগদানন্দ কহে প্রভুর ধরিয়া চরণ।
"পূর্ব হৈতে ইচ্ছা মোর যাইতে বৃন্দাবন ॥ ২৪ ॥

jagadānanda kahe prabhura dhariyā caraṇa
"pūrva haite icchā mora yāite vṛndāvana

SYNONYMS

jagadānanda—Jagadānanda Paṇḍita; *kahe*—said; *prabhura*—of Śrī Caitanya Mahāprabhu; *dhariyā caraṇa*—grasping the lotus feet; *pūrva haite*—for a very long time; *icchā*—desire; *mora*—my; *yāite vṛndāvana*—to go to Vṛndāvana.

TRANSLATION

Grasping the Lord's feet, Jagadānanda Paṇḍita then said, "For a long time I have desired to go to Vṛndāvana.

TEXT 25

প্রভু-আজ্ঞা নাহি, তাতে না পারি যাইতে ।
এবে আজ্ঞা দেহ', অবশ্য যাইমু নিশ্চিতে ॥" ২৫ ॥

prabhu-ājñā nāhi, tāte nā pāri yāite
ebe ājñā deha', avaśya yāimu niścite"

SYNONYMS

prabhu-ājñā—the permission of Your Lordship; *nāhi*—not; *tāte*—therefore; *nā pāri yāite*—I could not go; *ebe*—now; *ājñā*—permission; *deha'*—give; *avaśya*—certainly; *yāimu*—I shall go; *niścite*—without fail.

TRANSLATION

"I could not go without Your Lordship's permission. Now You must give me permission, and I shall certainly go there."

TEXT 26

প্রভু প্রীতে তাঁর গমন না করেন অঙ্গীকার ।
তেঁহো প্রভুর ঠাঞি আজ্ঞা মাগে বার বার ॥ ২৬ ॥

prabhu prīte tāṅra gamana nā karena aṅgīkāra
teṅho prabhura ṭhāñi ājñā māge bāra bāra

SYNONYMS

prabhu—Śrī Caitanya Mahāprabhu; *prīte*—out of affection; *tāṅra*—his; *gamana*—departure; *nā karena aṅgīkāra*—does not accept; *teṅho*—he; *prabhura ṭhāñi*—from Śrī Caitanya Mahāprabhu; *ājñā*—permission; *māge*—begs; *bāra bāra*—again and again.

TRANSLATION

Because of affection for Jagadānanda Paṇḍita, Śrī Caitanya Mahāprabhu would not permit him to depart, but Jagadānanda Paṇḍita repeatedly insisted that the Lord give him permission to go.

TEXT 27

স্বরূপ-গোসাঞিরে পণ্ডিত কৈলা নিবেদন ।
"পূর্ব হৈতে বৃন্দাবন যাইতে মোর মন ॥ ২৭ ॥

svarūpa-gosāñire paṇḍita kailā nivedana
"pūrva haite vṛndāvana yāite mora mana

SYNONYMS

svarūpa-gosāñire—to Svarūpa Dāmodara Gosvāmī; *paṇḍita*—Jagadānanda Paṇḍita; *kailā nivedana*—made his petition; *pūrva haite*—for a long time; *vṛndāvana yāite*—to go to Vṛndāvana; *mora mana*—my mind.

TRANSLATION

He then submitted a plea to Svarūpa Dāmodara Gosvāmī. "For a very long time," he said, "I have wanted to go to Vṛndāvana.

TEXT 28

প্রভু-আজ্ঞা বিনা তাহাঁ যাইতে না পারি ।
এবে আজ্ঞা না দেন মোরে, 'ক্রোধে যাহ' বলি ॥২৮॥

prabhu-ājñā vinā tāhāṅ yāite nā pāri
ebe ājñā nā dena more, 'krodhe yāha' bali

SYNONYMS

prabhu-ājñā—the permission of Śrī Caitanya Mahāprabhu; *vinā*—without; *tāhāṅ*—there; *yāite*—to go; *nā pāri*—I am unable; *ebe*—now; *ājñā*—permission; *nā dena*—does not give; *more*—me; *krodhe*—in anger; *yāha*—you go; *bali*—saying.

TRANSLATION

"I cannot go there, however, without the Lord's permission, which at present He denies me. He says, 'You are going because you are angry at Me.'

TEXT 29

সহজেই মোর তাহাঁ যাইতে মন হয় ।
প্রভু-আজ্ঞা লঞা দেহ', করিয়ে বিনয় ॥" ২৯ ॥

sahajei mora tāhāṅ yāite mana haya
prabhu-ājñā lañā deha', kariye vinaya"

SYNONYMS

sahejei—naturally; *mora*—my; *tāhāṅ*—there; *yāite*—to go; *mana*—mind; *haya*—is; *prabhu-ājñā*—permission from Śrī Caitanya Mahāprabhu; *lañā deha'*—kindly get; *kariye vinaya*—humbly requesting.

TRANSLATION

"Naturally I have a desire to go to Vṛndāvana; therefore please humbly request Him to grant His permission."

TEXT 30

তবে স্বরূপ-গোসাঞি কহে প্রভুর চরণে ।
"জগদানন্দের ইচ্ছা বড় যাইতে বৃন্দাবনে ॥ ৩০ ॥

tabe svarūpa-gosāñi kahe prabhura caraṇe
"jagadānandera icchā baḍa yāite vṛndāvane

SYNONYMS

tabe—thereafter; *svarūpa-gosāñi*—Svarūpa Dāmodara Gosvāmī; *kahe*—submits; *prabhura caraṇe*—at the lotus feet of Śrī Caitanya Mahāprabhu; *jagadānandera*—of Jagadānanda Paṇḍita; *icchā baḍa*—intense desire; *yāite vṛndāvane*—to go to Vṛndāvana.

TRANSLATION

Thereafter, Svarūpa Dāmodara Gosvāmī submitted this appeal at the lotus feet of Śrī Caitanya Mahāprabhu. "Jagadānanda Paṇḍita intensely desires to go to Vṛndāvana.

TEXT 31

তোমার ঠাঞি আজ্ঞা তেঁহো মাগে বার বার ।
আজ্ঞা দেহ',—মথুরা দেখি' আইসে একবার ॥ ৩১ ॥

tomāra ṭhāñi ājñā teṅho māge bāra bāra
ājñā deha',——mathurā dekhi' āise eka-bāra

SYNONYMS

tomāra ṭhāñi—from You; *ājñā*—permission; *teṅho*—he; *māge*—begs; *bāra bāra*—again and again; *ājñā deha'*—please give permission; *mathurā dekhi'*—after seeing Mathurā; *āise*—comes back; *eka-bāra*—once.

TRANSLATION

"He begs for Your permission again and again. Therefore, please permit him to go to Mathurā and then return.

TEXT 32

আইরে দেখিতে যৈছে গৌড়দেশে যায়।
তৈছে একবার বৃন্দাবন দেখি' আয় ॥" ৩২ ॥

āire dekhite yaiche gauḍa-deśe yāya
taiche eka-bāra vṛndāvana dekhi' āya"

SYNONYMS

āire—mother Śacī; *dekhite*—to see; *yaiche*—as; *gauḍa-deśe*—to Bengal; *yāya*—he went; *taiche*—similarly; *eka-bāra*—once; *vṛndāvana dekhi'*—after seeing Vṛndāvana; *āya*—he can come back.

TRANSLATION

"You permitted him to go see mother Śacī in Bengal, and You may similarly permit him to go see Vṛndāvana and then return here."

TEXT 33

স্বরূপ-গোসাঞির বোলে প্রভু আজ্ঞা দিলা।
জগদানন্দে বোলাঞা তাঁরে শিখাইলা ॥ ৩৩ ॥

svarūpa-gosāñira bole prabhu ājñā dilā
jagadānande bolāñā tāṅre śikhāilā

SYNONYMS

svarūpa-gosāñira—of Svarūpa Dāmodara Gosvāmī; *bole*—on the request; *prabhu*—Śrī Caitanya Mahāprabhu; *ājñā dilā*—gave permission; *jagadānande*—to Jagadānanda Paṇḍita; *bolāñā*—calling; *tāṅre*—to him; *śikhāilā*—gave instructions.

TRANSLATION

At the request of Svarūpa Dāmodara, Śrī Caitanya Mahāprabhu granted Jagadānanda Paṇḍita permission to go. The Lord sent for him and instructed him as follows.

TEXT 34

"বারাণসী পর্যন্ত স্বচ্ছন্দে যাইবা পথে।
আগে সাবধানে যাইবা ক্ষত্রিয়াদি-সাথে ॥ ৩৪ ॥

"vārāṇasī paryanta svacchande yāibā pathe
āge sāvadhāne yāibā kṣatriyādi-sāthe

SYNONYMS

vārāṇasī paryanta—up to Vārāṇasī; *svacchande*—without disturbance; *yāibā pathe*—you can go on the path; *āge*—after that; *sāvadhāne*—with great care; *yāibā*—you should go; *kṣatriya-ādi-sāthe*—with the *kṣatriyas.*

TRANSLATION

"You may go as far as Vārāṇasī without encountering disturbances, but beyond Vārāṇasī you should be very careful to travel on the path in the company of the kṣatriyas.

PURPORT

The path from Vārāṇasī to Vṛndāvana was infested with robbers, and therefore in those days there were *kṣatriyas* to protect travelers.

TEXT 35

কেবল গৌড়িয়া পাইলে 'বাটপাড়' করি' বান্ধে।
সব লুটি' বাঁধি' রাখে, যাইতে বিরোধে ॥ ৩৫ ॥

kevala gauḍiyā pāile 'bāṭapāḍa' kari' bāndhe
saba luṭi' bāṅdhi' rākhe, yāite virodhe

SYNONYMS

kevala—alone; *gauḍiyā*—Bengali; *pāile*—if gotten; *bāṭapāḍa*—plundering; *kari'*—doing; *bāndhe*—they arrest; *saba*—everything; *luṭi'*—taking; *bāṅdhi'*—arresting; *rākhe*—keep; *yāite virodhe*—do not release.

TRANSLATION

"As soon as the plunderers on the road see a Bengali traveling alone, they take everything from him, arrest him and do not let him go.

PURPORT

Bengalis are generally not very stout or strong. Therefore when a lone Bengali traverses the roads of Bihar, the plunderers on the road capture him, rob all his belongings and kidnap him for their own service. According to one opinion, the rogues of Bihar know very well that Bengalis are intelligent; therefore these thieves generally force the Bengalis into service requiring intelligence and do not allow them to leave.

TEXT 36

মথুরা গেলে সনাতন-সঙ্গেই রহিবা ।
মথুরার স্বামী সবের চরণ বন্দিবা ॥ ৩৬ ॥

mathurā gele sanātana-saṅgei rahibā
mathurāra svāmī sabera caraṇa vandibā

SYNONYMS

mathurā gele—when you go to Mathurā; *sanātana-saṅgei*—in the association of Sanātana Gosvāmī; *rahibā*—remain; *mathurāra svāmī*—the leading men of Mathurā; *sabera*—of all; *caraṇa vandibā*—worship the feet.

TRANSLATION

"When you reach Mathurā, you should remain with Sanātana Gosvāmī and offer respectful obeisances to the feet of all the leading men there.

TEXT 37

দূরে রহি' ভক্তি করিহ সঙ্গে না রহিবা ।
তাঁ-সবার আচার-চেষ্টা লইতে নারিবা ॥ ৩৭ ॥

dūre rahi' bhakti kariha saṅge nā rahibā
tāṅ-sabāra ācāra-ceṣṭā la-ite nāribā

SYNONYMS

dūre rahi'—keeping apart; *bhakti kariha*—show devotion; *saṅge*—in association; *nā rahibā*—do not stay; *tāṅ-sabāra*—their; *ācāra*—behavior; *ceṣṭā*—endeavors; *la-ite nāribā*—you cannot take up.

TRANSLATION

"Do not mix freely with the residents of Mathurā; show them respect from a distance. Because you are on a different platform of devotional service, you cannot adopt their behavior and practices.

PURPORT

The residents of Vṛndāvana and Mathurā are devotees of Kṛṣṇa in parental affection, and their feelings always conflict with the opinions of *smārta-brāhmaṇas.* Devotees who worship Kṛṣṇa in opulence cannot understand the parental devotional feelings of the residents of Mathurā and Vṛndāvana, who follow the path of spontaneous love. Devotees on the platform of *vidhi-mārga* (regulative devotional principles) may misunderstand the activities of those on the platform of *rāga-mārga* (devotional service in spontaneous love). Therefore Śrī Caitanya Mahāprabhu instructed Jagadānanda Paṇḍita to remain apart from the residents of Vṛndāvana, who were spontaneous devotees, so as not to become disrespectful toward them.

TEXT 38

সনাতন-সঙ্গে করিহ বন দরশন ।
সনাতনের সঙ্গ না ছাড়িবা একক্ষণ ॥ ৩৮ ॥

sanātana-saṅge kariha vana daraśana
sanātanera saṅga nā chāḍibā eka-kṣaṇa

SYNONYMS

sanātana-saṅge—with Sanātana Gosvāmī; *kariha*—do; *vana daraśana*—visiting the twelve forests; *sanātanera*—of Sanātana Gosvāmī; *saṅga*—association; *nā chāḍibā*—do not leave; *eka-kṣaṇa*—even for a moment.

TRANSLATION

"Visit all twelve forests of Vṛndāvana in the company of Sanātana Gosvāmī. Do not leave his association for even a moment.

TEXT 39

শীঘ্র আসিহ, তাহাঁ না রহিহ চিরকাল ।
গোবর্ধনে না চড়িহ দেখিতে 'গোপাল' ॥ ৩৯ ॥

śīghra āsiha, tāhāṅ nā rahiha cira-kāla
govardhane nā caḍiha dekhite 'gopāla'

SYNONYMS

śīghra—as soon as possible; *āsiha*—return; *tāhāṅ*—there; *nā rahiha*—do not remain; *cira-kāla*—for a long time; *govardhane*—on Govardhana Hill; *nā caḍiha*—do not climb; *dekhite gopāla*—to see the Gopāla Deity.

TRANSLATION

"You should remain in Vṛndāvana for only a short time and then return here as soon as possible. Also, do not climb Govardhana Hill to see the Gopāla Deity.

PURPORT

In his *Amṛta-pravāha-bhāṣya,* Śrīla Bhaktivinoda Ṭhākura advises that one avoid remaining in Vṛndāvana for a very long time. As the saying goes, "Familiarity breeds contempt." If one stays in Vṛndāvana for many days, he may fail to maintain proper respect for its inhabitants. Therefore those who have not attained the stage of spontaneous love for Kṛṣṇa should not live in Vṛndāvana very long. It is better for them to make short visits. One should also avoid climbing Govardhana Hill to see the Gopāla Deity. Since Govardhana Hill itself is identical with Gopāla, one should not step on the hill or touch it with his feet. One may see Gopāla when He goes elsewhere.

TEXT 40

আমিহ আসিতেছি,—কহিহ সনাতনে ।
আমার তরে একস্থান যেন করে বৃন্দাবনে ॥" ৪০ ॥

āmiha āsitechi,——kahiha sanātane
āmāra tare eka-sthāna yena kare vṛndāvane"

SYNONYMS

āmiha—I also; *āsitechi*—am coming; *kahiha sanātane*—inform Sanātana Gosvāmī; *āmāra tare*—for Me; *eka-sthāna*—one place; *yena*—so; *kare*—he may make; *vṛndāvane*—at Vṛndāvana.

TRANSLATION

"Inform Sanātana Gosvāmī that I am coming to Vṛndāvana for a second time and that he should therefore arrange a place for Me to stay."

TEXT 41

এত বলি' জগদানন্দে কৈলা আলিঙ্গন ।
জগদানন্দ চলিলা প্রভুর বন্দিয়া চরণ ॥ ৪১ ॥

eta bali' jagadānande kailā āliṅgana
jagadānanda calilā prabhura vandiyā caraṇa

SYNONYMS

eta bali'—saying this; *jagadānande*—to Jagadānanda Paṇḍita; *kailā*—did; *āliṅgana*—embracing; *jagadānanda*—Jagadānanda Paṇḍita; *calilā*—proceeded; *prabhura*—of Śrī Caitanya Mahāprabhu; *vandiyā caraṇa*—after worshiping the feet.

TRANSLATION

After saying this, the Lord embraced Jagadānanda Paṇḍita, who then worshiped the Lord's lotus feet and started for Vṛndāvana.

TEXT 42

সব ভক্তগণ-ঠাঞি আজ্ঞা মাগিলা ।
বনপথে চলি' চলি' বারাণসী আইলা ॥ ৪২ ॥

saba bhakta-gaṇa-ṭhāñi ājñā māgilā
vana-pathe cali' cali' vārāṇasī āilā

SYNONYMS

saba bhakta-gaṇa-ṭhāñi—from all the devotees; *ājñā māgilā*—asked permission; *vana-pathe cali' cali'*—traversing the forest path; *vārāṇasī āilā*—he reached Vārāṇasī.

TRANSLATION

He took permission from all the devotees and then departed. Traveling on the forest path, he soon reached Vārāṇasī.

TEXT 43

তপনমিশ্র, চন্দ্রশেখর,—দোঁহারে মিলিলা ।
তাঁর ঠাঞি প্রভুর কথা সকলই শুনিলা ॥ ৪৩ ॥

tapana-miśra, candraśekhara,——doṅhāre mililā
tāṅra ṭhāñi prabhura kathā sakala-i śunilā

SYNONYMS

tapana-miśra—Tapana Miśra; *candra-śekhara*—Candraśekhara; *doṅhāre mililā*—he met both; *tāṅra ṭhāñi*—from him; *prabhura*—of Śrī Caitanya Mahāprabhu; *kathā*—topics; *sakala-i*—all; *śunilā*—they heard.

TRANSLATION

When he met Tapana Miśra and Candraśekhara in Vārāṇasī, they both heard from him about topics concerning Śrī Caitanya Mahāprabhu.

TEXT 44

মথুরাতে আসি' মিলিলা সনাতনে ।
দুইজনের সঙ্গে দুঁহে আনন্দিত মনে ॥ ৪৪ ॥

mathurāte āsi' mililā sanātane
dui-janera saṅge duṅhe ānandita mane

SYNONYMS

mathurāte āsi'—when he reached Mathurā; *mililā sanātane*—he met Sanātana Gosvāmī; *dui-janera*—of both; *saṅge*—in association; *duṅhe*—both; *ānandita mane*—very pleased within their minds.

TRANSLATION

Finally Jagadānanda Paṇḍita reached Mathurā, where he met Sanātana Gosvāmī. They were very pleased to see each other.

TEXT 45

সনাতন করাইলা তাঁরে দ্বাদশ বন দরশন ।
গোকুলে রহিলা দুঁহে দেখি' মহাবন ॥ ৪৫ ॥

sanātana karāilā tāṅre dvādaśa vana daraśana
gokule rahilā duṅhe dekhi' mahāvana

SYNONYMS

sanātana—Sanātana Gosvāmī; *karāilā*—made; *tāṅre*—him; *dvādaśa*—twelve; *vana*—forests; *daraśana*—visiting; *gokule*—at Gokula; *rahilā*—remained; *duṅhe*—both; *dekhi'*—after seeing; *mahā-vana*—Mahāvana.

TRANSLATION

After Sanātana Gosvāmī had taken Jagadānanda to see all twelve forests of Vṛndāvana, concluding with Mahāvana, they both remained in Gokula.

TEXT 46

সনাতনের গোফাতে দুঁহে রহে একঠাঞি ।
পণ্ডিত পাক করেন দেবালয়ে যাই' ॥ ৪৬ ॥

sanātanera gophāte duṅhe rahe eka-ṭhāñi
paṇḍita pāka karena devālaye yāi'

SYNONYMS

sanātanera gophāte—in the cave where Sanātana Gosvāmī stayed; *duṅhe*—both; *rahe*—stay; *eka-ṭhāñi*—in one place; *paṇḍita*—Jagadānanda; *pāka karena*—cooks; *devālaye yāi'*—going to a temple.

TRANSLATION

They stayed in Sanātana Gosvāmī's cave, but Jagadānanda Paṇḍita would go cook for himself at a nearby temple.

TEXT 47

সনাতন ভিক্ষা করেন যাই' মহাবনে ।
কভু দেবালয়ে, কভু ব্রাহ্মণ-সদনে ॥ ৪৭ ॥

sanātana bhikṣā karena yāi' mahāvane
kabhu devālaye, kabhu brāhmaṇa-sadane

SYNONYMS

sanātana—Sanātana Gosvāmī; *bhikṣā karena*—begs alms; *yāi' mahā-vane*—going to the vicinity of Mahāvana; *kabhu*—sometimes; *devālaye*—in a temple; *kabhu*—sometimes; *brāhmaṇa-sadane*—in the house of a *brāhmaṇa.*

TRANSLATION

Sanātana Gosvāmī would beg alms from door to door in the vicinity of Mahāvana. Sometimes he would go to a temple and sometimes to a brāhmaṇa's house.

TEXT 48

সনাতন পণ্ডিতের করে সমাধান ।
মহাবনে দেন আনি' মাগি' অন্ন-পান ॥ ৪৮ ॥

sanātana paṇḍitera kare samādhāna
mahāvane dena āni' māgi' anna-pāna

SYNONYMS

sanātana—Sanātana Gosvāmī; *paṇḍitera*—of Jagadānanda Paṇḍita; *kare samādhāna*—gave all kinds of service; *mahā-vane*—at Mahāvana; *dena*—gives; *āni'*—bringing; *māgi'*—by begging; *anna-pāna*—food and drink.

TRANSLATION

Sanātana Gosvāmī attended to all of Jagadānanda Paṇḍita's needs. He begged in the area of Mahāvana and brought Jagadānanda all kinds of things to eat and drink.

TEXT 49

একদিন সনাতনে পণ্ডিত নিমন্ত্রিলা ।
নিত্যকৃত্য করি' তেঁহ পাক চড়াইলা ॥ ৪৯ ॥

eka-dina sanātane paṇḍita nimantrilā
nitya-kṛtya kari' teṅha pāka caḍāilā

SYNONYMS

eka-dina—one day; *sanātane*—Sanātana Gosvāmī; *paṇḍita nimantrilā*—Jagadānanda Paṇḍita invited; *nitya-kṛtya kari'*—after finishing his routine duties; *teṅha*—he; *pāka caḍāilā*—began to cook.

TRANSLATION

One day Jagadānanda Paṇḍita, having invited Sanātana to the nearby temple for lunch, finished his routine duties and began to cook.

TEXT 50

'মুকুন্দ সরস্বতী' নাম সন্ন্যাসী মহাজনে ।
এক বহির্বাস তেঁহো দিল সনাতনে ॥ ৫০ ॥

'mukunda sarasvatī' nāma sannyāsī mahā-jane
eka bahirvāsa teṅho dila sanātane

SYNONYMS

mukunda sarasvatī—Mukunda Sarasvatī; *nāma*—named; *sannyāsī*—a *sannyāsī; mahā-jane*—a great personality; *eka*—one; *bahirvāsa*—outward covering; *teṅho*—he; *dila*—gave; *sanātane*—to Sanātana Gosvāmī.

TRANSLATION

Previously, a great sannyāsī named Mukunda Sarasvatī had given Sanātana Gosvāmī an outer garment.

TEXT 51

সনাতন সেই বস্ত্র মস্তকে বান্ধিয়া ।
জগদানন্দের বাসা-দ্বারে বসিলা আসিয়া ॥ ৫১ ॥

sanātana sei vastra mastake bāndhiyā
jagadānandera vāsā-dvāre vasilā āsiyā

SYNONYMS

sanātana—Sanātana Gosvāmī; *sei*—that; *vastra*—cloth; *mastake*—on the head; *bāndhiyā*—binding; *jagadānandera*—of Jagadānanda Paṇḍita; *vāsā-dvāre*—at the door of the residence; *vasilā*—sat down; *āsiyā*—coming.

TRANSLATION

Sanātana Gosvāmī was wearing this cloth bound about his head when he came to Jagadānanda Paṇḍita's door and sat down.

TEXT 52

রাতুল বস্ত্র দেখি' পণ্ডিত প্রেমাবিষ্ট হইলা।
'মহাপ্রভুর প্রসাদ' জানি' তাঁহারে পুছিলা ॥ ৫২ ॥

rātula vastra dekhi' paṇḍita premāviṣṭa ha-ilā
'mahāprabhura prasāda' jāni' tāṅhāre puchilā

SYNONYMS

rātula—red; *vastra*—cloth; *dekhi'*—seeing; *paṇḍita*—Jagadānanda Paṇḍita; *prema-āviṣṭa ha-ilā*—became overwhelmed in ecstatic love; *mahāprabhura prasāda*—the blessed gift of Śrī Caitanya Mahāprabhu; *jāni'*—thinking; *tāṅhāre puchilā*—inquired from him.

TRANSLATION

Assuming the reddish cloth to be a gift from Caitanya Mahāprabhu, Jagadānanda Paṇḍita was overwhelmed with ecstatic love. Thus he questioned Sanātana Gosvāmī.

TEXT 53

"কাহাঁ পাইলা তুমি এই রাতুল বসন ?"
'মুকুন্দ-সরস্বতী' দিল,—কহে সনাতন ॥ ৫৩ ॥

"kāhāṅ pāilā tumi ei rātula vasana?"
'mukunda-sarasvatī' dila,— kahe sanātana

SYNONYMS

kāhāṅ—where; *pāilā*—did get; *tumi*—you; *ei*—this; *rātula vasana*—red cloth; *mukunda-sarasvatī dila*—Mukunda Sarasvatī gave; *kahe sanātana*—Sanātana replied.

TRANSLATION

"Where did you get that reddish cloth on your head?" Jagadānanda asked. Sanātana Gosvāmī replied, "Mukunda Sarasvatī gave it to me."

TEXT 54

শুনি' পণ্ডিতের মনে ক্রোধ উপজিল ।
ভাতের হাণ্ডি হাতে লঞা মারিতে আইল ॥ ৫৪ ॥

śuni' paṇḍitera mane krodha upajila
bhātera hāṇḍi hāte lañā mārite āila

SYNONYMS

śuni'—hearing; *paṇḍitera*—of Jagadānanda Paṇḍita; *mane*—in the mind; *krodha*—anger; *upajila*—arose; *bhātera hāṇḍi*—the cooking pot; *hāte*—in his hand; *lañā*—taking; *mārite āila*—was ready to beat.

TRANSLATION

Hearing this, Jagadānanda Paṇḍita was immediately very angry and took a cooking pot in his hand, intending to beat Sanātana Gosvāmī.

TEXT 55

সনাতন তাঁরে জানি' লজ্জিত হইলা ।
বলিতে লাগিলা পণ্ডিত হাণ্ডি চুলাতে ধরিলা ॥ ৫৫ ॥

sanātana tāṅre jāni' lajjita ha-ilā
balite lāgilā paṇḍita hāṇḍi culāte dharilā

SYNONYMS

sanātana—Sanātana Gosvāmī; *tāṅre*—him; *jāni'*—knowing; *lajjita ha-ilā*—became ashamed; *balite lāgilā*—began to speak; *paṇḍita*—Jagadānanda Paṇḍita; *hāṇḍi*—the cooking pot; *culāte*—on the stove; *dharilā*—kept.

TRANSLATION

Sanātana Gosvāmī, however, knew Jagadānanda Paṇḍita very well and was consequently somewhat ashamed. Jagadānanda therefore left the cooking pot on the stove and spoke as follows.

TEXT 56

"তুমি মহাপ্রভুর হও পার্ষদ-প্রধান।
তোমা-সম মহাপ্রভুর প্রিয় নাহি আন ॥ ৫৬ ॥

"tumi mahāprabhura hao pārṣada-pradhāna
tomā-sama mahāprabhura priya nāhi āna

SYNONYMS

tumi—you; *mahāprabhura*—of Śrī Caitanya Mahāprabhu; *hao*—are; *pārṣada-pradhāna*—one of the chief associates; *tomā-sama*—like you; *mahāprabhura*—of Śrī Caitanya Mahāprabhu; *priya*—dear; *nāhi*—is not; *āna*—other.

TRANSLATION

"You are one of the chief associates of Śrī Caitanya Mahāprabhu. Indeed, no one is dearer to Him than you.

TEXT 57

অন্য সন্ন্যাসীর বস্ত্র তুমি ধর শিরে।
কোন্ ঐছে হয়,—ইহা পারে সহিবারে ?"৫৭ ॥

anya sannyāsīra vastra tumi dhara śire
kon aiche haya,——ihā pāre sahibāre?"

SYNONYMS

anya sannyāsīra—of another *sannyāsī*; *vastra*—cloth; *tumi*—you; *dhara*—keep; *śire*—on the head; *kon*—who; *aiche haya*—is such; *ihā*—this; *pāre sahibāre*—can tolerate.

TRANSLATION

"Still, you have bound your head with a cloth given to you by another sannyāsī. Who can tolerate such behavior?"

TEXT 58

সনাতন কহে—"সাধু পণ্ডিত-মহাশয় !
তোমা-সম চৈতন্যের প্রিয় কেহ নয় ॥ ৫৮ ॥

sanātana kahe——"sādhu paṇḍita-mahāśaya!
tomā-sama caitanyera priya keha naya

SYNONYMS

sanātana kahe—Sanātana Gosvāmī said; *sādhu*—saint; *paṇḍita*—learned scholar; *mahāśaya*—a great soul; *tomā-sama*—like you; *caitanyera*—of Śrī Caitanya Mahāprabhu; *priya*—dear; *keha naya*—no one is.

TRANSLATION

Sanātana Gosvāmī said, "My dear Jagadānanda Paṇḍita, you are a greatly learned saint. No one is dearer to Śrī Caitanya Mahāprabhu than you.

TEXT 59

ঐছে চৈতন্যনিষ্ঠা যোগ্য তোমাতে ।
তুমি না দেখাইলে ইহা শিখিব কেমতে ? ৫৯ ॥

aiche caitanya-niṣṭhā yogya tomāte
tumi nā dekhāile ihā śikhiba ke-mate?

SYNONYMS

aiche—such; *caitanya-niṣṭhā*—faith in Śrī Caitanya Mahāprabhu; *yogya*—just befitting; *tomāte*—in you; *tumi nā dekhāile*—if you do not show; *ihā*—this; *śikhiba*—I shall learn; *ke-mate*—how.

TRANSLATION

"This faith in Śrī Caitanya Mahāprabhu fits you quite well. Unless you demonstrate it, how could I learn such faith?

TEXT 60

যাহা দেখিবারে বস্ত্র মস্তকে বান্ধিল ।
সেই অপূর্ব প্রেম এই প্রত্যক্ষ দেখিল ॥ ৬০ ॥

yāhā dekhibāre vastra mastake bāndhila
sei apūrva prema ei pratyakṣa dekhila

SYNONYMS

yāhā—which; *dekhibāre*—to see; *vastra*—the cloth; *mastake bāndhila*—I bound on my head; *sei*—that; *apūrva prema*—uncommon love; *ei*—this; *pratyakṣa*—by direct experience; *dekhila*—I have seen.

TRANSLATION

"My purpose in binding my head with the cloth has now been fulfilled because I have personally seen your uncommon love for Śrī Caitanya Mahāprabhu.

TEXT 61

রক্তবস্ত্র 'বৈষ্ণবের' পরিতে না যুয়ায় ।
কোন প্রবাসীরে দিমু, কি কায উহায় ? ৬১ ॥

rakta-vastra 'vaiṣṇavera' parite nā yuyāya
kona pravāsīre dimu, ki kāya uhāya?

SYNONYMS

rakta-vastra—saffron clothing; *vaiṣṇavera*—for a Vaiṣṇava; *parite nā yuyāya*—is not fit to put on; *kona pravāsīre*—to some outsider; *dimu*—I shall give; *ki*—what; *kāya*—business; *uhāya*—with that.

TRANSLATION

"This saffron cloth is unfit for a Vaiṣṇava to wear; therefore I have no use for it. I shall give it to a stranger."

PURPORT

Śrīla Bhaktisiddhānta Sarasvatī Ṭhākura comments on this incident as follows: Vaiṣṇavas are all liberated persons, unattached to anything material. Therefore a Vaiṣṇava need not accept the dress of a *sannyāsī* to prove his exalted position. Śrī Caitanya Mahāprabhu accepted the renounced order from a *sannyāsī* of the Māyāvāda school. Present-day Vaiṣṇava *sannyāsīs,* however, never think that by accepting the dress of the *sannyāsa* order they have become equal to Caitanya Mahāprabhu. In fact, a Vaiṣṇava accepts the *sannyāsa* order to remain an eternal servant of his spiritual master. He accepts the *sannyāsa* order knowing that he is unequal to his spiritual master, who is a *paramahaṁsa,* and he thinks that he is unfit to dress like a *paramahaṁsa.* Therefore a Vaiṣṇava accepts *sannyāsa* out of humility, not out of pride.

Sanātana Gosvāmī had adopted the dress of a *paramahaṁsa;* therefore it was inappropriate for him to wear the saffron cloth on his head. However, a Vaiṣṇava *sannyāsī* does not think himself fit to imitate the dress of a *paramahaṁsa* Vaiṣṇava. According to the principles set down by Śrī Caitanya Mahāprabhu (*tṛṇād api sunīcena*), one should always think himself in the lowest stage, not on the level of a *paramahaṁsa* Vaiṣṇava. Thus a Vaiṣṇava will sometimes accept the *sannyāsa* order just to keep himself below the level of a *paramahaṁsa* Vaiṣṇava. This is the instruction of Śrīla Bhaktisiddhānta Sarasvatī Ṭhākura.

TEXT 62

পাক করি' জগদানন্দ চৈতন্যে সমর্পিলা।
দুইজন বসি' তবে প্রসাদ পাইলা ॥ ৬২ ॥

pāka kari' jagadānanda caitanya samarpilā
dui-jana vasi' tabe prasāda pāilā

SYNONYMS

pāka kari'—after cooking; *jagadānanda*—Jagadānanda Paṇḍita; *caitanya samarpilā*—offered to Śrī Caitanya Mahāprabhu; *dui-jana*—two persons; *vasi'*—sitting; *tabe*—then; *prasāda*—remnants of food; *pāilā*—took.

TRANSLATION

When Jagadānanda Paṇḍita finished cooking, he offered the food to Śrī Caitanya Mahāprabhu. Then he and Sanātana Gosvāmī sat down and ate the prasāda.

TEXT 63

প্রসাদ পাই অন্যোন্যে কৈলা আলিঙ্গন।
চৈতন্যবিরহে দুঁহে করিলা ক্রন্দন ॥ ৬৩ ॥

prasāda pāi anyonye kailā āliṅgana
caitanya-virahe duṅhe karilā krandana

SYNONYMS

prasāda pāi—after eating the remnants of food; *anyonye*—one another; *kailā āliṅgana*—they embraced; *caitanya-virahe*—in separation from Lord Caitanya; *duṅhe*—both; *karilā krandana*—cried.

TRANSLATION

After eating the prasāda, they embraced each other and cried due to separation from Lord Caitanya.

TEXT 64

এইমত মাস দুই রহিলা বৃন্দাবনে ।
চৈতন্যবিরহ-দুঃখ না যায় সহনে ॥ ৬৪ ॥

ei-mata māsa dui rahilā vṛndāvane
caitanya-viraha-duḥkha nā yāya sahane

SYNONYMS

ei-mata—in this way; *māsa*—months; *dui*—two; *rahilā*—remained; *vṛndāvane*—in Vṛndāvana; *caitanya-viraha*—of separation from Śrī Caitanya Mahāprabhu; *duḥkha*—unhappiness; *nā yāya sahane*—could not tolerate.

TRANSLATION

They passed two months in Vṛndāvana in this way. Finally they could no longer tolerate the unhappiness of separation from Śrī Caitanya Mahāprabhu.

TEXT 65

মহাপ্রভুর সন্দেশ কহিলা সনাতনে ।
'আমিহ আসিতেছি, রহিতে করিহ একস্থানে' ॥৬৫॥

mahāprabhura sandeśa kahilā sanātane
'āmiha āsitechi, rahite kariha eka-sthāne'

SYNONYMS

mahāprabhura—of Śrī Caitanya Mahāprabhu; *sandeśa*—message; *kahilā*—said; *sanātane*—to Sanātana; *āmiha āsitechi*—I am also coming; *rahite*—for My stay; *kariha eka-sthāne*—arrange for one place.

TRANSLATION

Jagadānanda Paṇḍita therefore gave Sanātana Gosvāmī the message from the Lord: "I am also coming to Vṛndāvana; please arrange a place for Me to stay."

TEXT 66

জগদানন্দ-পণ্ডিত তবে আজ্ঞা মাগিলা ।
সনাতন প্রভুরে কিছু ভেটবস্তু দিলা ॥ ৬৬ ॥

jagadānanda-paṇḍita tabe ājñā māgilā
sanātana prabhure kichu bheṭa-vastu dilā

SYNONYMS

jagadānanda-paṇḍita—Jagadānanda Paṇḍita; *tabe*—at that time; *ājñā māgilā*—asked permission; *sanātana*—Sanātana Gosvāmī; *prabhure*—for Śrī Caitanya Mahāprabhu; *kichu*—some; *bheṭa-vastu*—gifts; *dilā*—presented.

TRANSLATION

When Sanātana Gosvāmī granted permission for Jagadānanda to return to Jagannātha Purī, he gave Jagadānanda some gifts for Lord Caitanya Mahāprabhu.

TEXT 67

রাসস্থলীর বালু আর গোবর্ধনের শিলা ।
শুষ্ক পক্ক পীলুফল আর গুঞ্জামালা ॥ ৬৭ ॥

rāsa-sthalīra vālu āra govardhanera śilā
śuṣka pakka pīlu-phala āra guñjā-mālā

SYNONYMS

rāsa-sthalīra vālu—sand from the place where Lord Kṛṣṇa held His *rāsa* dance; *āra*—and; *govardhanera śilā*—a stone from Govardhana Hill; *śuṣka*—dry; *pakka*—mature; *pīlu-phala*—*pīlu* fruit; *āra*—also; *guñjā-mālā*—a garland of small conchshells.

TRANSLATION

The gifts consisted of some sand from the site of the rāsa-līlā, a stone from Govardhana Hill, dry ripened pīlu fruits and a garland of small conchshells.

TEXT 68

জগদানন্দ-পণ্ডিত চলিলা সব লঞা ।
ব্যাকুল হৈলা সনাতন তাঁরে বিদায় দিয়া ॥ ৬৮ ॥

jagadānanda-paṇḍita calilā saba lañā
vyākula hailā sanātana tāṅre vidāya diyā

SYNONYMS

jagadānanda-paṇḍita—Jagadānanda Paṇḍita; *calilā*—proceeded; *saba*—all; *lañā*—taking; *vyākula hailā*—became very agitated; *sanātana*—Sanātana Gosvāmī; *tāṅre*—to him; *vidāya diyā*—bidding farewell.

TRANSLATION

Thus Jagadānanda Paṇḍita, bearing all these gifts, started on his journey. Sanātana Gosvāmī, however, was very agitated after bidding him farewell.

TEXT 69

প্রভুর নিমিত্ত একস্থান মনে বিচারিল।
দ্বাদশাদিত্য-টিলায় এক 'মঠ' পাইল ॥ ৬৯ ॥

prabhura nimitta eka-sthāna mane vicārila
dvādaśāditya-ṭilāya eka 'maṭha' pāila

SYNONYMS

prabhura nimitta—for Śrī Caitanya Mahāprabhu; *eka-sthāna*—one place; *mane*—within the mind; *vicārila*—considered; *dvādaśāditya-ṭilāya*—on the highland named Dvādaśāditya; *eka*—one; *maṭha*—temple; *pāila*—got.

TRANSLATION

Soon afterward, Sanātana Gosvāmī selected a place where Śrī Caitanya Mahāprabhu could stay while in Vṛndāvana. It was a temple in the highlands named Dvādaśāditya-ṭilā.

TEXT 70

সেই স্থান রাখিলা গোসাঞি সংস্কার করিয়া।
মঠের আগে রাখিলা এক ছাউনি বান্ধিয়া ॥ ৭০ ॥

sei sthāna rākhilā gosāñi saṁskāra kariyā
maṭhera āge rākhilā eka chāuni bāndhiyā

SYNONYMS

sei sthāna—that place; *rākhilā*—kept reserved; *gosāñi*—Sanātana Gosvāmī; *saṁskāra kariyā*—cleansing and repairing; *maṭhera āge*—in front of the temple; *rākhilā*—kept; *eka*—one; *chāuni*—small hut; *bāndhiyā*—erecting.

TRANSLATION

Sanātana Gosvāmī kept the temple very clean and in good repair. In front of it he erected a small hut.

TEXT 71

শীঘ্র চলি' নীলাচলে গেলা জগদানন্দ।
ভক্ত সহ গোসাঞি হৈলা পরম আনন্দ ॥ ৭১ ॥

śīghra cali' nīlācale gelā jagadānanda
bhakta saha gosāñi hailā parama ānanda

SYNONYMS

śīghra—very quickly; *cali'*—going; *nīlācale*—at Jagannātha Purī; *gelā*—arrived; *jagadānanda*—Jagadānanda Paṇḍita; *bhakta saha*—with His devotees; *gosāñi*—Śrī Caitanya Mahāprabhu; *hailā*—became; *parama ānanda*—very happy.

TRANSLATION

Meanwhile, traveling very quickly, Jagadānanda Paṇḍita soon arrived in Jagannātha Purī, much to the joy of Śrī Caitanya Mahāprabhu and His devotees.

TEXT 72

প্রভুর চরণ বন্দি' সবারে মিলিলা।
মহাপ্রভু তাঁরে দৃঢ় আলিঙ্গন কৈলা ॥ ৭২ ॥

prabhura caraṇa vandi' sabāre mililā
mahāprabhu tāṅre dṛḍha āliṅgana kailā

SYNONYMS

prabhura—of Śrī Caitanya Mahāprabhu; *caraṇa*—lotus feet; *vandi'*—offering prayers to; *sabāre mililā*—he met everyone; *mahāprabhu*—Śrī Caitanya Mahāprabhu; *tāṅre*—to him; *dṛḍha*—very strong; *āliṅgana*—embracing; *kailā*—did.

TRANSLATION

After offering prayers at the lotus feet of Śrī Caitanya Mahāprabhu, Jagadānanda Paṇḍita greeted everyone. Then the Lord embraced Jagadānanda very strongly.

TEXT 73

সনাতনের নামে পণ্ডিত দণ্ডবৎ কৈলা।
রাসস্থলীর ধূলি আদি সব ভেট দিলা ॥ ৭৩ ॥

sanātanera nāme paṇḍita daṇḍavat kailā
rāsa-sthalīra dhūli ādi saba bheṭa dilā

SYNONYMS

sanātanera—of Sanātana Gosvāmī; *nāme*—in the name; *paṇḍita*—Jagadānanda Paṇḍita; *daṇḍavat kailā*—offered obeisances; *rāsa-sthalīra*—the arena of the *rāsa* dance; *dhūli*—dust; *ādi*—and other things; *saba*—all; *bheṭa*—gifts; *dilā*—presented.

TRANSLATION

Jagadānanda Paṇḍita also offered obeisances to the Lord on behalf of Sanātana Gosvāmī. Then he gave the Lord the dust from the site of the rāsa dance and the other gifts.

TEXT 74

সব দ্রব্য রাখিলেন, পীলু দিলেন বাঁটিয়া।
'বৃন্দাবনের ফল' বলি' খাইলা হৃষ্ট হঞা ॥ ৭৪ ॥

saba dravya rākhilena, pīlu dilena bāṅṭiyā
'vṛndāvanera phala' bali' khāilā hṛṣṭa hañā

SYNONYMS

saba—all; *dravya*—gifts; *rākhilena*—kept; *pīlu*—the *pīlu* fruit; *dilena*—gave; *bāṅṭiyā*—distributing; *vṛndāvanera phala*—fruit from Vṛndāvana; *bali'*—because of; *khāilā*—ate; *hṛṣṭa hañā*—with great happiness.

TRANSLATION

Śrī Caitanya Mahāprabhu kept all the gifts except the pīlu fruits, which He distributed to the devotees. Because the fruits were from Vṛndāvana, everyone ate them with great happiness.

TEXT 75

যে কেহ জানে, আঁটি চুষিতে লাগিল।
যে না জানে গৌড়িয়া পীলু চাবাঞা খাইল ॥ ৭৫ ॥

ye keha jāne, āṅṭi cuṣite lāgila
ye nā jāne gauḍiyā pīlu cāvāñā khāila

SYNONYMS

ye—those who; *keha*—some; *jāne*—knew; *āṅṭi*—seeds; *cuṣite lāgila*—began to lick; *ye*—those who; *nā jāne*—did not know; *gauḍiyā*—Bengali devotees; *pīlu*—the *pīlu* fruit; *cāvāñā*—chewing; *khāila*—ate.

TRANSLATION

Those devotees who were familiar with pīlu fruits sucked on the seeds, but the Bengali devotees who did not know what they were chewed the seeds and swallowed them.

TEXT 76

মুখে তার ঝাল গেল, জিহ্বা করে জ্বালা।
বৃন্দাবনের 'পীলু' খাইতে এই এক লীলা ॥ ৭৬ ॥

mukhe tāra jhāla gela, jihvā kare jvālā
vṛndāvanera 'pīlu' khāite ei eka līlā

SYNONYMS

mukhe tāra—in their mouths; *jhāla*—the taste of chili; *gela*—went; *jihvā*—the tongue; *kare jvālā*—was burning; *vṛndāvanera*—of Vṛndāvana; *pīlu*—the *pīlu* fruit; *khāite*—eating; *ei*—this; *eka līlā*—a pastime.

TRANSLATION

The hot chili-like taste burned the tongues of those who chewed the seeds. The eating of pīlu fruits from Vṛndāvana was a pastime for Śrī Caitanya Mahāprabhu.

TEXT 77

জগদানন্দের আগমনে সবার উল্লাস।
এইমতে নীলাচলে প্রভুর বিলাস ॥ ৭৭ ॥

jagadānandera āgamane sabāra ullāsa
ei-mate nīlācale prabhura vilāsa

SYNONYMS

jagadānandera—of Jagadānanda Paṇḍita; *āgamane*—upon the return; *sabāra ullāsa*—everyone was jubilant; *ei-mate*—in this way; *nīlācale*—at Jagannātha Purī; *prabhura*—of Śrī Caitanya Mahāprabhu; *vilāsa*—pastime.

TRANSLATION

When Jagadānanda Paṇḍita returned from Vṛndāvana, everyone was jubilant. Thus Śrī Caitanya Mahāprabhu enjoyed His pastimes while residing at Jagannātha Purī.

TEXT 78

একদিন প্রভু যমেশ্বর-টোটা যাইতে।
সেইকালে দেবদাসী লাগিলা গাইতে ॥ ৭৮ ॥

eka-dina prabhu yameśvara-ṭoṭā yāite
sei-kāle deva-dāsī lāgilā gāite

SYNONYMS

eka-dina—one day; *prabhu*—Śrī Caitanya Mahāprabhu; *yameśvara-ṭoṭā*—to the temple of Yameśvara-ṭoṭā; *yāite*—when He was going; *sei-kāle*—at that time; *deva-dāsī*—a female singer of the Jagannātha temple; *lāgilā*—began; *gāite*—to sing.

TRANSLATION

One day when the Lord was going to the temple of Yameśvara, a female singer began to sing in the Jagannātha temple.

TEXT 79

গুজ্জরীরাগিণী লঞা সুমধুর-স্বরে ।
'গীতগোবিন্দ'-পদ গায় জগমন হরে ॥ ৭৯ ॥

gujjarī-rāgiṇī lañā sumadhura-svare
'gīta-govinda'-pada gāya jaga-mana hare

SYNONYMS

gujjarī-rāgiṇī—the *gujjarī* mode of singing; *lañā*—accompanied by; *su-madhura-svare*—in a very sweet voice; *gīta-govinda*—*Gīta-govinda,* by Jayadeva Gosvāmī; *pada*—verses; *gāya*—sings; *jaga-mana*—the mind of the entire world; *hare*—attracts.

TRANSLATION

She sang a gujjarī tune in a very sweet voice, and because the subject was Jayadeva Gosvāmī's Gīta-govinda, the song attracted the attention of the entire world.

TEXT 80

দূরে গান শুনি' প্রভুর হইল আবেশ ।
স্ত্রী, পুরুষ, কে গায়,—না জানে বিশেষ ॥ ৮০ ॥

dūre gāna śuni' prabhura ha-ila āveśa
strī, puruṣa, ke gāya,——nā jāne viśeṣa

SYNONYMS

dūre—from a distant place; *gāna*—song; *śuni'*—hearing; *prabhura*—of Śrī Caitanya Mahāprabhu; *ha-ila*—there was; *āveśa*—ecstatic emotion; *strī*—woman; *puruṣa*—man; *ke gāya*—who sings; *nā jāne*—could not understand; *viśeṣa*—particularly.

TRANSLATION

Hearing the song from a distance, Śrī Caitanya Mahāprabhu immediately became ecstatic. He did not know whether it was a man or a woman singing.

TEXT 81

তারে মিলিবারে প্রভু আবেশে ধাইলা ।
পথে 'সিজের বাড়ি' হয়, ফুটিয়া চলিলা ॥ ৮১ ॥

tāre milibāre prabhu āveśe dhāilā
pathe 'sijera bāḍi' haya, phuṭiyā calilā

SYNONYMS

tāre—the singer; *milibāre*—to meet; *prabhu*—Śrī Caitanya Mahāprabhu; *āveśe*—in ecstasy; *dhāilā*—ran; *pathe*—on the path; *sijera bāḍi*—thorny hedges; *haya*—were; *phuṭiyā*—pricking; *calilā*—He went on.

TRANSLATION

As the Lord ran in ecstasy to meet the singer, thorny hedges pricked His body.

TEXT 82

অঙ্গে কাঁটা লাগিল, কিছু না জানিলা !
আস্তে-ব্যস্তে গোবিন্দ তাঁর পাছেতে ধাইলা ॥ ৮২ ॥

aṅge kāṅṭā lāgila, kichu nā jānilā!
āste-vyaste govinda tāṅra pāchete dhāilā

SYNONYMS

aṅge—on the body; *kāṅṭā*—thorns; *lāgila*—touched; *kichu*—anything; *nā jānilā*—did not perceive; *āste-vyaste*—very hastily; *govinda*—His personal servant; *tāṅra*—Him; *pāchete*—behind; *dhāilā*—ran.

TRANSLATION

Govinda ran very quickly behind the Lord, who did not feel any pain from the pricking of the thorns.

TEXT 83

ধাঞা যায়েন প্রভু, স্ত্রী আছে অল্প দূরে ।
স্ত্রী গায়' বলি' গোবিন্দ প্রভুরে কৈলা কোলে ॥৮৩॥

dhāñā yāyena prabhu, strī āche alpa dūre
strī gāya' bali' govinda prabhure kailā kole

SYNONYMS

dhāñā—very hastily; *yāyena*—was going; *prabhu*—Śrī Caitanya Mahāprabhu; *strī*—the woman; *āche*—was; *alpa dūre*—within a short distance; *strī gāya'*—a woman is singing; *bali'*—saying; *govinda*—His personal servant; *prabhure*—Śrī Caitanya Mahāprabhu; *kailā kole*—held in his arms.

TRANSLATION

Śrī Caitanya Mahāprabhu was running very rapidly, and the girl was only a short distance away. Just then Govinda caught the Lord in his arms and cried, "It is a woman singing!"

TEXT 84

স্ত্রী-নাম শুনি' প্রভুর বাহ্য হইলা ।
পুনরপি সেই পথে বাহুড়ি' চলিলা ॥ ৮৪ ॥

strī-nāma śuni' prabhura bāhya ha-ilā
punarapi sei pathe bāhuḍi' calilā

SYNONYMS

strī-nāma—the word "woman"; *śuni'*—hearing; *prabhura*—of Śrī Caitanya Mahāprabhu; *bāhya*—external consciousness; *ha-ilā*—returned; *punarapi*—again; *sei pathe*—on that path; *bāhuḍi' calilā*—He turned back.

TRANSLATION

As soon as He heard the word "woman," the Lord became externally conscious and turned back.

TEXT 85

প্রভু কহে,—"গোবিন্দ, আজি রাখিলা জীবন।
স্ত্রী-পরশ হৈলে আমার হইত মরণ ॥ ৮৫ ॥

prabhu kahe,——"govinda, āji rākhilā jīvana
strī-paraśa haile āmāra ha-ita maraṇa

SYNONYMS

prabhu kahe—Lord Śrī Caitanya Mahāprabhu said; *govinda*—My dear Govinda; *āji*—today; *rākhilā jīvana*—you saved My life; *strī-paraśa haile*—if I had touched a woman; *āmāra*—My; *ha-ita*—there would have been; *maraṇa*—death.

TRANSLATION

"My dear Govinda," He said, "you have saved My life. If I had touched the body of a woman, I would certainly have died.

TEXT 86

এ-ঋণ শোধিতে আমি নারিমু তোমার।"
গোবিন্দ কহে,—'জগন্নাথ রাখেন মুই কোন্‌ছার'? ৮৬ ॥

e-ṛṇa śodhite āmi nārimu tomāra"
govinda kahe,——'jagannātha rākhena mui kon chāra'?

SYNONYMS

e-ṛṇa—this debt; *śodhite*—to repay; *āmi*—I; *nārimu*—shall not be able; *tomāra*—to you; *govinda kahe*—Govinda replied; *jagannātha*—Lord Jagannātha; *rākhena*—saves; *mui*—I; *kon chāra*—the most insignificant person.

TRANSLATION

"I shall never be able to repay My debt to you." Govinda replied, "Lord Jagannātha has saved You. I am insignificant."

TEXT 87

প্রভু কহে,—"গোবিন্দ, মোর সঙ্গে রহিবা।
যাহাঁ তাহাঁ মোর রক্ষায় সাবধান হইবা ॥" ৮৭ ॥

prabhu kahe,——"govinda, mora saṅge rahibā
yāhāṅ tāhāṅ mora rakṣāya sāvadhāna ha-ibā"

SYNONYMS

prabhu kahe—Śrī Caitanya Mahāprabhu said; *govinda*—My dear Govinda; *mora saṅge rahibā*—you should always remain with Me; *yāhāṅ tāhāṅ*—anywhere and everywhere; *mora*—My; *rakṣāya*—for protection; *sāvadhāna ha-ibā*—you should be very careful.

TRANSLATION

Śrī Caitanya Mahāprabhu replied, "My dear Govinda, you should stay with Me always. There is danger anywere and everywhere; therefore you should protect Me very carefully."

TEXT 88

এত বলি' লেউটি' প্রভু গেলা নিজ-স্থানে ।
শুনি' মহা-ভয় হইল স্বরূপাদি-মনে ॥ ৮৮ ॥

eta bali' leuṭi' prabhu gelā nija-sthāne
śuni' mahā-bhaya ha-ila svarūpādi-mane

SYNONYMS

eta bali'—saying this; *leuṭi'*—returning; *prabhu*—Śrī Caitanya Mahāprabhu; *gelā*—went; *nija-sthāne*—to His own place; *śuni'*—hearing; *mahā-bhaya*—great fear; *ha-ila*—there was; *svarūpa-ādi-mane*—in the minds of Svarūpa Dāmodara and other attendants.

TRANSLATION

After saying this, Śrī Caitanya Mahāprabhu returned home. When Svarūpa Gosvāmī and His other attendants heard about the incident, they were very afraid.

TEXT 89

এথা তপনমিশ্র-পুত্র রঘুনাথ-ভট্টাচার্য ।
প্রভুরে দেখিতে চলিলা ছাড়ি' সর্ব কার্য ॥ ৮৯ ॥

ethā tapana-miśra-putra raghunātha-bhaṭṭācārya
prabhure dekhite calilā chāḍi' sarva kārya

SYNONYMS

ethā—on the other hand; *tapana-miśra-putra*—the son of Tapana Miśra; *raghunātha-bhaṭṭācārya*—Raghunātha Bhaṭṭa; *prabhure*—Śrī Caitanya

Mahāprabhu; *dekhite*—to meet; *calilā*—proceeded; *chāḍi'*—giving up; *sarva kārya*—all duties.

TRANSLATION

During this time, Raghunātha Bhaṭṭācārya, the son of Tapana Miśra, gave up all his duties and left home, intending to meet Śrī Caitanya Mahāprabhu.

TEXT 90

কাশী হৈতে চলিলা তেঁহো গৌড়পথ দিয়া ।
সঙ্গে সেবক চলে তাঁর ঝালি বহিয়া ॥ ৯০ ॥

kāśī haite calilā teṅho gauḍa-patha diyā
saṅge sevaka cale tāṅra jhāli vahiyā

SYNONYMS

kāśī haite—from Kāśī; *calilā*—proceeded; *teṅho*—he; *gauḍa-patha diyā*—by the path through Bengal; *saṅge*—along with him; *sevaka*—one servant; *cale*—goes; *tāṅra*—his; *jhāli*—baggage; *vahiyā*—carrying.

TRANSLATION

Accompanied by one servant carrying his baggage, Raghunātha Bhaṭṭa started from Vārāṇasī and traveled along the path leading through Bengal.

TEXT 91

পথে তারে মিলিলা বিশ্বাস-রামদাস ।
বিশ্বাসখানার কায়স্থ তেঁহো রাজার বিশ্বাস ॥ ৯১ ॥

pathe tāre mililā viśvāsa-rāmadāsa
viśvāsa-khānāra kāyastha teṅho rājāra viśvāsa

SYNONYMS

pathe—on the path; *tāre*—him; *mililā*—met; *viśvāsa-rāmadāsa*—Rāmadāsa Viśvāsa; *viśvāsa-khānāra*—of the governmental accounting department; *kāyastha*—belonging to the *kāyastha* class; *teṅho*—he; *rājāra*—to the king; *viśvāsa*—secretary.

TRANSLATION

In Bengal he met Rāmadāsa Viśvāsa, who belonged to the kāyastha caste. He was one of the king's secretaries.

PURPORT

The word *viśvāsa-khānāra kāyastha* indicates a secretary or clerk belonging to the *kāyastha* caste. *Kāyasthas* were usually secretaries to kings, governors or other important persons. It is said that anyone working in the government secretariat at this time was a *kāyastha.*

TEXT 92

সর্বশাস্ত্রে প্রবীণ, কাব্যপ্রকাশ-অধ্যাপক ।
পরমবৈষ্ণব, রঘুনাথ-উপাসক ॥ ৯২ ॥

sarva-śāstre pravīṇa, kāvya-prakāśa-adhyāpaka
parama-vaiṣṇava, raghunātha-upāsaka

SYNONYMS

sarva-śāstre—in all revealed scriptures; *pravīṇa*—very learned scholar; *kāvya-prakāśa*—of the famous book *Kāvya-prakāśa; adhyāpaka*—a teacher; *parama-vaiṣṇava*—highly advanced devotee; *raghunātha-upāsaka*—worshiper of Lord Rāmacandra.

TRANSLATION

Rāmadāsa Viśvāsa was very learned in all the revealed scriptures. He was a teacher of the famous book Kāvya-prakāśa and was known as an advanced devotee and worshiper of Raghunātha [Lord Rāmacandra].

PURPORT

Commenting on the word *parama-vaiṣṇava,* Śrīla Bhaktivinoda Ṭhākura says that anyone who desires to merge into the existence of the Lord cannot be a pure Vaiṣṇava, but because Rāmadāsa Viśvāsa was a great devotee of Lord Rāmacandra, he was almost a Vaiṣṇava. In those days, no one could distinguish between a pure Vaiṣṇava and a pseudo Vaiṣṇava. Therefore Rāmadāsa Viśvāsa was known as a Vaiṣṇava because he worshiped Lord Rāmacandra.

TEXT 93

অষ্টপ্রহর রামনাম জপেন রাত্রি-দিনে ।
সর্ব ত্যজি' চলিলা জগন্নাথ-দরশনে ॥ ৯৩ ॥

aṣṭa-prahara rāma-nāma japena rātri-dine
sarva tyaji' calilā jagannātha-daraśane

SYNONYMS

aṣṭa-prahara—twenty-four hours a day; *rāma-nāma*—the holy name of Lord Rāma; *japena*—chants; *rātri-dine*—day and night; *sarva*—all; *tyaji'*—giving up; *calilā*—went; *jagannātha-daraśane*—to see Lord Jagannātha.

TRANSLATION

Rāmadāsa had renounced everything and was going to see Lord Jagannātha. While traveling, he chanted the holy name of Lord Rāma twenty-four hours a day.

TEXT 94

রঘুনাথ-ভট্টের সনে পথেতে মিলিলা ।
ভট্টের ঝালি মাথে করি' বহিয়া চলিলা ॥ ৯৪ ॥

raghunātha-bhaṭṭera sane pathete mililā
bhaṭṭera jhāli māthe kari' vahiyā calilā

SYNONYMS

raghunātha-bhaṭṭera—Raghunātha Bhaṭṭa; *sane*—with; *pathete*—on the way; *mililā*—he met; *bhaṭṭera*—of Raghunātha Bhaṭṭa; *jhāli*—baggage; *māthe kari'*—taking on the head; *vahiyā calilā*—carried.

TRANSLATION

When he met Raghunātha Bhaṭṭa on the way, he took Raghunātha's baggage on his head and carried it.

TEXT 95

নানা সেবা করি' করে পাদ-সম্বাহন ।
তাতে রঘুনাথের হয় সঙ্কুচিত মন ॥ ৯৫ ॥

nānā sevā kari' kare pāda-samvāhana
tāte raghunāthera haya saṅkucita mana

SYNONYMS

nānā sevā kari'—serving in various ways; *kare pāda-samvāhana*—massaged his legs; *tāte*—because of this; *raghunāthera*—of Raghunātha Bhaṭṭa; *haya*—there was; *saṅkucita mana*—hesitation in the mind.

TRANSLATION

Rāmadāsa served Raghunātha Bhaṭṭa in various ways, even massaging his legs. Raghunātha Bhaṭṭa felt some hesitation in accepting all this service.

TEXT 96

"তুমি বড় লোক, পণ্ডিত, মহাভাগবতে।
সেবা না করিহ, সুখে চল মোর সাথে॥" ৯৬॥

"tumi baḍa loka, paṇḍita, mahā-bhāgavate
sevā nā kariha, sukhe cala mora sāthe"

SYNONYMS

tumi—you; *baḍa loka*—a great personality; *paṇḍita*—a learned scholar; *mahā-bhāgavate*—a great devotee; *sevā nā kariha*—please do not serve; *sukhe*—happily; *cala*—go; *mora sāthe*—with me.

TRANSLATION

"You are a respectable gentleman, a learned scholar and a great devotee," he said. "Please do not try to serve me. Just come with me in a happy mood."

TEXT 97

রামদাস কহে,—"আমি শূদ্র অধম!
'ব্রাহ্মণের সেবা',—এই মোর নিজ-ধর্ম॥ ৯৭॥

rāmadāsa kahe,—"āmi śūdra adhama!
'brāhmaṇera sevā',—ei mora nija-dharma

SYNONYMS

rāmadāsa kahe—Rāmadāsa said; *āmi*—I; *śūdra*—a *śūdra; adhama*—most fallen; *brāhmaṇera sevā*—to serve a *brāhmaṇa; ei*—this; *mora nija-dharma*—my own religious duty.

TRANSLATION

Rāmadāsa replied, "I am a śūdra, a fallen soul. To serve a brāhmaṇa is my duty and religious principle.

TEXT 98

সঙ্কোচ না কর তুমি, আমি—তোমার 'দাস'।
তোমার সেবা করিলে হয় হৃদয়ে উল্লাস॥" ৯৮॥

saṅkoca nā kara tumi, āmi——tomāra 'dāsa'
tomāra sevā karile haya hṛdaye ullāsa"

SYNONYMS

saṅkoca—hesitation; *nā*—not; *kara*—do; *tumi*—you; *āmi*—I; *tomāra*—your; *dāsa*—servant; *tomāra*—your; *sevā*—service; *karile*—by rendering; *haya*—there is; *hṛdaye*—within the heart; *ullāsa*—jubilation.

TRANSLATION

"Therefore please do not be hesitant. I am your servant, and when I serve you my heart becomes jubilant."

TEXT 99

এত বলি' ঝালি বহেন, করেন সেবনে।
রঘুনাথের তারকমন্ত্র জপেন রাত্রি-দিনে ॥ ৯৯ ॥

eta bali' jhāli vahena, karena sevane
raghunāthera tāraka-mantra japena rātri-dine

SYNONYMS

eta bali'—saying this; *jhāli vahena*—carries the baggage; *karena sevane*—serves; *raghunāthera*—of Lord Rāmacandra; *tāraka*—deliverer; *mantra*—chanting of the holy name; *japena*—chants; *rātri-dine*—day and night.

TRANSLATION

Thus Rāmadāsa carried the baggage of Raghunātha Bhaṭṭa and served him sincerely. He constantly chanted the holy name of Lord Rāmacandra day and night.

TEXT 100

এইমতে রঘুনাথ আইলা নীলাচলে।
প্রভুর চরণে যাঞা মিলিলা কুতুহলে ॥ ১০০ ॥

ei-mate raghunātha āilā nīlācale
prabhura caraṇe yāñā mililā kutūhale

SYNONYMS

ei-mate—in this way; *raghunātha*—Raghunātha Bhaṭṭa; *āilā*—came; *nīlācale*—to Jagannātha Purī; *prabhura caraṇe*—to the lotus feet of Śrī Caitanya Mahāprabhu; *yāñā*—going; *mililā*—met; *kutūhale*—in great delight.

TRANSLATION

Traveling in this way, Raghunātha Bhaṭṭa soon arrived at Jagannātha Purī. There, with great delight, he met Śrī Caitanya Mahāprabhu and fell at His lotus feet.

TEXT 101

দণ্ডপরণাম করি' ভট্ট পড়িলা চরণে ।
প্রভু 'রঘুনাথ' জানি কৈলা আলিঙ্গনে ॥ ১০১ ॥

daṇḍa-paraṇāma kari' bhaṭṭa paḍilā caraṇe
prabhu 'raghunātha' jāni kailā āliṅgane

SYNONYMS

daṇḍa-paraṇāma kari'—offering obeisances by falling down on the ground; *bhaṭṭa*—Raghunātha Bhaṭṭa; *paḍilā caraṇe*—fell at the lotus feet; *prabhu*—Śrī Caitanya Mahāprabhu; *raghunātha*—Raghunātha Bhaṭṭa; *jāni*—knowing; *kailā āliṅgane*—embraced.

TRANSLATION

Raghunātha Bhaṭṭa fell straight as a rod at the lotus feet of Śrī Caitanya Mahāprabhu. Then the Lord embraced him, knowing well who he was.

TEXT 102

মিশ্র আর শেখরের দণ্ডবৎ জানাইলা ।
মহাপ্রভু তাঁ-সবার বার্তা পুছিলা ॥ ১০২ ॥

miśra āra śekharera daṇḍavat jānāilā
mahāprabhu tāṅ-sabāra vārtā puchilā

SYNONYMS

miśra—of Tapana Miśra; *āra*—and; *śekharera*—of Candraśekhara; *daṇḍavat*—obeisances; *jānāilā*—he informed; *mahāprabhu*—Śrī Caitanya Mahāprabhu; *tāṅ-sabāra*—of all of them; *vārtā*—news; *puchilā*—inquired.

TRANSLATION

Raghunātha offered respectful obeisances to Śrī Caitanya Mahāprabhu on behalf of Tapana Miśra and Candraśekhara, and the Lord also inquired about them.

TEXT 103

"ভাল হইল আইলা, দেখ 'কমললোচন'।
আজি আমার এথা করিবা প্রসাদ ভোজন ॥" ১০৩ ॥

"bhāla ha-ila āilā, dekha 'kamala-locana'
āji āmāra ethā karibā prasāda bhojana"

SYNONYMS

bhāla ha-ila—it is very good; *āilā*—you have come; *dekha*—see; *kamala-locana*—the lotus-eyed Lord Jagannātha; *āji*—today; *āmāra ethā*—at My place; *karibā prasāda bhojana*—you will accept *prasāda.*

TRANSLATION

"It is very good that you have come here," the Lord said. "Now go see the lotus-eyed Lord Jagannātha. Today you will accept prasāda here at My place."

TEXT 104

গোবিন্দেরে কহি' এক বাসা দেওয়াইলা।
স্বরূপাদি ভক্তগণ-সনে মিলাইলা ॥ ১০৪ ॥

govindere kahi' eka vāsā deoyāilā
svarūpādi bhakta-gaṇa-sane milāilā

SYNONYMS

govindere—to Govinda; *kahi'*—speaking; *eka*—one; *vāsā*—residential place; *deoyāilā*—caused to be given; *svarūpa-ādi*—headed by Svarūpa Dāmodara Gosvāmī; *bhakta-gaṇa-sane*—with the devotees; *milāilā*—introduced.

TRANSLATION

The Lord asked Govinda to arrange for Raghunātha Bhaṭṭa's accomodations and then introduced him to all the devotees, headed by Svarūpa Dāmodara Gosvāmī.

TEXT 105

এইমত প্রভু-সঙ্গে রহিলা অষ্টমাস।
দিনে দিনে প্রভুর কৃপায় বাড়য়ে উল্লাস ॥ ১০৫ ॥

ei-mata prabhu-saṅge rahilā aṣṭa-māsa
dine dine prabhura kṛpāya bāḍaye ullāsa

SYNONYMS

ei-mata—in this way; *prabhu-saṅge*—along with Śrī Caitanya Mahāprabhu; *rahilā*—remained; *aṣṭa-māsa*—eight months; *dine dine*—day after day; *prabhura*—of Śrī Caitanya Mahāprabhu; *kṛpāya*—by the mercy; *bāḍaye ullāsa*—felt increased jubilation.

TRANSLATION

Thus Raghunātha Bhaṭṭa lived with Śrī Caitanya Mahāprabhu continuously for eight months, and by the Lord's mercy he felt increased transcendental happiness every day.

TEXT 106

মধ্যে মধ্যে মহাপ্রভুর করেন নিমন্ত্রণ ।
ঘর-ভাত করেন, আর বিবিধ ব্যঞ্জন ॥ ১০৬ ॥

madhye madhye mahāprabhura karena nimantraṇa
ghara-bhāta karena, āra vividha vyañjana

SYNONYMS

madhye madhye—at intervals; *mahāprabhura*—to Śrī Caitanya Mahāprabhu; *karena nimantraṇa*—he makes invitations; *ghara-bhāta karena*—he cooks rice at home; *āra*—and; *vividha vyañjana*—various kinds of vegetables.

TRANSLATION

He would periodically cook rice with various vegetables and invite Śrī Caitanya Mahāprabhu to his home.

TEXT 107

রঘুনাথ-ভট্ট—পাকে অতি সুনিপুণ ।
যেই রান্ধে, সেই হয় অমৃতের সম ॥ ১০৭ ॥

raghunātha-bhaṭṭa——pāke ati sunipuṇa
yei rāndhe, sei haya amṛtera sama

SYNONYMS

raghunātha-bhaṭṭa—Raghunātha Bhaṭṭa; *pāke*—in cooking; *ati su-nipuṇa*—very expert; *yei rāndhe*—whatever he cooked; *sei*—that; *haya*—is; *amṛtera sama*—like nectar.

TRANSLATION

Raghunātha Bhaṭṭa was an expert cook. Whatever he prepared tasted just like nectar.

TEXT 108

পরম সন্তোষে প্রভু করেন ভোজন ।
প্রভুর অবশিষ্ট-পাত্র ভট্টের ভক্ষণ ॥ ১০৮ ॥

parama santoṣe prabhu karena bhojana
prabhura avaśiṣṭa-pātra bhaṭṭera bhakṣaṇa

SYNONYMS

parama santoṣe—in great satisfaction; *prabhu*—Śrī Caitanya Mahāprabhu; *karena bhojana*—eats; *prabhura*—of Śrī Caitanya Mahāprabhu; *avaśiṣṭa-pātra*—the plate of remnants; *bhaṭṭera*—of Raghunātha Bhaṭṭa; *bhakṣaṇa*—the eatables.

TRANSLATION

Śrī Caitanya Mahāprabhu would accept with great satisfaction all the food he prepared. After the Lord was satisfied, Raghunātha Bhaṭṭa would eat His remnants.

TEXT 109

রামদাস যদি প্রথম প্রভুরে মিলিলা ।
মহাপ্রভু অধিক তাঁরে কৃপা না করিলা ॥ ১০৯ ॥

rāmadāsa yadi prathama prabhure mililā
mahāprabhu adhika tāṅre kṛpā nā karilā

SYNONYMS

rāmadāsa—the devotee Rāmadāsa Viśvāsa; *yadi*—when; *prathama*—for the first time; *prabhure mililā*—met Śrī Caitanya Mahāprabhu; *mahāprabhu*—Śrī Caitanya Mahāprabhu; *adhika*—much; *tāṅre*—unto him; *kṛpā*—mercy; *nā karilā*—did not show.

TRANSLATION

When Rāmadāsa Viśvāsa met Śrī Caitanya Mahāprabhu, the Lord did not show him any special mercy, although this was their first meeting.

TEXT 110

অন্তরে মুমুক্ষু তেঁহো, বিদ্যা-গর্ববান্ ।
সর্বচিত্ত-জ্ঞাতা প্রভু – সর্বজ্ঞ ভগবান্ ॥ ১১০ ॥

antare mumukṣu teṅho, vidyā-garvavān
sarva-citta-jñātā prabhu——sarvajña bhagavān

SYNONYMS

antare—within his heart; *mumukṣu*—desiring liberation; *teṅho*—he; *vidyā-garvavān*—very proud of his learning; *sarva-citta-jñātā*—one who knows the heart of everyone; *prabhu*—Śrī Caitanya Mahāprabhu; *sarva-jña bhagavān*—the omniscient Supreme Personality of Godhead.

TRANSLATION

Within his heart, Rāmadāsa Viśvāsa was an impersonalist who desired to merge into the existence of the Lord, and he was very proud of his learning. Being the omniscient Supreme Personality of Godhead, Śrī Caitanya Mahāprabhu can understand the heart of everyone, and thus He knew all these things.

TEXT 111

রামদাস কৈলা তবে নীলাচলে বাস ।
পট্টনায়ক-গোষ্ঠীকে পড়ায় 'কাব্যপ্রকাশ' ॥ ১১১ ॥

rāmadāsa kailā tabe nīlācale vāsa
paṭṭanāyaka-goṣṭhīke paḍāya 'kāvya-prakāśa'

SYNONYMS

rāmadāsa—Rāmadāsa Viśvāsa; *kailā*—did; *tabe*—then; *nīlācale vāsa*—residence at Jagannātha Purī; *paṭṭanāyaka-goṣṭhīke*—to the Paṭṭanāyaka family (the descendants of Bhavānanda Rāya); *paḍāya*—teaches; *kāvya-prakāśa*—on the book *Kāvya-prakāśa*.

TRANSLATION

Rāmadāsa Viśvāsa then took up residence in Jagannātha Purī and taught the Kāvya-prakāśa to the Paṭṭanāyaka family [the descendants of Bhavānanda Rāya].

TEXT 112

অষ্টমাস রহি' প্রভু ভট্টে বিদায় দিলা ।
'বিবাহ না করিহ' বলি' নিষেধ করিলা ॥ ১১২ ॥

aṣṭa-māsa rahi' prabhu bhaṭṭe vidāya dilā
'vivāha nā kariha' bali' niṣedha karilā

SYNONYMS

aṣṭa-māsa—for eight months; *rahi'*—staying; *prabhu*—Śrī Caitanya Mahāprabhu; *bhaṭṭe*—to Raghunātha Bhaṭṭa; *vidāya dilā*—bid farewell; *vivāha nā kariha*—do not marry; *bali'*—saying; *niṣedha karilā*—he forbade.

TRANSLATION

After eight months, when Śrī Caitanya Mahāprabhu bade farewell to Raghunātha Bhaṭṭa, the Lord flatly forbade him to marry. "Do not marry," the Lord said.

PURPORT

Raghunātha Bhaṭṭācārya had become a greatly advanced devotee while still unmarried. Śrī Caitanya Mahāprabhu could see this, and therefore He advised him not to begin the process of material sense gratification. Marriage is a concession for people who are unable to control their senses. Raghunātha, however, being an advanced devotee of Kṛṣṇa, naturally had no desire for sense gratification. Therefore Śrī Caitanya Mahāprabhu advised him not to enter the bondage of marriage. Generally a person cannot make much advancement in spiritual consciousness if he is married. He becomes attached to his family and is prone to sense gratification. Thus his spiritual advancement is very slow or almost nil.

TEXT 113

বৃদ্ধ মাতা-পিতার যাই' করহ সেবন ।
বৈষ্ণব-পাশ ভাগবত কর অধ্যয়ন ॥ ১১৩ ॥

vṛddha mātā-pitāra yāi' karaha sevana
vaiṣṇava-pāśa bhāgavata kara adhyayana

SYNONYMS

vṛddha—old; *mātā-pitāra*—of the mother and father; *yāi'*—going back; *karaha sevana*—engage in service; *vaiṣṇava-pāśa*—from a pure Vaiṣṇava; *bhāgavata*—*Śrīmad-Bhāgavatam; kara adhyayana*—study.

TRANSLATION

Śrī Caitanya Mahāprabhu said to Raghunātha Bhaṭṭa, "When you return home, serve your aged father and mother, who are devotees, and try to study Śrīmad-Bhāgavatam from a pure Vaiṣṇava who has realized God."

PURPORT

One should note how Śrī Caitanya Mahāprabhu, the Supreme Personality of Godhead, advised Raghunātha Bhaṭṭācārya to learn *Śrīmad-Bhāgavatam*. He advised him to understand *Śrīmad-Bhāgavatam* not from professional men but from a real *bhāgavata,* devotee. He also advised Raghunātha Bhaṭṭa to serve his mother and father because they were both His devotees. Anyone who wishes to advance in Kṛṣṇa consciousness must try to serve the devotees of Kṛṣṇa. As Narottama dāsa Ṭhākura says, *chāḍiyā vaiṣṇava-sevā nistāra pāyeche kebā:* "Without serving a self-realized Vaiṣṇava, no one has ever been released from the materialistic way of life." Śrī Caitanya Mahāprabhu would have never advised Raghunātha Bhaṭṭa to serve ordinary parents, but since his parents were Vaiṣṇavas, the Lord advised him to serve them.

One might ask "Why shouldn't ordinary parents be served?" As stated in *Śrīmad-Bhāgavatam* (5.5.18):

gurur na sa syāt svajano na sa syāt
pitā na sa syāj jananī na sā syāt
daivaṁ na tat syāt na patiś ca sa syān
na mocayed yaḥ samupeta-mṛtyum

"One who cannot deliver his dependent from the path of birth and death should never become a spiritual master, a relative, a father or mother, or a worshipable demigod, nor should such a person become a husband." Everyone naturally gets a father and mother at the time of birth, but the real father and mother are they who can release their offspring from the clutches of imminent death. This is possible only for parents advanced in Kṛṣṇa consciousness. Therefore any parents who cannot enlighten their offspring in Kṛṣṇa consciousness cannot be accepted as a real father and mother. The following verse from the *Bhakti-rasāmṛta-sindhu* (1.2.200) confirms the uselessness of serving ordinary parents:

laukikī vaidikī vāpi
yā kriyā kriyate mune
hari-sevānukūlaiva
sa kāryā bhaktim icchatā

"One should perform only those activities—either worldly or prescribed by Vedic rules and regulations—which are favorable for the cultivation of Kṛṣṇa consciousness."

Concerning the study of *Śrīmad-Bhāgavatam,* Śrī Caitanya Mahāprabhu clearly advises that one avoid hearing from a non-Vaiṣṇava professional reciter. In this connection Sanātana Gosvāmī quotes a verse from the *Padma Purāṇa:*

avaiṣṇava-mukhodgīrṇaṁ
pūtaṁ hari-kathāmṛtam
śravaṇaṁ naiva kartavyaṁ
sarpocchiṣṭaṁ yathā payaḥ

"No one should hear or take lessons from a person who is not a Vaiṣṇava. Even if he speaks about Kṛṣṇa, such a lesson should not be accepted, for it is like milk touched by the lips of a serpent." Nowadays it is fashionable to observe Bhāgavata-saptāha and hear *Śrīmad-Bhāgavatam* from persons who are anything but advanced devotees or self-realized souls. There are even many Māyāvādīs who read *Śrīmad-Bhāgavatam* to throngs of people. Many Māyāvādīs have recently begun reciting *Śrīmad-Bhāgavatam* in Vṛndāvana, and because they can present the *Bhāgavatam* with word jugglery, twisting the meaning by grammatical tricks, materialistic persons who go to Vṛndāvana as a matter of spiritual fashion like to hear them. All this is clearly forbidden by Śrī Caitanya Mahāprabhu. We should note carefully that since these Māyāvādīs cannot personally know the meaning of *Śrīmad-Bhāgavatam,* they can never deliver others by reciting it. On the other hand, an advanced devotee of the Lord is free from material bondage. He personifies the *Śrīmad-Bhāgavatam* in life and action. Therefore we advise that anyone who wants to learn the *Śrīmad-Bhāgavatam* must approach such a realized soul.

TEXT 114

পুনরপি একবার আসিহ নীলাচলে ।"
এত বলি' কণ্ঠ-মালা দিলা তাঁর গলে ॥ ১১৪ ॥

punarapi eka-bāra āsiha nīlācale"
eta bali' kaṇṭha-mālā dilā tāṅra gale

SYNONYMS

punarapi—again, also; *eka-bāra*—once; *āsiha nīlācale*—come to Jagannātha Purī; *eta bali'*—saying this; *kaṇṭha-mālā*—neck beads; *dilā*—gave; *tāṅra gale*—on his neck.

TRANSLATION

Śrī Caitanya Mahāprabhu concluded, "Come again to Nīlācala [Jagannātha Purī]." After saying this, the Lord put His own neck beads on Raghunātha Bhaṭṭa's neck.

TEXT 115

আলিঙ্গন করি' প্রভু বিদায় তাঁরে দিলা ।
প্রেমে গর গর ভট্ট কান্দিতে লাগিলা ॥ ১১৫ ॥

āliṅgana kari' prabhu vidāya tāṅre dilā
preme gara gara bhaṭṭa kāndite lāgilā

SYNONYMS

āliṅgana kari'—embracing; *prabhu*—Śrī Caitanya Mahāprabhu; *vidāya tāṅre dilā*—bade him farewell; *preme*—in ecstatic love; *gara gara*—overwhelmed; *bhaṭṭa*—Raghunātha Bhaṭṭa; *kāndite lāgilā*—began to cry.

TRANSLATION

Then the Lord embraced him and bade him farewell. Overwhelmed with ecstatic love, Raghunātha Bhaṭṭa began to cry due to imminent separation from Śrī Caitanya Mahāprabhu.

TEXT 116

স্বরূপ-আদি ভক্ত-ঠাঞি আজ্ঞা মাগিয়া ।
বারাণসী আইলা ভট্ট প্রভুর আজ্ঞা পাঞা ॥ ১১৬ ॥

svarūpa-ādi bhakta-ṭhāñi ājñā māgiyā
vārāṇasī āilā bhaṭṭa prabhura ājñā pāñā

SYNONYMS

svarūpa-ādi—headed by Svarūpa Dāmodara Gosvāmī; *bhakta-ṭhāñi*—from the devotees; *ājñā māgiyā*—asking permission; *vārāṇasī āilā*—returned to Vārāṇasī; *bhaṭṭa*—Raghunātha Bhaṭṭa; *prabhura*—of Śrī Caitanya Mahāprabhu; *ājñā pāñā*—getting permission.

TRANSLATION

After taking permission from Śrī Caitanya Mahāprabhu and all the devotees, headed by Svarūpa Dāmodara, Raghunātha Bhaṭṭa returned to Vārāṇasī.

TEXT 117

চারিবৎসর ঘরে পিতা-মাতার সেবা কৈলা ।
বৈষ্ণব-পণ্ডিত-ঠাঞি ভাগবত পড়িলা ॥ ১১৭ ॥

cāri-vatsara ghare pitā-mātāra sevā kailā
vaiṣṇava-paṇḍita-ṭhāñi bhāgavata paḍilā

SYNONYMS

cāri-vatsara—for four years; *ghare*—at home; *pitā-mātāra*—of the father and mother; *sevā kailā*—rendered service; *vaiṣṇava-paṇḍita-ṭhāñi*—from a self-realized, advanced Vaiṣṇava; *bhāgavata paḍilā*—he studied *Śrīmad-Bhāgavatam.*

TRANSLATION

In accordance with the instructions of Śrī Caitanya Mahāprabhu, he continuously rendered service to his mother and father for four years. He also regularly studied the Śrīmad-Bhāgavatam from a self-realized Vaiṣṇava.

TEXT 118

পিতা-মাতা কাশী পাইলে উদাসীন হঞা ।
পুনঃ প্রভুর ঠাঞি আইলা গৃহাদি ছাড়িয়া ॥ ১১৮ ॥

pitā-mātā kāśī pāile udāsīna hañā
punaḥ prabhura ṭhāñi āilā gṛhādi chāḍiyā

SYNONYMS

pitā-mātā—the father and mother; *kāśī pāile*—when they passed away at Kāśī (Vārāṇasī); *udāsīna hañā*—being indifferent; *punaḥ*—again; *prabhura ṭhāñi*—to Śrī Caitanya Mahāprabhu; *āilā*—returned; *gṛha-ādi chāḍiyā*—leaving all relationships with home.

TRANSLATION

Then his parents died at Kāśī [Vārāṇasī], and he became detached. He therefore returned to Śrī Caitanya Mahāprabhu, giving up all relationships with his home.

TEXT 119

পূর্ববৎ অষ্টমাস প্রভু-পাশ ছিলা ।
অষ্টমাস রহি' পুনঃ প্রভু আজ্ঞা দিলা ॥ ১১৯ ॥

pūrvavat aṣṭa-māsa prabhu-pāśa chilā
aṣṭa-māsa rahi' punaḥ prabhu ājñā dilā

SYNONYMS

pūrva-vat—as previously; *aṣṭa-māsa*—for eight months; *prabhu-pāśa chilā*—remained with Śrī Caitanya Mahāprabhu; *aṣṭa-māsa rahi'*—after staying for eight months; *punaḥ*—again; *prabhu*—Śrī Caitanya Mahāprabhu; *ājñā dilā*—ordered him.

TRANSLATION

As previously, Raghunātha remained continuously with Śrī Caitanya Mahāprabhu for eight months. Then the Lord gave him the following order.

TEXT 120

"আমার আজ্ঞায়, রঘুনাথ, যাহ বৃন্দাবনে ।
তাহাঁ যাঞা রহ রূপ-সনাতন-স্থানে ॥ ১২০ ॥

"āmāra ājñāya, raghunātha, yāha vṛndāvane
tāhāṅ yāñā raha rūpa-sanātana-sthāne

SYNONYMS

āmāra ājñāya—upon My order; *raghunātha*—My dear Raghunātha; *yāha vṛndāvane*—go to Vṛndāvana; *tāhāṅ yāñā*—going there; *raha*—remain; *rūpa-sanātana-sthāne*—in the care of Rūpa Gosvāmī and Sanātana Gosvāmī.

TRANSLATION

"My dear Raghunātha, go to Vṛndāvana, following My instructions, and place yourself under the care of Rūpa and Sanātana Gosvāmīs.

TEXT 121

ভাগবত পড়, সদা লহ কৃষ্ণনাম ।
অচিরে করিবেন কৃপা কৃষ্ণ ভগবান্ ॥" ১২১ ॥

bhāgavata paḍa, sadā laha kṛṣṇa-nāma
acire karibena kṛpā kṛṣṇa bhagavān"

SYNONYMS

bhāgavata paḍa—read *Śrīmad-Bhāgavatam; sadā*—always; *laha kṛṣṇa-nāma*—chant the Hare Kṛṣṇa *mantra; acire*—very soon; *karibena*—will bestow; *kṛpā*—mercy; *kṛṣṇa*—Lord Kṛṣṇa; *bhagavān*—the Supreme Personality of Godhead.

TRANSLATION

"In Vṛndāvana you should chant the Hare Kṛṣṇa mantra twenty-four hours a day and read Śrīmad-Bhāgavatam continuously. Kṛṣṇa, the Supreme Personality of Godhead, will very soon bestow His mercy upon you."

TEXT 122

এত বলি' প্রভু তাঁরে আলিঙ্গন কৈলা ।
প্রভুর কৃপাতে কৃষ্ণপ্রেমে মত্ত হৈলা ॥ ১২২ ॥

eta bali' prabhu tāṅre āliṅgana kailā
prabhura kṛpāte kṛṣṇa-preme matta hailā

SYNONYMS

eta bali'—saying this; *prabhu*—Śrī Caitanya Mahāprabhu; *tāṅre*—Raghunātha Bhaṭṭa; *āliṅgana kailā*—embraced; *prabhura*—of Śrī Caitanya Mahāprabhu; *kṛpāte*—by the mercy; *kṛṣṇa-preme*—in love of Kṛṣṇa; *matta hailā*—became enlivened.

TRANSLATION

After saying this, Śrī Caitanya Mahāprabhu embraced Raghunātha Bhaṭṭa, and by the Lord's mercy Raghunātha was enlivened with ecstatic love for Kṛṣṇa.

TEXT 123

চৌদ্দ-হাত জগন্নাথের তুলসীর মালা ।
ছুটা-পান-বিড়া মহোৎসবে পাঞাছিলা ॥ ১২৩ ॥

caudda-hāta jagannāthera tulasīra mālā
chuṭā-pāna-viḍā mahotsave pāñāchilā

SYNONYMS

caudda-hāta—fourteen cubits long; *jagannāthera*—of Lord Jagannātha; *tulasīra mālā*—a garland made of *tulasī* leaves; *chuṭā-pāna-viḍā*—unspiced betel; *mahotsave*—at a festival; *pāñāchilā*—got.

TRANSLATION

At a festival Śrī Caitanya Mahāprabhu had been given some unspiced betel and a garland of tulasī leaves fourteen cubits long. The garland had been worn by Lord Jagannātha.

TEXT 124

সেই মালা, ছুটা পান প্রভু তাঁরে দিলা ।
'ইষ্টদেব' করি' মালা ধরিয়া রাখিলা ॥ ১২৪ ॥

sei mālā, chuṭā pāna prabhu tāṅre dilā
'iṣṭa-deva' kari' mālā dhariyā rākhilā

SYNONYMS

sei mālā—that garland; *chuṭā pāna*—the betel; *prabhu*—Śrī Caitanya Mahāprabhu; *tāṅre dilā*—delivered to him; *iṣṭa-deva*—his worshipable Deity; *kari'*—accepting as; *mālā*—that garland; *dhariyā rākhilā*—kept.

TRANSLATION

Śrī Caitanya Mahāprabhu gave the garland and betel to Raghunātha Bhaṭṭa, who accepted them as a worshipable Deity, preserving them very carefully.

TEXT 125

প্রভুর ঠাঞি আজ্ঞা লঞা গেলা বৃন্দাবনে ।
আশ্রয় করিলা আসি' রূপ-সনাতনে ॥ ১২৫ ॥

prabhura ṭhāñi ājñā lañā gelā vṛndāvane
āśraya karilā āsi' rūpa-sanātane

SYNONYMS

prabhura ṭhāñi—from Śrī Caitanya Mahāprabhu; *ājñā lañā*—taking permission; *gelā vṛndāvane*—went to Vṛndāvana; *āśraya karilā*—took shelter; *āsi'*—coming; *rūpa-sanātane*—of Rūpa Gosvāmī and Sanātana Gosvāmī.

TRANSLATION

Taking permission from Śrī Caitanya Mahāprabhu, Raghunātha Bhaṭṭa then departed for Vṛndāvana. When he arrived there, he put himself under the care of Rūpa and Sanātana Gosvāmīs.

TEXT 126

রূপ-গোসাঞির সভায় করেন ভাগবত-পঠন ।
ভাগবত পড়িতে প্রেমে আউলায় তাঁর মন ॥ ১২৬ ॥

rūpa-gosāñira sabhāya karena bhāgavata-paṭhana
bhāgavata paḍite preme āulāya tāṅra mana

SYNONYMS

rūpa-gosāñira sabhāya—in the assembly of Rūpa, Sanātana and other Vaiṣṇavas; *karena*—performs; *bhāgavata-paṭhana*—recitation of *Śrīmad-Bhāgavatam; bhāgavata paḍite*—while reciting *Śrīmad-Bhāgavatam; preme*—in ecstatic love; *āulāya*—becomes overwhelmed; *tāṅra mana*—his mind.

TRANSLATION

When reciting Śrīmad-Bhāgavatam in the company of Rūpa and Sanātana, Raghunātha Bhaṭṭa would be overwhelmed with ecstatic love for Kṛṣṇa.

TEXT 127

অশ্রু, কম্প, গদ্গদ প্রভুর কৃপাতে ।
নেত্র কণ্ঠ রোধে বাষ্প, না পারে পড়িতে ॥ ১২৭ ॥

aśru, kampa, gadgada prabhura kṛpāte
netra kaṇṭha rodhe bāṣpa, nā pāre paḍite

SYNONYMS

aśru—tears; *kampa*—trembling; *gadgada*—faltering of the voice; *prabhura*—of Śrī Caitanya Mahāprabhu; *kṛpāte*—by the mercy; *netra*—eyes; *kaṇṭha*—neck; *rodhe*—choked up; *bāṣpa*—tears; *nā pāre paḍite*—could not recite.

TRANSLATION

By the mercy of Śrī Caitanya Mahāprabhu, he experienced the symptoms of ecstatic love—tears, trembling, and faltering of the voice. His eyes filled with tears, his throat became choked, and thus he could not recite Śrīmad-Bhāgavatam.

TEXT 128

পিকস্বর-কণ্ঠ, তাতে রাগের বিভাগ ।
একশ্লোক পড়িতে ফিরায় তিন-চারি রাগ ॥ ১২৮ ॥

pika-svara-kaṇṭha, tāte rāgera vibhāga
eka-śloka paḍite phirāya tina-cāri rāga

SYNONYMS

pika-svara-kaṇṭha—a very sweet voice like a cuckoo's; *tāte*—above that; *rāgera*—of tunes; *vibhāga*—division; *eka-śloka*—one verse; *paḍite*—reciting; *phirāya*—changes; *tina-cāri rāga*—three or four different tunes.

TRANSLATION

His voice was as sweet as a cuckoo's, and he would recite each verse of Śrīmad-Bhāgavatam in three or four tunes. Thus his recitations were very sweet to hear.

TEXT 129

কৃষ্ণের সৌন্দর্য-মাধুর্য যবে পড়ে, শুনে ।
প্রেমেতে বিহ্বল তবে, কিছুই না জানে ॥ ১২৯ ॥

kṛṣṇera saundarya-mādhurya yabe paḍe, śune
premete vihvala tabe, kichui nā jāne

SYNONYMS

kṛṣṇera—of Kṛṣṇa; *saundarya*—beauty; *mādhurya*—sweetness; *yabe*—when; *paḍe*—recites; *śune*—hears; *premete*—in ecstatic love of Kṛṣṇa; *vihvala*—overwhelmed; *tabe*—then; *kichui*—anything; *nā jāne*—does not know.

TRANSLATION

When he recited or heard about the beauty and sweetness of Kṛṣṇa, he would be overwhelmed with ecstatic love and become oblivious to everything.

TEXT 130

গোবিন্দ-চরণে কৈলা আত্মসমর্পণ ।
গোবিন্দ-চরণারবিন্দ—যাঁর প্রাণধন ॥ ১৩০ ॥

govinda-caraṇe kailā ātma-samarpaṇa
govinda-caraṇāravinda——yāṅra prāṇa-dhana

SYNONYMS

govinda-caraṇe—at the lotus feet of Lord Govinda; *kailā ātma-samarpaṇa*—he surrendered himself fully; *govinda-caraṇa-aravinda*—the lotus feet of Lord Govinda; *yāṅra*—of whom; *prāṇa-dhana*—the life and soul.

TRANSLATION

Thus Raghunātha Bhaṭṭa surrendered fully at the lotus feet of Lord Govinda, and those lotus feet became his life and soul.

TEXT 131

নিজ শিষ্যে কহি' গোবিন্দের মন্দির করাইলা ।
বংশী, মকর, কুণ্ডলাদি 'ভূষণ' করি' দিলা ॥ ১৩১ ॥

nija śiṣye kahi' govindera mandira karāilā
vaṁśī, makara, kuṇḍalādi 'bhūṣaṇa' kari' dilā

SYNONYMS

nija śiṣye—to his own disciples; *kahi'*—by speaking; *govindera*—of Lord Govinda; *mandira karāilā*—constructed a temple; *vaṁśī*—flute; *makara kuṇḍala-ādi*—earrings shaped like sharks, etc.; *bhūṣaṇa*—ornaments; *kari'*—preparing; *dilā*—gave.

TRANSLATION

Subsequently Raghunātha Bhaṭṭa ordered his disciples to construct a temple for Govinda. He prepared various ornaments for Govinda, including a flute and earrings shaped like sharks.

TEXT 132

গ্রাম্যবার্তা না শুনে, না কহে জিহ্বায় ।
কৃষ্ণকথা-পূজাদিতে অষ্টপ্রহর যায় ॥ ১৩২ ॥

grāmya-vārtā nā śune, nā kahe jihvāya
kṛṣṇa-kathā-pūjādite aṣṭa-prahara yāya

SYNONYMS

grāmya-vārtā—common topics; *nā śune*—he never heard; *nā*—not; *kahe*—utters; *jihvāya*—with his tongue; *kṛṣṇa-kathā*—topics on Kṛṣṇa; *pūjā-ādite*—and in worshiping and so on; *aṣṭa-prahara yāya*—he passed the whole day and night.

TRANSLATION

Raghunātha Bhaṭṭa would neither hear nor speak about anything of the material world. He would simply discuss Kṛṣṇa and worship the Lord day and night.

TEXT 133

বৈষ্ণবের নিন্দ্য-কর্ম নাহি পাড়ে কাণে ।
সবে কৃষ্ণ ভজন করে,—এইমাত্র জানে ॥ ১৩৩ ॥

vaiṣṇavera nindya-karma nāhi pāḍe kāṇe
sabe kṛṣṇa bhajana kare,——ei-mātra jāne

SYNONYMS

vaiṣṇavera—of the Vaiṣṇava; *nindya-karma*—reproachable activities; *nāhi pāḍe kāṇe*—he does not hear; *sabe*—all; *kṛṣṇa bhajana kare*—are engaged in Kṛṣṇa's service; *ei-mātra*—only this; *jāne*—he understands.

TRANSLATION

He would not listen to blasphemy of a Vaiṣṇava, nor would he listen to talk of a Vaiṣṇava's misbehavior. He knew only that everyone was engaged in Kṛṣṇa's service; he did not understand anything else.

PURPORT

Raghunātha Bhaṭṭa never did anything harmful to a Vaiṣṇava. In other words, he was never inattentive in the service of the Lord, nor did he ever violate the rules and regulations of a pure Vaiṣṇava. It is the duty of a Vaiṣṇava *ācārya* to prevent his disciples and followers from violating the principles of Vaiṣṇava behavior. He should always advise them to strictly follow the regulative principles, which will protect them from falling down. Although a Vaiṣṇava preacher may sometimes criticize others, Raghunātha Bhaṭṭa avoided this. Even if another Vaiṣṇava was actually at fault, Raghunātha Bhaṭṭa would not criticize him; he saw only that everyone was engaged in Kṛṣṇa's service. That is the position of a *mahā-bhāgavata.* Actually, even if one is serving *māyā,* in a higher sense he is also a servant of Kṛṣṇa. Because *māyā* is the servant of Kṛṣṇa, anyone serving *māyā* serves Kṛṣṇa indirectly. Therefore it is said:

keha māne, keha nā māne, saba tāṅra dāsa
ye nā māne, tāra haya sei pāpe nāśa

"Some accept Him, whereas others do not, yet everyone is His servant. One who does not accept Him, however, will be ruined by his sinful activities." (Cc. *Ādi.* 6.85)

TEXT 134

মহাপ্রভুর দত্ত মালা মননের কালে ।
প্রসাদ-কড়ার-সহ বান্ধি লেন গলে ॥ ১৩৪ ॥

mahāprabhura datta mālā mananera kāle
prasāda-kaḍāra saha bāndhi lena gale

SYNONYMS

mahāprabhura—by Śrī Caitanya Mahāprabhu; *datta*—given; *mālā*—*tulasī* garland; *mananera*—of remembering; *kāle*—at the time; *prasāda-kaḍāra*—the remnants of Lord Jagannātha; *saha*—with; *bāndhi*—binding together; *lena*—takes; *gale*—on his neck.

TRANSLATION

When Raghunātha Bhaṭṭa Gosvāmī was absorbed in remembrance of Lord Kṛṣṇa, he would take the tulasī garland and the prasāda of Lord Jagannātha given to him by Śrī Caitanya Mahāprabhu, bind them together and wear them on his neck.

TEXT 135

মহাপ্রভুর কৃপায় কৃষ্ণপ্রেম অনর্গল ।
এই ত' কহিলুঁ তাতে চৈতন্য-কৃপাফল ॥ ১৩৫ ॥

mahāprabhura kṛpāya kṛṣṇa-prema anargala
ei ta' kahiluṅ tāte caitanya-kṛpā-phala

SYNONYMS

mahāprabhura kṛpāya—by the mercy of Śrī Caitanya Mahāprabhu; *kṛṣṇa-prema anargala*—incessantly overwhelmed with ecstatic love of Kṛṣṇa; *ei ta'*—thus; *kahiluṅ*—I have described; *tāte*—thereby; *caitanya-kṛpā-phala*—the result of Śrī Caitanya Mahāprabhu's mercy.

TRANSLATION

Thus I have described the powerful mercy of Śrī Caitanya Mahāprabhu, by which Raghunātha Bhaṭṭa Gosvāmī remained constantly overwhelmed with ecstatic love for Kṛṣṇa.

TEXTS 136-137

জগদানন্দের কহিলুঁ বৃন্দাবনগমন ।
তার মধ্যে দেবদাসীর গান-শ্রবণ ॥ ১৩৬ ॥
মহাপ্রভুর রঘুনাথে কৃপা-প্রেম-ফল ।
একপরিচ্ছেদে তিন কথা কহিলুঁ সকল ॥ ১৩৭ ॥

jagadānandera kahiluṅ vṛndāvana-gamana
tāra madhye deva-dāsīra gāna-śravaṇa

mahāprabhura raghunāthe kṛpā-prema-phala
eka-paricchede tina kathā kahiluṅ sakala

SYNONYMS

jagadānandera—of Jagadānanda Paṇḍita; *kahiluṅ*—I have described; *vṛndāvana-gamana*—going to Vṛndāvana; *tāra madhye*—within that; *deva-dāsīra*—of the female singer in the temple of Jagannātha; *gāna-śravaṇa*—hearing of the song; *mahāprabhura*—of Śrī Caitanya Mahāprabhu; *raghunāthe*—unto Raghunātha Bhaṭṭa; *kṛpā*—by mercy; *prema*—love; *phala*—result; *eka-paricchede*—in one chapter; *tina kathā*—three topics; *kahiluṅ*—I have described; *sakala*—all.

TRANSLATION

In this chapter I have spoken about three topics: Jagadānanda Paṇḍita's visit to Vṛndāvana, Śrī Caitanya Mahāprabhu's listening to the song of the deva-dāsī at the temple of Jagannātha, and how Raghunātha Bhaṭṭa Gosvāmī achieved ecstatic love of Kṛṣṇa by the mercy of Śrī Caitanya Mahāprabhu.

TEXT 138

যে এইসকল কথা শুনে শ্রদ্ধা করি'।
তাঁরে কৃষ্ণপ্রেমধন দেন গৌরহরি ॥ ১৩৮ ॥

ye ei-sakala kathā śune śraddhā kari'
tāṅre kṛṣṇa-prema-dhana dena gaurahari

SYNONYMS

ye—one who; *ei-sakala*—all these; *kathā*—topics; *śune*—hears; *śraddhā kari'*—with faith and love; *tāṅre*—unto him; *kṛṣṇa-prema-dhana*—the wealth of ecstatic love of Lord Kṛṣṇa; *dena*—delivers; *gaurahari*—Śrī Caitanya Mahāprabhu.

TRANSLATION

Śrī Caitanya Mahāprabhu [Gaurahari] bestows ecstatic love for Kṛṣṇa upon anyone who hears all these topics with faith and love.

TEXT 139

শ্রীরূপ-রঘুনাথ-পদে যার আশ।
চৈতন্যচরিতামৃত কহে কৃষ্ণদাস ॥ ১৩৯ ॥

śrī-rūpa-raghunātha-pade yāra āśa
caitanya-caritāmṛta kahe kṛṣṇadāsa

SYNONYMS

śrī-rūpa—Śrīla Rūpa Gosvāmī; *raghunātha*—Śrīla Raghunātha dāsa Gosvāmī; *pade*—at the lotus feet; *yāra*—whose; *āśa*—expectation; *caitanya-caritāmṛta*—the book named *Caitanya-caritāmṛta;* *kahe*—describes; *kṛṣṇadāsa*—Śrīla Kṛṣṇadāsa Kavirāja Gosvāmī.

TRANSLATION

Praying at the lotus feet of Śrī Rūpa and Śrī Raghunātha, always desiring their mercy, I, Kṛṣṇadāsa, narrate Śrī Caitanya-caritāmṛta, following in their footsteps.

Thus end the Bhaktivedanta purports to the Śrī Caitanya-caritāmṛta, Antya-līlā, *Thirteenth Chapter, describing Jagadānanda Paṇḍita's visit to Vṛndāvana, the Lord's hearing the song of the deva-dāsī, and Raghunātha Bhaṭṭa Gosvāmī's achieving love of Kṛṣṇa.*

CHAPTER 14

Lord Śrī Caitanya Mahāprabhu's Feelings of Separation from Kṛṣṇa

Śrīla Bhaktivinoda Ṭhākura gives the following summary of the Fourteenth Chapter of *Antya-līlā*. Śrī Caitanya Mahāprabhu's feelings of separation from Kṛṣṇa resulted in highly elevated transcendental madness. When He was standing near the Garuḍa-stambha and praying to Lord Jagannātha, a woman from Orissa put her foot on the Lord's shoulder in her great eagerness to see Lord Jagannātha. Govinda chastised her for this, but Caitanya Mahāprabhu praised her eagerness. When Caitanya Mahāprabhu went to the temple of Lord Jagannātha, He was absorbed in ecstatic love and saw only Kṛṣṇa. As soon as He perceived this woman, however, His external consciousness immediately returned, and He saw Jagannātha, Baladeva and Subhadrā. Caitanya Mahāprabhu also saw Kṛṣṇa in a dream, and He was overwhelmed with ecstatic love. When He could no longer see Kṛṣṇa, Śrī Caitanya Mahāprabhu compared Himself to a *yogī* and described how that *yogī* was seeing Vṛndāvana. Sometimes all the transcendental ecstatic symptoms were manifest in Him. One night, Govinda and Svarūpa Dāmodara noticed that although the three doors to the Lord's room were closed and locked, the Lord was not present inside. Seeing this, Svarūpa Dāmodara and the other devotees went outside and saw the Lord lying unconscious by the gate known as Siṁha-dvāra. His body had become unusually long, and the joints of His bones were loose. The devotees gradually brought Śrī Caitanya Mahāprabhu back to His senses by chanting the Hare Kṛṣṇa *mantra,* and then they took Him back to His residence. Once Śrī Caitanya Mahāprabhu mistook Caṭaka-parvata for Govardhana-parvata. As He ran toward it, He became stunned, and then the eight ecstatic transformations appeared in His body due to great love for Kṛṣṇa. At that time all the devotees chanted the Hare Kṛṣṇa *mantra* to pacify Him.

TEXT 1

কৃষ্ণবিচ্ছেদবিভ্রান্ত্যা মনসা বপুষা ধিয়া ।
যদ্‌যদ্ব্যধত্ত গৌরাঙ্গস্তল্লেশঃ কথ্যতেঽধুনা ॥ ১ ॥

kṛṣṇa-viccheda-vibhrāntyā
manasā vapuṣā dhiyā

yad yad vyadhatta gaurāṅgas
tal-leśaḥ kathyate 'dhunā

SYNONYMS

kṛṣṇa-viccheda—of separation from Kṛṣṇa; *vibhrāntyā*—by the bewilderment; *manasā*—by the mind; *vapuṣā*—by the body; *dhiyā*—by the intelligence; *yat yat*—whatever; *vyadhatta*—performed; *gaurāṅgaḥ*—Śrī Caitanya Mahāprabhu; *tat*—of that; *leśaḥ*—a very small fragment; *kathyate*—is being described; *adhunā*—now.

TRANSLATION

I shall now describe a very small portion of the activities performed by Śrī Caitanya Mahāprabhu with His mind, intelligence and body when He was bewildered by strong feelings of separation from Kṛṣṇa.

TEXT 2

জয় জয় শ্রীচৈতন্য স্বয়ং ভগবান্ ।
জয় জয় গৌরচন্দ্র ভক্তগণ-প্রাণ ॥ ২ ॥

jaya jaya śrī-caitanya svayaṁ bhagavān
jaya jaya gauracandra bhakta-gaṇa-prāṇa

SYNONYMS

jaya jaya—all glories; *śrī-caitanya*—to Śrī Caitanya Mahāprabhu; *svayam bhagavān*—the Personality of Godhead Himself; *jaya jaya*—all glories; *gaura-candra*—to Śrī Caitanya Mahāprabhu; *bhakta-gaṇa-prāṇa*—the life and soul of the devotees.

TRANSLATION

All glories to Śrī Caitanya Mahāprabhu, the Supreme Personality of Godhead! All glories to Lord Gauracandra, the life and soul of His devotees.

TEXT 3

জয় জয় নিত্যানন্দ চৈতন্য-জীবন ।
জয়াদ্বৈতাচার্য জয় গৌরপ্রিয়তম ॥ ৩ ॥

jaya jaya nityānanda caitanya-jīvana
jayādvaitācārya jaya gaura-priyatama

SYNONYMS

jaya jaya—all glories; *nityānanda*—to Lord Nityānanda; *caitanya-jīvana*—the life of Śrī Caitanya Mahāprabhu; *jaya*—all glories; *advaita-ācārya*—to Advaita Ācārya; *jaya*—all glories; *gaura-priya-tama*—very, very dear to Śrī Caitanya Mahāprabhu.

TRANSLATION

All glories to Lord Nityānanda, who is Śrī Caitanya Mahāprabhu's very life. And all glories to Advaita Ācārya, who is extremely dear to Śrī Caitanya Mahāprabhu.

TEXT 4

জয় স্বরূপ, শ্রীবাসাদি প্রভুভক্তগণ।
শক্তি দেহ',—করি যেন চৈতন্যবর্ণন ॥ ৪ ॥

jaya svarūpa, śrīvāsādi prabhu-bhakta-gaṇa
śakti deha',——kari yena caitanya-varṇana

SYNONYMS

jaya—all glories; *svarūpa*—to Svarūpa Dāmodara; *śrīvāsa-ādi*—headed by Śrīvāsa Ṭhākura; *prabhu-bhakta-gaṇa*—to the devotees of the Lord; *śakti deha'*—please give strength; *kari*—I can make; *yena*—so that; *caitanya-varṇana*—description of Lord Caitanya Mahāprabhu.

TRANSLATION

All glories to Svarūpa Dāmodara and the devotees, headed by Śrīvāsa Ṭhākura. Please give me the strength to describe the character of Śrī Caitanya Mahāprabhu.

TEXT 5

প্রভুর বিরহোন্মাদ-ভাব গম্ভীর।
বুঝিতে না পারে কেহ, যদ্যপি হয় 'ধীর' ॥ ৫ ॥

prabhura virahonmāda-bhāva gambhīra
bujhite nā pāre keha, yadyapi haya 'dhīra'

SYNONYMS

prabhura—of Śrī Caitanya Mahāprabhu; *viraha-unmāda*—of the transcendental madness of separation from Kṛṣṇa; *bhāva*—emotion; *gambhīra*—very deep and mysterious; *bujhite*—to understand; *nā pāre keha*—no one is able; *yadyapi*—although; *haya*—is; *dhīra*—a very learned and gentle scholar.

TRANSLATION

Śrī Caitanya Mahāprabhu's emotion of transcendental madness in separation from Kṛṣṇa is very deep and mysterious. Even though one is very advanced and learned, he cannot understand it.

TEXT 6

বুঝিতে না পারি যাহা, বর্ণিতে কে পারে ?
সেই বুঝে, বর্ণে, চৈতন্য শক্তি দেন যাঁরে ॥ ৬ ॥

bujhite nā pāri yāhā, varṇite ke pāre?
sei bujhe, varṇe, caitanya śakti dena yāṅre

SYNONYMS

bujhite—to understand; *nā pāri*—not being able; *yāhā*—subject which; *varṇite ke pāre*—who can describe; *sei bujhe*—he can understand; *varṇe*—can describe; *caitanya*—Śrī Caitanya Mahāprabhu; *śakti*—capacity; *dena*—gives; *yāṅre*—to whom.

TRANSLATION

How can one describe unfathomable subject matters? It is possible only if Śrī Caitanya Mahāprabhu gives him the capability.

TEXT 7

স্বরূপ-গোসাঞি আর রঘুনাথ-দাস ।
এই দুইর কড়চাতে এ-লীলা প্রকাশ ॥ ৭ ॥

svarūpa-gosāñi āra raghunātha-dāsa
ei duira kaḍacāte e-līlā prakāśa

SYNONYMS

svarūpa-gosāñi—Svarūpa Dāmodara Gosvāmī; *āra*—and; *raghunātha-dāsa*—Raghunātha dāsa Gosvāmī; *ei duira*—of these two; *kaḍacāte*—in the notebooks; *e-līlā*—these pastimes; *prakāśa*—described.

TRANSLATION

Svarūpa Dāmodara Gosvāmī and Raghunātha dāsa Gosvāmī recorded all these transcendental activities of Śrī Caitanya Mahāprabhu in their notebooks.

PURPORT

Śrī Caitanya Mahāprabhu's transcendental feelings of separation from Kṛṣṇa and His consequent madness are not at all understandable by a person on the material platform. Nonetheless, a so-called party of devotees named *nadīyā-nāgarī* has sprung up and introduced the worship of Viṣṇupriyā. This certainly indicates their ignorance concerning Śrī Caitanya Mahāprabhu's pastimes. In the opinion of Bhaktisiddhānta Sarasvatī Ṭhākura, such worship is a product of the imagination. Many other methods of worshiping Caitanya Mahāprabhu have also been introduced, but they have all been rejected by stalwart devotees like Bhaktivinoda Ṭhākura. The groups practicing such unauthorized worship have been listed by Śrīla Bhaktivinoda Ṭhākura:

āula, bāula, kartābhajā, neḍā, daraveśa, sāṅi
sahajiyā, sakhībhekī, smārta, jāta-gosāñi
ativāḍī, cūḍādhārī, gaurāṅga-nāgarī

Svarūpa Dāmodara Gosvāmī and Raghunātha dāsa Gosvāmī witnessed Caitanya Mahāprabhu's activities firsthand, and they recorded them in two notebooks. Therefore, without reference to these notebooks, one cannot understand the activities of Śrī Caitanya Mahāprabhu. Anyone inventing some new method for worshiping Śrī Caitanya Mahāprabhu is certainly unable to understand the Lord's pastimes, for he is bereft of the real process of approaching the Lord.

TEXT 8

সেকালে এ-দুই রহেন মহাপ্রভুর পাশে ।
আর সব কড়চা-কর্তা রহেন দূরদেশে ॥ ৮ ॥

se-kāle e-dui rahena mahāprabhura pāśe
āra saba kaḍacā-kartā rahena dūra-deśe

SYNONYMS

se-kāle—in those days; *e-dui*—these two; *rahena*—stayed; *mahāprabhura pāśe*—with Śrī Caitanya Mahāprabhu; *āra*—other; *saba*—all; *kaḍacā-kartā*—commentators; *rahena*—remained; *dūra-deśe*—far away.

TRANSLATION

In those days, Svarūpa Dāmodara and Raghunātha dāsa Gosvāmī lived with Śrī Caitanya Mahāprabhu, whereas all other commentators lived far away from Him.

PURPORT

Besides Svarūpa Dāmodara and Raghunātha dāsa Gosvāmī, there were many others who also recorded Śrī Caitanya Mahāprabhu's activities. Śrīla Bhaktisiddhānta Sarasvatī Ṭhākura believes that the people of the world would benefit greatly if such notes were available. It is a most unfortunate situation for human society that none of these notebooks are still extant.

TEXT 9

ক্ষণে ক্ষণে অনুভবি' এই দুইজন ।
সংক্ষেপে বাহুল্যে করেন কড়চা-গ্রন্থন ॥ ৯ ॥

kṣaṇe kṣaṇe anubhavi' ei dui-jana
saṅkṣepe bāhulye karena kaḍacā-granthana

SYNONYMS

kṣaṇe kṣaṇe—moment by moment; *anubhavi'*—understanding; *ei dui-jana*—these two persons; *saṅkṣepe*—in brief; *bāhulye*—elaborately; *karena*—do; *kaḍacā-granthana*—compiling the notebooks.

TRANSLATION

These two great personalities [Svarūpa Dāmodara and Raghunātha dāsa Gosvāmī] recorded the activities of Śrī Caitanya Mahāprabhu moment by moment. They described these activities briefly as well as elaborately in their notebooks.

PURPORT

For future reference, we should remember that Svarūpa Dāmodara Gosvāmī recorded the pastimes briefly, whereas Raghunātha dāsa Gosvāmī recorded them elaborately. These two great personalities simply recorded the facts; they did not create any descriptive literary embellishments.

TEXT 10

স্বরূপ—'সূত্রকর্তা', রঘুনাথ—'বৃত্তিকার' ।
তার বাহুল্য বর্ণি—পাঁজি-টীকা-ব্যবহার ॥ ১০ ॥

svarūpa——'sūtra-kartā', raghunātha——'vṛttikāra'
tāra bāhulya varṇi——pāṅji-ṭīkā-vyavahāra

SYNONYMS

svarūpa—Svarūpa Dāmodara Gosvāmī; *sūtra-kartā*—maker of short codes; *raghunātha*—Raghunātha dāsa Gosvāmī; *vṛttikāra*—maker of elaborate explanations; *tāra*—of those; *bāhulya*—more elaborately; *varṇi*—I shall describe; *pāṅji*—fluffing out (as of cotton); *ṭīkā*—explanation; *vyavahāra*—behavior.

TRANSLATION

Svarūpa Dāmodara wrote short codes, whereas Raghunātha dāsa Gosvāmī wrote elaborate descriptions. I shall now describe Śrī Caitanya Mahāprabhu's activities more elaborately, as if fluffing out compressed cotton.

PURPORT

Pāṅji-ṭīkā means further explanations of a subject. Writing such explanations is likened to the process of fluffing out cotton.

TEXT 11

তাতে বিশ্বাস করি' শুন ভাবের বর্ণন ।
হইবে ভাবের জ্ঞান, পাইবা প্রেমধন ॥ ১১ ॥

tāte viśvāsa kari' śuna bhāvera varṇana
ha-ibe bhāvera jñāna, pāibā prema-dhana

SYNONYMS

tāte—therefore; *viśvāsa kari'*—having faith; *śuna*—please hear; *bhāvera varṇana*—description of ecstatic emotions; *ha-ibe*—there will be; *bhāvera*—of ecstatic emotions; *jñāna*—knowledge; *pāibā*—you will get; *prema-dhana*—love of Kṛṣṇa.

TRANSLATION

Please hear faithfully this description of Caitanya Mahāprabhu's ecstatic emotions. Thus you will come to know of His ecstatic love, and ultimately you will achieve love of Godhead.

TEXT 12

কৃষ্ণ মথুরায় গেলে, গোপীর যে দশা হৈল ।
কৃষ্ণবিচ্ছেদে প্রভুর সে দশা উপজিল ॥ ১২ ॥

kṛṣṇa mathurāya gele, gopīra ye daśā haila
kṛṣṇa-vicchede prabhura se daśā upajila

SYNONYMS

kṛṣṇa mathurāya gele—when Lord Kṛṣṇa departed for Mathurā; *gopīra*—of the *gopīs; ye daśā*—which condition; *haila*—was; *kṛṣṇa-vicchede*—by separation from Kṛṣṇa; *prabhura*—of Śrī Caitanya Mahāprabhu; *se daśā*—that situation; *upajila*—happened.

TRANSLATION

When Śrī Caitanya Mahāprabhu felt separation from Kṛṣṇa, His condition exactly corresponded to the condition of the gopīs in Vṛndāvana after Kṛṣṇa's departure for Mathurā.

TEXT 13

উদ্ধব-দর্শনে যৈছে রাধার বিলাপ ।
ক্রমে ক্রমে হৈল প্রভুর সে উন্মাদ-বিলাপ ॥ ১৩ ॥

uddhava-darśane yaiche rādhāra vilāpa
krame krame haila prabhura se unmāda-vilāpa

SYNONYMS

uddhava-darśane—by seeing Uddhava; *yaiche*—as; *rādhāra*—of Śrīmatī Rādhārāṇī; *vilāpa*—lamentation; *krame krame*—gradually; *haila*—became; *prabhura*—of Śrī Caitanya Mahāprabhu; *se*—that; *unmāda-vilāpa*—lamentation in madness.

TRANSLATION

The lamentation of Śrīmatī Rādhārāṇī when Uddhava visited Vṛndāvana gradually became a feature of Śrī Caitanya Mahāprabhu's transcendental madness.

TEXT 14

রাধিকার ভাবে প্রভুর সদা 'অভিমান' ।
সেই ভাবে আপনাকে হয় 'রাধা'-জ্ঞান ॥ ১৪ ॥

rādhikāra bhāve prabhura sadā 'abhimāna'
sei bhāve āpanāke haya 'rādhā'-jñāna

SYNONYMS

rādhikāra bhāve—in the emotion of Śrīmatī Rādhārāṇī; *prabhura*—of Śrī Caitanya Mahāprabhu; *sadā*—always; *abhimāna*—conception; *sei bhāve*—under such a conception; *āpanāke*—upon Himself; *haya*—becomes; *rādhā-jñāna*—consideration as Śrīmatī Rādhārāṇī.

TRANSLATION

Śrīmatī Rādhārāṇī's emotions after seeing Uddhava exactly correspond to those of Śrī Caitanya Mahāprabhu. He always conceived of Himself in Her position and sometimes thought that He was Śrīmatī Rādhārāṇī Herself.

PURPORT

Śrīla Bhaktisiddhānta Sarasvatī Ṭhākura explains that the purport of the word *abhimāna*, or "self-conception," is that Śrī Caitanya Mahāprabhu thought Himself to be in the position of Śrīmatī Rādhārāṇī and was always ready to render service in that way. Although Śrī Caitanya Mahāprabhu is Kṛṣṇa Himself, He assumed the complexion and emotions of Śrīmatī Rādhārāṇī and remained in that status. He never assumed the complexion or status of Lord Kṛṣṇa. Of course, Kṛṣṇa wanted to experience the role of Śrīmatī Rādhārāṇī; that is the original cause of His assuming the body of Śrī Caitanya Mahāprabhu. Therefore pure Vaiṣṇavas never disturb Śrī Caitanya Mahāprabhu's conception of being Śrīmatī Rādhārāṇī.

Unfortunately, at the present time a group of so-called devotees maintain that Śrī Caitanya Mahāprabhu is the enjoyer and that they are enjoyers as well. They have actually deviated from devotional service to the Lord. Śrī Caitanya Mahāprabhu manifested Himself to show that cultivation of love for Kṛṣṇa in separation is the easiest way of success for all living entities. Despite this fact, there are some theosophists who declare that because Śrī Caitanya Mahāprabhu is the Supreme Personality of Godhead, such cultivation is easy for Him but difficult for the living entity and that one can therefore approach Kṛṣṇa in any way he likes. To nullify this idea, Śrī Caitanya Mahāprabhu demonstrated practically how one can achieve love of Kṛṣṇa by adopting Śrīmatī Rādhārāṇī's mood in separation from Kṛṣṇa.

TEXT 15

দিব্যোন্মাদে ঐছে হয়, কি ইহা বিস্ময় ?
অধিরূঢ়-ভাবে দিব্যোন্মাদ-প্রলাপ হয় ॥ ১৫ ॥

divyonmāde aiche haya, ki ihā vismaya?
adhirūḍha-bhāve divyonmāda-pralāpa haya

SYNONYMS

divya-unmāde—in transcendental madness; *aiche*—such; *haya*—is; *ki ihā vismaya*—what is the wonder; *adhirūḍha-bhāve*—in highly elevated love of Kṛṣṇa; *divya-unmāda*—in transcendental madness; *pralāpa*—talking; *haya*—there is.

TRANSLATION

Such is the state of transcendental madness. Why is it difficult to understand? When one is highly elevated in love of Kṛṣṇa, he becomes transcendentally mad and talks like a madman.

TEXT 16

এতস্য মোহনাখ্যস্য গতিং কামপ্যুপেয়ুষঃ ।
ভ্রমাভা কাপি বৈচিত্রী দিব্যোন্মাদ ইতীর্যতে ।
উদ্ঘূর্ণা-চিত্রজল্পাদ্যাস্তদ্ভেদা বহবো মতাঃ ॥ ১৬ ॥

etasya mohanākhyasya
gatiṁ kāmapy upeyuṣaḥ
bhramābhā kāpi vaicitrī
divyonmāda itīryate
udghūrṇā-citra-jalpādyās
tad-bhedā bahavo matāḥ

SYNONYMS

etasya—of this; *mohana-ākhyasya*—mood known as *mohana,* or enchanting; *gatim*—progress; *kāmapi*—inexplicable; *upeyuṣaḥ*—having obtained; *bhrama-ābhā*—resembling bewilderment; *kāpi*—some; *vaicitrī*—condition bringing about astonishment; *divya-unmāda*—transcendental madness; *iti*—thus; *īryate*—it is called; *udghūrṇā*—of the name *udghūrṇā; citra-jalpa*—of the name *citra-jalpa; ādyāḥ*—and so on; *tat-bhedāḥ*—different features of that; *bahavaḥ*—many; *matāḥ*—described.

TRANSLATION

"When the ecstatic emotion of enchantment gradually progresses, it becomes similar to bewilderment. Then one reaches the stage of astonishment [vaicitrī], which awakens transcendental madness. Udghūrṇā and citra-jalpa are two among the many divisions of transcendental madness."

PURPORT

This is a quotation from the *Ujjvala-nīlamaṇi* (*Sthāyibhāva-prakaraṇa,* 190).

TEXT 17

একদিন মহাপ্রভু করিয়াছেন শয়ন ।
কৃষ্ণ রাসলীলা করে,—দেখিলা স্বপন ॥ ১৭ ॥

eka-dina mahāprabhu kariyāchena śayana
kṛṣṇa rāsa-līlā kare,——dekhilā svapana

SYNONYMS

eka-dina—one day; *mahāprabhu*—Śrī Caitanya Mahāprabhu; *kariyāchena śayana*—was taking rest; *kṛṣṇa*—Lord Kṛṣṇa; *rāsa-līlā kare*—performs *rāsa-līlā* dance; *dekhilā*—He saw; *svapana*—a dream.

TRANSLATION

One day while He was resting, Śrī Caitanya Mahāprabhu dreamed He saw Kṛṣṇa performing His rāsa dance.

TEXT 18

ত্রিভঙ্গ-সুন্দর-দেহ, মুরলীবদন ।
পীতাম্বর, বনমালা, মদনমোহন ॥ ১৮ ॥

tribhaṅga-sundara-deha, muralī-vadana
pītāmbara, vana-mālā, madana-mohana

SYNONYMS

tri-bhaṅga—curved in three places; *sundara*—beautiful; *deha*—body; *muralī-vadana*—with a flute to the mouth; *pīta-ambara*—with yellow garments; *vana-mālā*—forest flower garlands; *madana-mohana*—enchanting Cupid.

TRANSLATION

Śrī Caitanya Mahāprabhu saw Lord Kṛṣṇa standing with His beautiful body curved in three places, holding His flute to His lips. Wearing yellow garments and garlands of forest flowers, He was enchanting even to Cupid.

TEXT 19

মণ্ডলীবন্ধে গোপীগণ করেন নর্ত্তন ।
মধ্যে রাধা-সহ নাচে ব্রজেন্দ্রনন্দন ॥ ১৯ ॥

maṇḍalī-bandhe gopī-gaṇa karena nartana
madhye rādhā-saha nāce vrajendra-nandana

SYNONYMS

maṇḍalī-bandhe—in a circle; *gopī-gaṇa*—the *gopīs;* *karena nartana*—engaged in dancing; *madhye*—in the middle; *rādhā-saha*—with Śrīmatī Rādhārāṇī; *nāce*—dances; *vrajendra-nandana*—Kṛṣṇa, the son of Mahārāja Nanda.

TRANSLATION

The gopīs were dancing in a circle, and in the middle of that circle, Kṛṣṇa, the son of Mahārāja Nanda, danced with Rādhārāṇī.

TEXT 20

দেখি' প্রভু সেই রসে আবিষ্ট হৈলা ।
'বৃন্দাবনে কৃষ্ণ পাইনু'—এই জ্ঞান কৈলা ॥ ২০ ॥

dekhi' prabhu sei rase āviṣṭa hailā
'vṛndāvane kṛṣṇa pāinu'——ei jñāna kailā

SYNONYMS

dekhi'—seeing; *prabhu*—Śrī Caitanya Mahāprabhu; *sei*—that; *rase*—in the transcendental mellow; *āviṣṭa hailā*—became overwhelmed; *vṛndāvane*—in Vṛndāvana; *kṛṣṇa pāinu*—I have gotten Kṛṣṇa; *ei*—this; *jñāna kailā*—He thought.

TRANSLATION

Seeing this, Śrī Caitanya Mahāprabhu was overwhelmed with the transcendental mellow of the rāsa dance, and He thought, "Now I am with Kṛṣṇa in Vṛndāvana."

TEXT 21

প্রভুর বিলম্ব দেখি' গোবিন্দ জাগাইলা ।
জাগিলে 'স্বপ্ন'-জ্ঞান হৈল, প্রভু দুঃখী হৈলা ॥ ২১ ॥

prabhura vilamba dekhi' govinda jāgāilā
jāgile 'svapna'-jñāna haila, prabhu duḥkhī hailā

SYNONYMS

prabhura—of Śrī Caitanya Mahāprabhu; *vilamba*—delay; *dekhi'*—seeing; *govinda jāgāilā*—caused to awaken; *jāgile*—when He awoke; *svapna-jñāna haila*—could understand that it was a dream; *prabhu*—Śrī Caitanya Mahāprabhu; *duḥkhī hailā*—became unhappy.

TRANSLATION

When Govinda saw that the Lord had not yet risen, he awakened Him. Understanding that He had only been dreaming, the Lord was somewhat unhappy.

TEXT 22

দেহাভ্যাসে নিত্যকৃত্য করি' সমাপন ।
কালে যাই' কৈলা জগন্নাথ দরশন ॥ ২২ ॥

dehābhyāse nitya-kṛtya kari' samāpana
kāle yāi' kailā jagannātha daraśana

SYNONYMS

deha-abhyāse—as a habit; *nitya-kṛtya*—the daily duties; *kari' samāpana*—finishing; *kāle*—at the proper time; *yāi'*—going; *kailā*—performed; *jagannātha daraśana*—seeing Lord Jagannātha.

TRANSLATION

Śrī Caitanya Mahāprabhu performed His customary daily duties, and at the usual time He went to see Lord Jagannātha in the temple.

TEXT 23

যাবৎ কাল দর্শন করেন গরুড়ের পাছে ।
প্রভুর আগে দর্শন করে লোক লাখে লাখে ॥ ২৩ ॥

yāvat kāla darśana karena garuḍera pāche
prabhura āge darśana kare loka lākhe lākhe

SYNONYMS

yāvat kāla—as long as; *darśana*—seeing; *karena*—performs; *garuḍera pāche*—from the back of the Garuḍa column; *prabhura āge*—in front of Śrī Caitanya Mahāprabhu; *darśana kare*—see; *loka*—people; *lākhe lākhe*—in hundreds of thousands.

TRANSLATION

As He viewed Lord Jagannātha from behind the Garuḍa column, hundreds and thousands of people in front of Him were seeing the Deity.

TEXT 24

উড়িয়া এক স্ত্রী ভীড়ে দর্শন না পাঞা ।
গরুড়ে চড়ি' দেখে প্রভুর স্কন্ধে পদ দিয়া ॥ ২৪ ॥

uḍiyā eka strī bhīḍe darśana nā pāñā
garuḍe caḍi' dekhe prabhura skandhe pada diyā

SYNONYMS

uḍiyā—a native of Orissa; *eka*—one; *strī*—woman; *bhīḍe*—in the crowd; *darśana nā pāñā*—being unable to see; *garuḍe caḍi'*—climbing up the column of Garuḍa; *dekhe*—sees; *prabhura*—of Śrī Caitanya Mahāprabhu; *skandhe*—on the shoulder; *pada*—her foot; *diyā*—placing.

TRANSLATION

Suddenly, a woman from Orissa, unable to see Lord Jagannātha because of the crowd, climbed the column of Garuḍa, placing her foot on Śrī Caitanya Mahāprabhu's shoulder.

TEXT 25

দেখিয়া গোবিন্দ আস্তে-ব্যস্তে স্ত্রীকে বর্জিলা ।
তারে নামাইতে প্রভু গোবিন্দে নিষেধিলা ॥ ২৫ ॥

dekhiyā govinda āste-vyaste strīke varjilā
tāre nāmāite prabhu govinde niṣedhilā

SYNONYMS

dekhiyā—seeing; *govinda*—the personal servant of Śrī Caitanya Mahāprabhu; *āste-vyaste*—with great haste; *strīke*—the woman; *varjilā*—got down; *tāre*—her; *nāmāite*—to get down; *prabhu*—Śrī Caitanya Mahāprabhu; *govinde*—Govinda; *niṣedhilā*—forbade.

TRANSLATION

When he saw this, Caitanya Mahāprabhu's personal secretary, Govinda, hastily got her down from her position. Śrī Caitanya Mahāprabhu, however, chastised him for this.

PURPORT

Because Garuḍa is the carrier of Lord Viṣṇu, he is the supreme Vaiṣṇava. Therefore to touch his body with one's feet or to climb the column of Garuḍa is certainly a *vaiṣṇava-aparādha,* an offense to a Vaiṣṇava. The woman was also offensive to Kṛṣṇa by putting her foot on the shoulder of Śrī Caitanya Mahāprabhu. Seeing all these offenses, Govinda very hastily made her get down.

TEXT 26

'আদিবস্যা' এই স্ত্রীরে না কর বর্জন ।
করুক যথেষ্ট জগন্নাথ দরশন ॥ ২৬ ॥

'ādi-vasyā' ei strīre nā kara varjana
karuka yatheṣṭa jagannātha daraśana

SYNONYMS

ādi-vasyā—uncivilized; *ei*—this; *strīre*—woman; *nā kara varjana*—do not forbid; *karuka*—let her do; *yathā-iṣṭa*—as desired; *jagannātha daraśana*—seeing Lord Jagannātha.

TRANSLATION

Śrī Caitanya Mahāprabhu said to Govinda, "O ādi-vasyā [uncivilized man], do not forbid this woman to climb the Garuḍa-stambha. Let her see Lord Jagannātha to her satisfaction."

PURPORT

For an explanation of the word *ādi-vasyā,* refer to *Antya-līlā,* Chapter Ten, verse 116.

TEXT 27

আস্তে-ব্যস্তে সেই নারী ভূমেতে নামিলা ।
মহাপ্রভুরে দেখি' তাঁর চরণ বন্দিলা ॥ ২৭ ॥

āste-vyaste sei nārī bhūmete nāmilā
mahāprabhure dekhi' tāṅra caraṇa vandilā

SYNONYMS

āste-vyaste—in great haste; *sei nārī*—that woman; *bhūmete*—on the ground; *nāmilā*—got down; *mahāprabhure dekhi'*—seeing Śrī Caitanya Mahāprabhu; *tāṅra*—His; *caraṇa vandilā*—begged pardon at the lotus feet.

TRANSLATION

When the woman came to her senses, however, she quickly climbed back down to the ground and, seeing Śrī Caitanya Mahāprabhu, immediately begged at His lotus feet for forgiveness.

TEXT 28

তার আর্তি দেখি' প্রভু কহিতে লাগিলা।
"এত আর্তি জগন্নাথ মোরে নাহি দিলা! ২৮ ॥

tāra ārti dekhi' prabhu kahite lāgilā
"eta ārti jagannātha more nāhi dilā!

SYNONYMS

tāra—her; *ārti*—eagerness; *dekhi'*—seeing; *prabhu*—Śrī Caitanya Mahāprabhu; *kahite lāgilā*—began to speak; *eta ārti*—so much eagerness; *jagannātha*—Lord Jagannātha; *more*—unto Me; *nāhi dilā*—did not bestow.

TRANSLATION

Seeing the woman's eagerness, Śrī Caitanya Mahāprabhu said, "Lord Jagannātha has not bestowed so much eagerness upon Me.

PURPORT

The woman was so eager to see Lord Jagannātha that she forgot she was offending the feet of a Vaiṣṇava by climbing the column of Garuḍa. She also neglected to consider that by putting her foot on the shoulder of Śrī Caitanya Mahāprabhu, she offended the Supreme Personality of Godhead. These are both grievous offenses that displease the Supreme Lord and Vaiṣṇavas. She was so eager to see Lord Jagannātha, however, that she committed all these offenses obliviously. Śrī Caitanya Mahāprabhu praised her eagerness; He regretted that Lord Jagannātha had not bestowed such great eagerness upon Him.

TEXT 29

জগন্নাথে আবিষ্ট ইহার তনু-মন-প্রাণে।
মোর স্কন্ধে পদ দিয়াছে, তাহো নাহি জানে ॥ ২৯ ॥

jagannāthe āviṣṭa ihāra tanu-mana-prāṇe
mora skandhe pada diyāche, tāho nāhi jāne

SYNONYMS

jagannāthe—in Lord Jagannātha; *āviṣṭa*—fully absorbed; *ihāra*—of this woman; *tanu*—body; *mana*—mind; *prāṇe*—life; *mora skandhe*—upon My shoulder; *pada*—foot; *diyāche*—has put; *tāho*—she; *nāhi jāne*—did not understand.

PURPORT

This is a quotation from *Śrīmad-Bhāgavatam* (10.21.18). It was spoken by the *gopīs* when Lord Kṛṣṇa and Balarāma entered the forest in the autumn. The *gopīs* spoke among themselves and glorified Kṛṣṇa and Balarāma for Their pastimes.

TEXT 87

এই শ্লোক পড়ি' প্রভু চলেন বায়ুবেগে ।
গোবিন্দ ধাইল পাছে, নাহি পায় লাগে ॥ ৮৭ ॥

ei śloka paḍi' prabhu calena vāyu-vege
govinda dhāila pāche, nāhi pāya lāge

SYNONYMS

ei śloka—this verse; *paḍi'*—reciting; *prabhu*—Śrī Caitanya Mahāprabhu; *calena*—goes; *vāyu-vege*—at the speed of the wind; *govinda*—Govinda; *dhāila*—ran; *pāche*—behind; *nāhi pāya lāge*—could not catch.

TRANSLATION

Reciting this verse, Śrī Caitanya Mahāprabhu ran toward the sand dune as fast as the wind. Govinda ran after Him, but he could not approach Him.

TEXT 88

ফুকার পড়িল, মহা-কোলাহল হইল ।
যেই যাহাঁ ছিল সেই উঠিয়া ধাইল ॥ ৮৮ ॥

phukāra paḍila, mahā-kolāhala ha-ila
yei yāhāṅ chila sei uṭhiyā dhāila

SYNONYMS

phu-kāra—a loud call; *paḍila*—arose; *mahā-kolāhala*—a tumultuous sound; *ha-ila*—there was; *yei*—whoever; *yāhāṅ*—wherever; *chila*—was; *sei*—he; *uṭhiyā dhāila*—got up and began to run.

TRANSLATION

First one devotee shouted loudly, and then a tumultuous uproar arose as all the devotees stood up and began to run after the Lord.

TEXT 89

স্বরূপ, জগদানন্দ, পণ্ডিত-গদাধর ।
রামাই, নন্দাই, আর পণ্ডিত-শঙ্কর ॥ ৮৯ ॥

svarūpa, jagadānanda, paṇḍita-gadādhara
rāmāi, nandāi, āra paṇḍita śaṅkara

SYNONYMS

svarūpa—Svarūpa Dāmodara Gosvāmī; *jagadānanda*—Jagadānanda Paṇḍita; *paṇḍita-gadādhara*—Gadādhara Paṇḍita; *rāmāi*—Rāmāi; *nandāi*—Nandāi; *āra*—and; *paṇḍita-śaṅkara*—Śaṅkara Paṇḍita.

TRANSLATION

Svarūpa Dāmodara Gosvāmī, Jagadānanda Paṇḍita, Gadādhara Paṇḍita, Rāmāi, Nandāi and Śaṅkara Paṇḍita are some of the devotees who ran after Śrī Caitanya Mahāprabhu.

TEXT 90

পুরী-ভারতী-গোসাঞি আইলা সিন্ধুতীরে ।
ভগবান্-আচার্য খঞ্জ চলিলা ধীরে ধীরে ॥ ৯০ ॥

purī-bhāratī-gosāñi āilā sindhu-tīre
bhagavān-ācārya khañja calilā dhīre dhīre

SYNONYMS

purī—Paramānanda Purī; *bhāratī-gosāñi*—Brahmānanda Bhāratī; *āilā*—came; *sindhu-tīre*—on the shore of the sea; *bhagavān-ācārya*—Bhagavān Ācārya; *khañja*—lame; *calilā*—ran; *dhīre dhīre*—very slowly.

TRANSLATION

Paramānanda Purī and Brahmānanda Bhāratī also went toward the beach, and Bhagavān Ācārya, who was lame, followed them very slowly.

TEXT 91

প্রথমে চলিলা প্রভু,—যেন বায়ুগতি ।
স্তম্ভভাব পথে হৈল, চলিতে নাহি শক্তি ॥ ৯১ ॥

prathame calilā prabhu,—yena vāyu-gati
stambha-bhāva pathe haila, calite nāhi śakti

SYNONYMS

prathame—in the beginning; *calilā*—went; *prabhu*—Śrī Caitanya Mahāprabhu; *yena*—like; *vāyu-gati*—the speed of the wind; *stambha-bhāva*—the emotion of being stunned; *pathe*—on the way; *haila*—there was; *calite*—to move; *nāhi*—no; *śakti*—power.

TRANSLATION

Śrī Caitanya Mahāprabhu was running with the speed of the wind, but He suddenly became stunned in ecstasy and lost all strength to proceed further.

TEXT 92

প্রতি-রোমকূপে মাংস— ব্রণের আকার ।
তার উপরে রোমোদ্গম—কদম্বপ্রকার ॥ ৯২ ॥

prati-roma-kūpe māṁsa——vraṇera ākāra
tāra upare romodgama——kadamba-prakāra

SYNONYMS

prati-roma-kūpe—in every hair hole; *māṁsa*—the flesh; *vraṇera ākāra*—like pimples; *tāra upare*—upon that; *roma-udgama*—standing of the hair; *kadamba-prakāra*—like the *kadamba* flowers.

TRANSLATION

The flesh at each of His pores erupted like pimples, and His hair, standing on end, appeared like kadamba flowers.

TEXT 93

প্রতি-রোমে প্রস্বেদ পড়ে রুধিরের ধার ।
কণ্ঠে ঘর্ঘর, নাহি বর্ণের উচ্চার ॥ ৯৩ ॥

prati-rome prasveda paḍe rudhirera dhāra
kaṇṭhe gharghara, nāhi varṇera uccāra

SYNONYMS

prati-rome—from each hair; *prasveda*—sweat; *paḍe*—drops; *rudhirera*—of blood; *dhāra*—flow; *kaṇṭhe*—in the throat; *gharghara*—gargling sound; *nāhi*—not; *varṇera*—of letters; *uccāra*—pronunciation.

TRANSLATION

Blood and perspiration flowed incessantly from every pore of His body, and He could not speak a word but simply produced a gargling sound within His throat.

TEXT 94

দুই নেত্রে ভরি' অশ্রু বহয়ে অপার ।
সমুদ্রে মিলিলা যেন গঙ্গা-যমুনা-ধার ॥ ৯৪ ॥

dui netre bhari' aśru vahaye apāra
samudre mililā yena gaṅgā-yamunā-dhāra

SYNONYMS

dui netre—in the two eyes; *bhari'*—filling; *aśru*—tears; *vahaye*—flow; *apāra*—unlimited; *samudre*—the ocean; *mililā*—met; *yena*—as if; *gaṅgā*—of the Ganges; *yamunā*—of the Yamunā; *dhāra*—flow.

TRANSLATION

The Lord's eyes filled up and overflowed with unlimited tears, like the Ganges and Yamunā meeting in the sea.

TEXT 95

বৈবর্ণ্যে শঙ্খপ্রায় শ্বেত হৈল অঙ্গ ।
তবে কম্প উঠে,—যেন সমুদ্রে তরঙ্গ ॥ ৯৫ ॥

vaivarṇye śaṅkha-prāya śveta haila aṅga
tabe kampa uṭhe,——yena samudre taraṅga

SYNONYMS

vaivarṇye—by fading; *śaṅkha-prāya*—like a conchshell; *śveta*—white; *haila*—became; *aṅga*—body; *tabe*—at that time; *kampa*—shivering; *uṭhe*—arises; *yena*—as if; *samudre*—in the ocean; *taraṅga*—waves.

TRANSLATION

His entire body faded to the color of a white conchshell, and then He began to quiver, like the waves in the ocean.

TEXT 96

কাঁপিতে কাঁপিতে প্রভু ভূমেতে পড়িলা ।
তবে ত' গোবিন্দ প্রভুর নিকটে আইলা ॥ ৯৬ ॥

kāṅpite kāṅpite prabhu bhūmete paḍilā
tabe ta' govinda prabhura nikaṭe āilā

SYNONYMS

kāṅpite kāṅpite—while shivering; *prabhu*—Śrī Caitanya Mahāprabhu; *bhūmete*—on the ground; *paḍilā*—fell down; *tabe*—at that time; *ta'*—certainly; *govinda*—Govinda; *prabhura*—to Śrī Caitanya Mahāprabhu; *nikaṭe*—near; *āilā*—came.

TRANSLATION

While quivering in this way, Śrī Caitanya Mahāprabhu fell down on the ground. Then Govinda approached Him.

TEXT 97

করঙ্গের জলে করে সর্বাঙ্গ সিঞ্চন ।
বহির্বাস লঞা করে অঙ্গ সংবীজন ॥ ৯৭ ॥

karaṅgera jale kare sarvāṅga siñcana
bahirvāsa lañā kare aṅga saṁvījana

SYNONYMS

karaṅgera jale—with water from a *karaṅga* waterpot; *kare*—does; *sarva-aṅga*—all parts of the body; *siñcana*—sprinkling; *bahirvāsa*—covering cloth; *lañā*—taking; *kare*—does; *aṅga*—the body; *saṁvījana*—fanning.

TRANSLATION

Govinda sprinkled water from a karaṅga waterpot all over the Lord's body, and then, taking His own outer garment, he began to fan Śrī Caitanya Mahāprabhu.

TEXT 98

স্বরূপাদিগণ তাহাঁ আসিয়া মিলিলা ।
প্রভুর অবস্থা দেখি' কান্দিতে লাগিলা ॥ ৯৮ ॥

svarūpādi-gaṇa tāhāṅ āsiyā mililā
prabhura avasthā dekhi' kāndite lāgilā

SYNONYMS

svarūpa-ādi-gaṇa—the devotees, headed by Svarūpa Dāmodara Gosvāmī; *tāhāṅ*—there; *āsiyā*—coming; *mililā*—met; *prabhura*—of Lord Śrī Caitanya Mahāprabhu; *avasthā*—condition; *dekhi'*—seeing; *kāndite lāgilā*—began to cry.

TRANSLATION

When Svarūpa Dāmodara and the other devotees reached the spot and saw the condition of Śrī Caitanya Mahāprabhu, they began to cry.

TEXT 99

প্রভুর অঙ্গে দেখে অষ্টসাত্ত্বিক বিকার।
আশ্চর্য সাত্ত্বিক দেখি' হৈলা চমৎকার ॥ ৯৯ ॥

prabhura aṅge dekhe aṣṭa-sāttvika vikāra
āścarya sāttvika dekhi' hailā camatkāra

SYNONYMS

prabhura—of Śrī Caitanya Mahāprabhu; *aṅge*—in the body; *dekhe*—they see; *aṣṭa-sāttvika vikāra*—eight kinds of transcendental transformations; *āścarya*—wonderful; *sāttvika*—transcendental; *dekhi'*—seeing; *hailā camatkāra*—they became struck with wonder.

TRANSLATION

All eight kinds of transcendental transformations were visible in the Lord's body. All the devotees were struck with wonder to see such a sight.

PURPORT

The eight ecstatic symptoms are the state of being stunned, perspiration, standing of the hairs on end, faltering of the voice, trembling, fading of the body's color, tears and devastation.

TEXT 100

উচ্চ সঙ্কীর্তন করে প্রভুর শ্রবণে।
শীতল জলে করে প্রভুর অঙ্গ সম্মার্জনে ॥ ১০০ ॥

ucca saṅkīrtana kare prabhura śravaṇe
śītala jale kare prabhura aṅga sammārjane

SYNONYMS

ucca—loud; *saṅkīrtana*—chanting of the Hare Kṛṣṇa *mantra; kare*—do; *prabhura*—of Śrī Caitanya Mahāprabhu; *śravaṇe*—within the hearing; *śītala*—cold; *jale*—with water; *kare*—do; *prabhura*—of Śrī Caitanya Mahāprabhu; *aṅga*—body; *sammārjane*—washing.

TRANSLATION

The devotees loudly chanted the Hare Kṛṣṇa mantra near Śrī Caitanya Mahāprabhu and washed His body with cold water.

TEXT 101

এইমত বহুবার কীর্তন করিতে।
'হরিবোল' বলি' প্রভু উঠে আচম্বিতে ॥ ১০১ ॥

ei-mata bahu-bāra kīrtana karite
'hari-bola' bali' prabhu uṭhe ācambite

SYNONYMS

ei-mata—in this way; *bahu-bāra*—for a long time; *kīrtana karite*—chanting; *hari-bola bali'*—uttering Hari bol; *prabhu*—Śrī Caitanya Mahāprabhu; *uṭhe*—stands up; *ācambite*—suddenly.

TRANSLATION

After the devotees had been chanting for a long time, Śrī Caitanya Mahāprabhu suddenly stood up, shouting, "Hari bol!"

TEXT 102

সানন্দে সকল বৈষ্ণব বলে 'হরি' 'হরি'।
উঠিল মঙ্গলধ্বনি চতুর্দিক ভরি' ॥ ১০২ ॥

sānande sakala vaiṣṇava bale 'hari' 'hari'
uṭhila maṅgala-dhvani catur-dik bhari'

SYNONYMS

sa-ānande—with great pleasure; *sakala*—all; *vaiṣṇava*—devotees; *bale*—chanted; *hari hari*—the holy name of the Lord; *uṭhila*—there arose; *maṅgala-dhvani*—an auspicious sound; *catuḥ-dik* —all directions; *bhari'*—filling.

TRANSLATION

When Śrī Caitanya Mahāprabhu stood up, all the Vaiṣṇavas loudly chanted, "Hari! Hari!" in great jubilation. The auspicious sound filled the air in all directions.

TEXT 103

উঠি' মহাপ্রভু বিস্মিত, ইতি উতি চায়।
যে দেখিতে চায়, তাহা দেখিতে না পায়॥ ১০৩॥

uṭhi' mahāprabhu vismita, iti uti cāya
ye dekhite cāya, tāhā dekhite nā pāya

SYNONYMS

uṭhi'—standing up; *mahāprabhu*—Śrī Caitanya Mahāprabhu; *vismita*—astonished; *iti uti*—here and there; *cāya*—looks; *ye*—what; *dekhite cāya*—He wanted to see; *tāhā*—that; *dekhite nā pāya*—He could not see.

TRANSLATION

Astonished, Śrī Caitanya Mahāprabhu stood up and began looking here and there, trying to see something. But He could not catch sight of it.

TEXT 104

'বৈষ্ণব' দেখিয়া প্রভুর অর্ধবাহ্য হইল।
স্বরূপ-গোসাঞিরে কিছু কহিতে লাগিল॥ ১০৪॥

'vaiṣṇava' dekhiyā prabhura ardha-bāhya ha-ila
svarūpa-gosāñire kichu kahite lāgila

SYNONYMS

vaiṣṇava dekhiyā—seeing the devotees; *prabhura*—of Śrī Caitanya Mahāprabhu; *ardha-bāhya*—half-external consciousness; *ha-ila*—there was; *svarūpa-gosāñire*—unto Svarūpa Gosāñi; *kichu*—something; *kahite lāgila*—began to speak.

TRANSLATION

When Śrī Caitanya Mahāprabhu saw all the Vaiṣṇavas, He returned to partial external consciousness and spoke to Svarūpa Dāmodara.

TEXT 105

"গোবর্ধন হৈতে মোরে কে ইহাঁ আনিল ?
পাঞা কৃষ্ণের লীলা দেখিতে না পাইল ॥ ১০৫ ॥

"govardhana haite more ke ihāṅ ānila?
pāñā kṛṣṇera līlā dekhite nā pāila

SYNONYMS

govardhana haite—from Govardhana Hill; *more*—Me; *ke*—who; *ihāṅ*—here; *ānila*—brought; *pāñā*—getting; *kṛṣṇera līlā*—pastimes of Kṛṣṇa; *dekhite nā pāila*—I could not see.

TRANSLATION

Śrī Caitanya Mahāprabhu said, "Who has brought Me here from Govardhana Hill? I was seeing Lord Kṛṣṇa's pastimes, but now I cannot see them.

TEXT 106

ইহাঁ হৈতে আজি মুই গেনু গোবর্ধনে ।
দেখোঁ,—যদি কৃষ্ণ করেন গোধন-চারণে ॥ ১০৬ ॥

ihāṅ haite āji mui genu govardhane
dekhoṅ,——yadi kṛṣṇa karena godhana-cāraṇe

SYNONYMS

ihāṅ haite—from here; *āji*—today; *mui*—I; *genu*—went; *govardhane*—to Govardhana Hill; *dekhoṅ*—I was searching; *yadi*—if; *kṛṣṇa*—Lord Kṛṣṇa; *karena*—does; *godhana-cāraṇe*—tending the cows.

TRANSLATION

"Today I went from here to Govardhana Hill to find out if Kṛṣṇa were tending His cows there.

TEXT 107

গোবর্ধনে চড়ি' কৃষ্ণ বাজাইলা বেণু ।
গোবর্ধনের চৌদিকে চরে সব ধেনু ॥ ১০৭ ॥

govardhane caḍi' kṛṣṇa bājāilā veṇu
govardhanera caudike care saba dhenu

SYNONYMS

govardhane—on Govardhana Hill; *caḍi'*—going up; *kṛṣṇa*—Lord Kṛṣṇa; *bājāilā veṇu*—played the flute; *govardhanera*—of Govardhana Hill; *cau-dike*—in four directions; *care*—graze; *saba*—all; *dhenu*—cows.

TRANSLATION

"I saw Lord Kṛṣṇa climbing Govardhana Hill and playing His flute, surrounded on all sides by grazing cows.

TEXT 108

বেণুনাদ শুনি' আইলা রাধা-ঠাকুরাণী।
সব সখীগণ-সঙ্গে করিয়া সাজনি ॥ ১০৮ ॥

veṇu-nāda śuni' āilā rādhā-ṭhākurāṇī
saba sakhī-gaṇa-saṅge kariyā sājani

SYNONYMS

veṇu-nāda—the vibration of the flute; *śuni'*—hearing; *āilā*—came; *rādhā-ṭhākurāṇī*—Śrīmatī Rādhārāṇī; *saba*—all; *sakhī-gaṇa-saṅge*—accompanied by *gopīs; kariyā sājani*—nicely dressed.

TRANSLATION

"Hearing the vibration of Kṛṣṇa's flute, Śrīmatī Rādhārāṇī and all Her gopī friends came there to meet Him. They were all very nicely dressed.

TEXT 109

রাধা লঞা কৃষ্ণ প্রবেশিলা কন্দরাতে।
সখীগণ কহে মোরে ফুল উঠাইতে ॥ ১০৯ ॥

rādhā lañā kṛṣṇa praveśilā kandarāte
sakhī-gaṇa kahe more phula uṭhāite

SYNONYMS

rādhā lañā—taking Śrīmatī Rādhārāṇī along; *kṛṣṇa*—Lord Kṛṣṇa; *praveśilā*—entered; *kandarāte*—a cave; *sakhī-gaṇa*—the *gopīs; kahe*—said; *more*—unto Me; *phula*—flowers; *uṭhāite*—to pick up.

TRANSLATION

"When Kṛṣṇa and Śrīmatī Rādhārāṇī entered a cave together, the other gopīs asked Me to pick some flowers.

TEXT 110

হেনকালে তুমি-সব কোলাহল কৈলা ।
তাহাঁ হৈতে ধরি' মোরে ইহাঁ লঞা আইলা ॥ ১১০ ॥

hena-kāle tumi-saba kolāhala kailā
tāhāṅ haite dhari' more ihāṅ lañā āilā

SYNONYMS

hena-kāle—at this time; *tumi-saba*—all of you; *kolāhala kailā*—made a tumultuous sound; *tāhāṅ haite*—from there; *dhari'*—catching; *more*—Me; *ihāṅ*—here; *lañā āilā*—you have brought.

TRANSLATION

"Just then, all of you made a tumultuous sound and carried Me from there to this place.

TEXT 111

কেনে বা আনিলা মোরে বৃথা দুঃখ দিতে ।
পাঞা কৃষ্ণের লীলা, না পাইনু দেখিতে !"১১১॥

kene vā ānilā more vṛthā duḥkha dite
pāñā kṛṣṇera līlā, nā pāinu dekhite

SYNONYMS

kene—why; *vā*—then; *ānilā*—brought; *more*—Me; *vṛthā*—unnecessarily; *duḥkha dite*—to give pain; *pāñā*—getting; *kṛṣṇera līlā*—the pastimes of Kṛṣṇa; *nā pāinu dekhite*—I could not see.

TRANSLATION

"Why have you brought Me here, causing Me unnecessary pain? I had a chance to see Kṛṣṇa's pastimes, but I could not see them."

TEXT 112

এত বলি' মহাপ্রভু করেন ক্রন্দন ।
তাঁর দশা দেখি' বৈষ্ণব করেন রোদন ॥ ১১২ ॥

eta bali' mahāprabhu karena krandana
tāṅra daśā dekhi' vaiṣṇava karena rodana

SYNONYMS

eta bali'—saying this; *mahāprabhu*—Śrī Caitanya Mahāprabhu; *karena krandana*—began to cry; *tāṅra daśā*—His state; *dekhi'*—seeing; *vaiṣṇava*—the Vaiṣṇavas; *karena rodana*—began to cry.

TRANSLATION

Saying this, Śrī Caitanya Mahāprabhu began to weep. When all the Vaiṣṇavas saw the Lord's condition, they also wept.

TEXT 113

হেনকালে আইলা পুরী, ভারতী,—দুইজন ।
দুঁহে দেখি' মহাপ্রভুর হইল সম্ভ্রম ॥ ১১৩ ॥

hena-kāle āilā purī, bhāratī,——dui-jana
duṅhe dekhi' mahāprabhura ha-ila sambhrama

SYNONYMS

hena-kāle—at this time; *āilā*—came; *purī*—Paramānanda Purī; *bhāratī*—Brahmānanda Bhāratī; *dui-jana*—two persons; *duṅhe dekhi'*—seeing both of them; *mahāprabhura*—of Śrī Caitanya Mahāprabhu; *ha-ila*—there was; *sambhrama*—respect.

TRANSLATION

At that time, Paramānanda Purī and Brahmānanda Bhāratī arrived. Seeing them, Śrī Caitanya Mahāprabhu became somewhat respectful.

TEXT 114

নিপট্ট-বাহ্য হইলে প্রভু দুঁহারে বন্দিলা ।
মহাপ্রভুরে দুইজন প্রেমালিঙ্গন কৈলা ॥ ১১৪ ॥

nipaṭṭa-bāhya ha-ile prabhu duṅhāre vandilā
mahāprabhure dui-jana premāliṅgana kailā

SYNONYMS

nipaṭṭa-bāhya—complete external consciousness; *ha-ile*—when there was; *prabhu*—Śrī Caitanya Mahāprabhu; *duṅhāre*—to both of them; *vandilā*—offered prayers; *mahāprabhure*—Śrī Caitanya Mahāprabhu; *dui-jana*—both persons; *prema-āliṅgana kailā*—embraced with love and affection.

TRANSLATION

Śrī Caitanya Mahāprabhu returned to complete external consciousness and immediately offered prayers to them. Then these two elderly gentlemen both embraced the Lord with loving affection.

TEXT 115

প্রভু কহে,—'দুঁহে কেনে আইলা এত দূরে' ?
পুরীগোসাঞি কহে,—'তোমার নৃত্য দেখিবারে' ॥

prabhu kahe,——'duṅhe kene āilā eta dūre'?
purī-gosāñi kahe,——'tomāra nṛtya dekhibāre'

SYNONYMS

prabhu kahe—Śrī Caitanya Mahāprabhu said; *duṅhe*—both of you; *kene*—why; *āilā*—have come; *eta dūre*—so far; *purī-gosāñi kahe*—Purī Gosāñi said; *tomāra nṛtya*—Your dancing; *dekhibāre*—to see.

TRANSLATION

Śrī Caitanya Mahāprabhu said to Purī Gosvāmī and Brahmānanda Bhāratī, "Why have you both come so far?" Purī Gosvāmī replied, "Just to see Your dancing."

TEXT 116

লজ্জিত হইলা প্রভু পুরীর বচনে ।
সমুদ্রঘাট আইলা সব বৈষ্ণব-সনে ॥ ১১৬ ॥

lajjita ha-ilā prabhu purīra vacane
samudra-ghāṭa āilā saba vaiṣṇava-sane

SYNONYMS

lajjita—ashamed; *ha-ilā*—became; *prabhu*—Śrī Caitanya Mahāprabhu; *purīra vacane*—by the words of Paramānanda Purī; *samudra*—of the sea; *ghāṭa*—to the bathing place; *āilā*—came; *saba vaiṣṇava-sane*—with all the Vaiṣṇavas.

TRANSLATION

When He heard this, Śrī Caitanya Mahāprabhu was somewhat ashamed. Then He went to bathe in the sea with all the Vaiṣṇavas.

TEXT 117

স্নান করি' মহাপ্রভু ঘরেতে আইলা ।
সবা লঞা মহাপ্রসাদ ভোজন করিলা ॥ ১১৭ ॥

snāna kari' mahāprabhu gharete āilā
sabā lañā mahā-prasāda bhojana karilā

SYNONYMS

snāna kari'—after taking a bath; *mahāprabhu*—Śrī Caitanya Mahāprabhu; *gharete āilā*—returned home; *sabā lañā*—taking everyone with Him; *mahā-prasāda*—remnants of food from Jagannātha; *bhojana karilā*—ate.

TRANSLATION

After bathing in the sea, Śrī Caitanya Mahāprabhu returned to His residence with all the devotees. Then they all lunched on the remnants of food offered to Lord Jagannātha.

TEXT 118

এই ত' কহিলুঁ প্রভুর দিব্যোন্মাদ-ভাব ।
ব্রহ্মাও কহিতে নারে যাহার প্রভাব ॥ ১১৮ ॥

ei ta' kahiluṅ prabhura divyonmāda-bhāva
brahmāo kahite nāre yāhāra prabhāva

SYNONYMS

ei ta'—thus; *kahiluṅ*—I have described; *prabhura*—of Śrī Caitanya Mahāprabhu; *divya-unmāda-bhāva*—transcendental ecstatic emotions; *brahmāo*—even Lord Brahmā; *kahite nāre*—cannot speak; *yāhāra*—of which; *prabhāva*—the influence.

TRANSLATION

Thus I have described the transcendental ecstatic emotions of Śrī Caitanya Mahāprabhu. Even Lord Brahmā cannot describe their influence.

TEXT 119

'চটক'-গিরি-গমন-লীলা রঘুনাথদাস ।
'গৌরাঙ্গস্তবকল্পবৃক্ষে' করিয়াছেন প্রকাশ ॥ ১১৯ ॥

'caṭaka'-giri-gamana-līlā raghunātha-dāsa
'gaurāṅga-stava-kalpavṛkṣe' kariyāchena prakāśa

SYNONYMS

caṭaka-giri—the sand hill known as Caṭaka-parvata; *gamana*—of going to; *līlā*—pastime; *raghunātha-dāsa*—Raghunātha dāsa Gosvāmī; *gaurāṅga-stava-kalpa-vṛkṣe*—in the book known as *Gaurāṅga-stava-kalpavṛkṣa; kariyāchena prakāśa*—has described.

TRANSLATION

In his book Gaurāṅga-stava-kalpavṛkṣa, Raghunātha dāsa Gosvāmī has very vividly described Śrī Caitanya Mahāprabhu's pastime of running toward the Caṭaka-parvata sand dune.

TEXT 120

সমীপে নীলাদ্রেশ্চটকগিরিরাজস্য কলনা-
দয়ে গোষ্ঠে গোবর্ধনগিরিপতিং লোকিতুমিতঃ।
ব্রজন্নস্মীত্যুক্ত্বা প্রমদ ইব ধাবন্নবধৃতো
গণৈঃ স্বৈর্গৌরাঙ্গো হৃদয় উদয়ন্মাং মদয়তি ॥ ১২০ ॥

samīpe nīlādreś caṭaka-giri-rājasya kalanād
aye goṣṭhe govardhana-giri-patiṁ lokitum itaḥ
vrajann asmīty uktvā pramada iva dhāvann avadhṛto
gaṇaiḥ svair gaurāṅgo hṛdaya udayan māṁ madayati

SYNONYMS

samīpe—near; *nīlādreḥ*—Jagannātha Purī; *caṭaka*—named Caṭaka; *giri-rājasya*—the king of sand hills; *kalanāt*—account of seeing; *aye*—oh; *goṣṭhe*—to the place for pasturing cows; *govardhana-giri-patim*—Govardhana, the king of hills; *lokitum*—to see; *itaḥ*—from here; *vrajan*—going; *asmi*—I am; *iti*—thus; *uktvā*—saying; *pramadaḥ*—maddened; *iva*—as if; *dhāvan*—running; *avadhṛtaḥ*—being followed; *gaṇaiḥ*—by the devotees; *svaiḥ*—own; *gaurāṅgaḥ*—Lord Śrī Caitanya Mahāprabhu; *hṛdaye*—in the heart; *udayan*—awakening; *mām*—me; *madayati*—maddens.

TRANSLATION

"Near Jagannātha Purī was a great sand dune known as Caṭaka-parvata. Seeing that hill, Śrī Caitanya Mahāprabhu said, 'Oh, I shall go to the land of

Vraja to see Govardhana Hill.' Then He began running madly toward it, and all the Vaiṣṇavas ran after Him. This scene awakens in my heart and maddens me."

PURPORT

This verse is quoted from the *Gaurāṅga-stava-kalpavṛkṣa* (8).

TEXT 121

এবে প্রভু যত কৈলা অলৌকিক-লীলা ।
কে বর্ণিতে পারে সেই মহাপ্রভুর খেলা ? ১২১ ॥

ebe prabhu yata kailā alaukika-līlā
ke varṇite pāre sei mahāprabhura khelā?

SYNONYMS

ebe—now; *prabhu*—Śrī Caitanya Mahāprabhu; *yata*—all that; *kailā*—performed; *alaukika-līlā*—uncommon pastimes; *ke*—who; *varṇite pāre*—can describe; *sei*—they; *mahāprabhura khelā*—the play of Śrī Caitanya Mahāprabhu.

TRANSLATION

Who can properly describe all the uncommon pastimes of Śrī Caitanya Mahāprabhu? They are all simply His play.

TEXT 122

সংক্ষেপে কহিয়া করি দিক্ দরশন ।
যেই ইহা শুনে, পায় কৃষ্ণের চরণ ॥ ১২২ ॥

saṅkṣepe kahiyā kari dik daraśana
yei ihā śune, pāya kṛṣṇera caraṇa

SYNONYMS

saṅkṣepe—in brief; *kahiyā*—describing; *kari dik daraśana*—I show an indication; *yei*—anyone who; *ihā*—this; *śune*—hears; *pāya*—gets; *kṛṣṇera caraṇa*—the shelter of the lotus feet of Lord Kṛṣṇa.

TRANSLATION

I have briefly described them just to give an indication of His transcendental pastimes. Nevertheless, anyone who hears this will certainly attain the shelter of Lord Kṛṣṇa's lotus feet.

TEXT 123

শ্রীরূপ-রঘুনাথ-পদে যার আশ।
চৈতন্যচরিতামৃত কহে কৃষ্ণদাস ॥ ১২৩ ॥

śrī-rūpa-raghunātha-pade yāra āśa
caitanya-caritāmṛta kahe kṛṣṇadāsa

SYNONYMS

śrī-rūpa—Śrīla Rūpa Gosvāmī; *raghunātha*—Śrīla Raghunātha dāsa Gosvāmī; *pade*—at the lotus feet; *yāra*—whose; *āśa*—expectation; *caitanya-caritāmṛta*—the book named *Caitanya-caritāmṛta;* *kahe*—describes; *kṛṣṇadāsa*—Śrīla Kṛṣṇadāsa Kavirāja Gosvāmī.

TRANSLATION

Praying at the lotus feet of Śrī Rūpa and Śrī Raghunātha, always desiring their mercy, I, Kṛṣṇadāsa, narrate Śrī Caitanya-caritāmṛta, following in their footsteps.

Thus end the Bhaktivedanta purports to the Śrī Caitanya-caritāmṛta, Antya-līlā, *Fourteenth Chapter, describing Śrī Caitanya Mahāprabhu's transcendental ecstatic emotions and His mistaking Caṭaka-parvata for Govardhana Hill.*

CHAPTER 15

The Transcendental Madness of Lord Śrī Caitanya Mahāprabhu

The following is a summary of the Fifteenth Chapter of *Antya-līlā.* After seeing the *upala-bhoga* ceremony of Lord Jagannātha, Śrī Caitanya Mahāprabhu once more began to feel ecstatic emotions. When He saw the garden on the beach by the sea, He again thought that He was in Vṛndāvana, and when He began to think of Kṛṣṇa engaging in His different pastimes, transcendental emotions excited Him again. On the night of the *rāsa* dance, the *gopīs,* bereaved by Kṛṣṇa's absence, searched for Kṛṣṇa from one forest to another. Śrī Caitanya Mahāprabhu adopted the same transcendental thoughts as the *gopīs* and was filled with ecstatic emotion. Svarūpa Dāmodara Gosvāmī recited a verse from *Gīta-govinda* just suitable to the Lord's emotions. Caitanya Mahāprabhu then exhibited the ecstatic transformations known as *bhāvodaya, bhāva-sandhi, bhāva-śābalya* and so on. The Lord experienced all eight kinds of ecstatic transformations, and He relished them very much.

TEXT 1

দুর্গমে কৃষ্ণভাবাব্ধৌ নিমগ্নোন্মগ্নচেতসা ।
গৌরেণ হরিণা প্রেমমর্যাদা ভূরি দর্শিতা ॥ ১ ॥

durgame kṛṣṇa-bhāvābdhau
nimagnonmagna-cetasā
gaureṇa hariṇā prema-
maryādā bhūri darśitā

SYNONYMS

durgame—very difficult to understand; *kṛṣṇa-bhāva-abdhau*—in the ocean of ecstatic love for Kṛṣṇa; *nimagna*—submerged; *unmagna-cetasā*—His heart being absorbed; *gaureṇa*—by Śrī Caitanya Mahāprabhu; *hariṇā*—by the Supreme Personality of Godhead; *prema-maryādā*—the exalted position of transcendental love; *bhūri*—in various ways; *darśitā*—was exhibited.

TRANSLATION

The ocean of ecstatic love for Kṛṣṇa is very difficult to understand, even for such demigods as Lord Brahmā. By enacting His pastimes, Śrī Caitanya

Mahāprabhu submerged Himself in that ocean, and His heart was absorbed in that love. Thus He exhibited in various ways the exalted position of transcendental love for Kṛṣṇa.

TEXT 2

জয় জয় শ্রীকৃষ্ণচৈতন্য অধীশ্বর।
জয় নিত্যানন্দ পূর্ণানন্দ-কলেবর॥ ২॥

jaya jaya śrī-kṛṣṇa-caitanya adhīśvara
jaya nityānanda pūrṇānanda-kalevara

SYNONYMS

jaya jaya—all glories; *śrī-kṛṣṇa-caitanya*—to Lord Caitanya Mahāprabhu; *adhīśvara*—the Supreme Personality of Godhead; *jaya*—all glories; *nityānanda*—to Lord Nityānanda; *pūrṇa-ānanda*—filled with transcendental pleasure; *kalevara*—His body.

TRANSLATION

All glories to Śrī Kṛṣṇa Caitanya, the Supreme Personality of Godhead! All glories to Lord Nityānanda, whose body is always filled with transcendental bliss!

TEXT 3

জয়াদ্বৈতাচার্য কৃষ্ণচৈতন্য-প্রিয়তম।
জয় শ্রীবাস-আদি প্রভুর ভক্তগণ॥ ৩॥

jayādvaitācārya kṛṣṇa-caitanya-priyatama
jaya śrīvāsa-ādi prabhura bhakta-gaṇa

SYNONYMS

jaya—all glories; *advaita-ācārya*—to Advaita Ācārya; *kṛṣṇa-caitanya*—to Lord Caitanya Mahāprabhu; *priya-tama*—very dear; *jaya*—all glories; *śrīvāsa-ādi*—headed by Śrīvāsa Ṭhākura; *prabhura*—of Lord Śrī Caitanya Mahāprabhu; *bhakta-gaṇa*—to the devotees.

TRANSLATION

All glories to Śrī Advaita Ācārya, who is very dear to Lord Caitanya! And all glories to the devotees of the Lord, headed by Śrīvāsa Ṭhākura!

TEXT 4

এইমত মহাপ্রভু রাত্রি-দিবসে ।
আত্মস্ফূর্তি নাহি কৃষ্ণভাবাবেশে ॥ ৪ ॥

ei-mata mahāprabhu rātri-divase
ātma-sphūrti nāhi kṛṣṇa-bhāvāveśe

SYNONYMS

ei-mata—in this way; *mahāprabhu*—Śrī Caitanya Mahāprabhu; *rātri-divase*—night and day; *ātma-sphūrti nāhi*—forgot Himself; *kṛṣṇa-bhāva-āveśe*—being merged in ecstatic love for Kṛṣṇa.

TRANSLATION

Thus Śrī Caitanya Mahāprabhu forgot Himself throughout the entire day and night, being merged in an ocean of ecstatic love for Kṛṣṇa.

TEXT 5

কভু ভাবে মগ্ন, কভু অর্ধ-বাহ্যস্ফূর্তি ।
কভু বাহ্যস্ফূর্তি,— তিন রীতে প্রভুস্থিতি ॥ ৫ ॥

kabhu bhāve magna, kabhu ardha-bāhya-sphūrti
kabhu bāhya-sphūrti,——tina rīte prabhu-sthiti

SYNONYMS

kabhu—sometimes; *bhāve*—in ecstatic emotion; *magna*—merged; *kabhu*—sometimes; *ardha*—half; *bāhya-sphūrti*—in external consciousness; *kabhu*—sometimes; *bāhya-sphūrti*—in full external consciousness; *tina rīte*—in three ways; *prabhu-sthiti*—the situation of the Lord.

TRANSLATION

The Lord would maintain Himself in three kinds of consciousness: sometimes He merged totally in ecstatic emotion, sometimes He was in partial external consciousness and sometimes in full external consciousness.

TEXT 6

স্নান, দর্শন, ভোজন দেহ-স্বভাবে হয় ।
কুমারের চাক যেন সতত ফিরয় ॥ ৬ ॥

snāna, darśana, bhojana deha-svabhāve haya
kumārera cāka yena satata phiraya

SYNONYMS

snāna—bathing; *darśana*—visiting the temple; *bhojana*—taking lunch; *deha-svabhāve*—by the nature of the body; *haya*—are; *kumārera cāka*—the potter's wheel; *yena*—as; *satata*—always; *phiraya*—revolves.

TRANSLATION

Actually, Śrī Caitanya Mahāprabhu was always merged in ecstatic emotion, but just as a potter's wheel turns without the potter's touching it, the Lord's bodily activities, like bathing, going to the temple to see Lord Jagannātha, and taking lunch, went on automatically.

TEXT 7

একদিন করেন প্রভু জগন্নাথ দরশন ।
জগন্নাথে দেখে সাক্ষাৎ ব্রজেন্দ্রনন্দন ॥ ৭ ॥

eka-dina karena prabhu jagannātha daraśana
jagannāthe dekhe sākṣāt vrajendra-nandana

SYNONYMS

eka-dina—one day; *karena*—does; *prabhu*—Śrī Caitanya Mahāprabhu; *jagannātha*—Lord Jagannātha; *daraśana*—visiting; *jagannāthe*—Lord Jagannātha; *dekhe*—He sees; *sākṣāt*—personally; *vrajendra-nandana*—the son of Mahārāja Nanda.

TRANSLATION

One day, while Śrī Caitanya Mahāprabhu was looking at Lord Jagannātha in the temple, Lord Jagannātha appeared to be personally the son of Nanda Mahārāja, Śrī Kṛṣṇa.

TEXT 8

একবারে স্ফুরে প্রভুর কৃষ্ণের পঞ্চগুণ ।
পঞ্চগুণে করে পঞ্চেন্দ্রিয় আকর্ষণ ॥ ৮ ॥

eka-bāre sphure prabhura kṛṣṇera pañca-guṇa
pañca-guṇe kare pañcendriya ākarṣaṇa

SYNONYMS

eka-bāre—at one time; *sphure*—manifest; *prabhura*—of Śrī Caitanya Mahāprabhu; *kṛṣṇera*—of Lord Kṛṣṇa; *pañca-guṇa*—five attributes; *pañca-guṇe*—five attributes; *kare*—do; *pañca-indriya*—of the five senses; *ākarṣaṇa*—attraction.

TRANSLATION

When He realized Lord Jagannātha to be Kṛṣṇa Himself, Śrī Caitanya Mahāprabhu's five senses were immediately absorbed in attraction for the five attributes of Lord Kṛṣṇa.

PURPORT

Śrī Kṛṣṇa's beauty attracted the eyes of Lord Caitanya Mahāprabhu. Kṛṣṇa's singing and the vibration of His flute attracted the Lord's ears, the transcendental fragrance of Kṛṣṇa's lotus feet attracted His nostrils, Kṛṣṇa's transcendental sweetness attracted His tongue, and Kṛṣṇa's bodily touch attracted the Lord's sensation of touch. Thus each of Śrī Caitanya Mahāprabhu's five senses was attracted by one of the five attributes of Lord Kṛṣṇa.

TEXT 9

একমন পঞ্চদিকে পঞ্চগুণ টানে ।
টানাটানি প্রভুর মন হৈল অগেয়ানে ॥ ৯ ॥

eka-mana pañca-dike pañca-guṇa ṭāne
ṭānāṭāni prabhura mana haila ageyāne

SYNONYMS

eka-mana—one mind; *pañca-dike*—in five directions; *pañca-guṇa*—the five attributes; *ṭāne*—attracted; *ṭānāṭāni*—by a tug-of-war; *prabhura*—of Śrī Caitanya Mahāprabhu; *mana*—the mind; *haila*—became; *ageyāne*—unconscious.

TRANSLATION

Just as in a tug-of-war, the single mind of Lord Caitanya was attracted in five directions by the five transcendental attributes of Lord Kṛṣṇa. Thus the Lord became unconscious.

TEXT 10

হেনকালে ঈশ্বরের উপলভোগ সরিল ।
ভক্তগণ মহাপ্রভুরে ঘরে লঞা আইল ॥ ১০ ॥

hena-kāle īśvarera upala-bhoga sarila
bhakta-gaṇa mahāprabhure ghare lañā āila

SYNONYMS

hena-kāle—at this time; *īśvarera*—of Lord Jagannātha; *upala-bhoga*—the *upala-bhoga* ceremony; *sarila*—was finished; *bhakta-gaṇa*—the devotees; *mahāprabhure*—Śrī Caitanya Mahāprabhu; *ghare*—home; *lañā āila*—brought.

TRANSLATION

Just then, the upala-bhoga ceremony of Lord Jagannātha concluded, and the devotees who had accompanied Lord Caitanya to the temple brought Him back home.

TEXT 11

স্বরূপ, রামানন্দ,— এই দুইজন লঞা।
বিলাপ করেন দুঁহার কণ্ঠেতে ধরিয়া ॥ ১১ ॥

svarūpa, rāmānanda,——ei dui-jana lañā
vilāpa karena duṅhāra kaṇṭhete dhariyā

SYNONYMS

svarūpa—Svarūpa Dāmodara Gosvāmī; *rāmānanda*—Rāmānanda Rāya; *ei dui-jana*—these two personalities; *lañā*—with; *vilāpa karena*—laments; *duṅhāra*—of both; *kaṇṭhete*—the necks; *dhariyā*—holding.

TRANSLATION

That night, Śrī Caitanya Mahāprabhu was attended by Svarūpa Dāmodara Gosvāmī and Rāmānanda Rāya. Keeping His hands around their necks, the Lord began to lament.

TEXT 12

কৃষ্ণের বিয়োগে রাধার উৎকণ্ঠিত মন।
বিশাখারে কহে আপন উৎকণ্ঠা-কারণ ॥ ১২ ॥

kṛṣṇera viyoge rādhāra utkaṇṭhita mana
viśākhāre kahe āpana utkaṇṭhā-kāraṇa

SYNONYMS

kṛṣṇera—from Lord Kṛṣṇa; *viyoge*—in separation; *rādhāra*—of Śrīmatī Rādhārāṇī; *utkaṇṭhita*—very agitated; *mana*—mind; *viśākhāre*—to Viśākhā;

kahe—spoke; *āpana*—own; *utkaṇṭhā-kāraṇa*—the cause of great anxiety and restlessness.

TRANSLATION

When Śrīmatī Rādhārāṇī was very agitated due to feeling great separation from Kṛṣṇa, She spoke a verse to Viśākhā explaining the cause of Her great anxiety and restlessness.

TEXT 13

সেই শ্লোক পড়ি' আপনে করে মনস্তাপ।
শ্লোকের অর্থ শুনায় দুঁহারে করিয়া বিলাপ ॥১৩॥

sei śloka paḍi' āpane kare manastāpa
ślokera artha śunāya duṅhāre kariyā vilāpa

SYNONYMS

sei śloka—that verse; *paḍi'*—reciting; *āpane*—personally; *kare*—does; *manaḥ-tāpa*—burning of the mind; *ślokera*—of the verse; *artha*—meaning; *śunāya*—causes to hear; *duṅhāre*—both; *kariyā vilāpa*—lamenting.

TRANSLATION

Reciting that verse, Śrī Caitanya Mahāprabhu expressed His burning emotions. Then, with great lamentation, He explained the verse to Svarūpa Dāmodara and Rāmānanda Rāya.

TEXT 14

সৌন্দর্যামৃতসিন্ধুভঙ্গললনা-চিত্তাদ্রিসংপ্লাবকঃ
কর্ণানন্দি-সনর্মরম্যবচনঃ কোটীন্দুশীতাঙ্গকঃ।
সৌরভ্যামৃতসংপ্লবাবৃতজগৎ পীযূষরম্যাধরঃ
শ্রীগোপেন্দ্রসুতঃ স কর্ষতি বলাৎ পঞ্চেন্দ্রিয়াণ্যালি মে ॥১৪॥

saundaryāmṛta-sindhu-bhaṅga-lalanā-cittādri-saṁplāvakaḥ
karṇānandi-sanarma-ramya-vacanaḥ koṭīndu-śītāṅgakaḥ
saurabhyāmṛta-samplavāvṛta-jagat pīyūṣa-ramyādharaḥ
śrī-gopendra-sutaḥ sa karṣati balāt pañcendriyāṇy āli me

SYNONYMS

saundarya—His beauty; *amṛta-sindhu*—of the ocean of nectar; *bhaṅga*—by the waves; *lalanā*—of women; *citta*—the hearts; *adri*—hills; *saṁplāvakaḥ*—inundating; *karṇa*—through the ears; *ānandi*—giving pleasure; *sanarma*—joyful; *ramya*—beautiful; *vacanaḥ*—whose voice; *koṭi-indu*—than ten million moons; *śīta*—more cooling; *aṅgakaḥ*—whose body; *saurabhya*—His fragrance; *amṛta*—of nectar; *samplava*—by the inundation; *āvṛta*—covered; *jagat*—the entire universe; *pīyūṣa*—nectar; *ramya*—beautiful; *adharaḥ*—whose lips; *śrī-gopa-indra*—of Nanda Mahārāja; *sutaḥ*—the son; *saḥ*—He; *karṣati*—attracts; *balāt*—by force; *pañca-indriyāṇi*—the five senses; *āli*—O dear friend; *me*—My.

TRANSLATION

Śrī Caitanya Mahāprabhu said: " 'Though the hearts of the gopīs are like high-standing hills, they are inundated by the waves of the nectarean ocean of Kṛṣṇa's beauty. His sweet voice enters their ears and gives them transcendental bliss. The touch of His body is cooler than millions and millions of moons together, and the nectar of His bodily fragrance overfloods the entire world. O My dear friend, that Kṛṣṇa, who is the son of Nanda Mahārāja and whose lips are exactly like nectar, is attracting My five senses by force.'

PURPORT

This verse is found in *Govinda-līlāmṛta* (8.3).

TEXT 15

কৃষ্ণ-রূপ-শব্দ-স্পর্শ, সৌরভ্য-অধর-রস,
যার মাধুর্য কহন না যায় ।
দেখি' লোভে পঞ্চজন, এক অশ্ব —মোর মন,
চড়ি' পঞ্চ পাঁচদিকে ধায় ॥ ১৫ ॥

kṛṣṇa-rūpa-śabda-sparśa, saurabhya-adhara-rasa,
yāra mādhurya kahana nā yāya
dekhi' lobhe pañca-jana, eka aśva——mora mana,
caḍi' pañca pāṅca-dike dhāya

SYNONYMS

kṛṣṇa—of Lord Kṛṣṇa; *rūpa*—beauty; *śabda*—sound; *sparśa*—touch; *saurabhya*—fragrance; *adhara*—of lips; *rasa*—taste; *yāra*—whose; *mādhurya*—sweetness; *kahana*—describing; *nā yāya*—is not possible; *dekhi'*—seeing; *lobhe*—in greed; *pañca-jana*—five men; *eka*—one; *aśva*—horse; *mora*—My; *mana*—mind; *caḍi'*—riding on; *pañca*—all five; *pāṅca-dike*—in five directions; *dhāya*—run.

TRANSLATION

"Lord Śrī Kṛṣṇa's beauty, the sound of His words and the vibration of His flute, His touch, His fragrance and the taste of His lips are full of an indescribable sweetness. When all these features attract My five senses at once, My senses all ride together on the single horse of My mind but want to go in five different directions.

TEXT 16

সখি হে, শুন মোর দুঃখের কারণ।
মোর পঞ্চেন্দ্রিয়গণ, মহা-লম্পট দস্যুগণ,
সবে কহে,—হর' পরধন ॥ ১৬ ॥ ধ্রু ॥

sakhi he, śuna mora duḥkhera kāraṇa
mora pañcendriya-gaṇa, mahā-lampaṭa dasyu-gaṇa,
sabe kahe,——hara' para-dhana

SYNONYMS

sakhi—My dear friend; *he*—O; *śuna*—please hear; *mora*—My; *duḥkhera kāraṇa*—the cause of unhappiness; *mora*—My; *pañca-indriya-gaṇa*—five senses of perception; *mahā*—very; *lampaṭa*—extravagant; *dasyu-gaṇa*—rogues; *sabe kahe*—they all say; *hara'*—plunder; *para-dhana*—another's property.

TRANSLATION

"O My dear friend, please hear the cause of My misery. My five senses are actually extravagant rogues. They know very well that Kṛṣṇa is the Supreme Personality of Godhead, but they still want to plunder Kṛṣṇa's property.

TEXT 17

এক অশ্ব একক্ষণে, পাঁচ পাঁচ দিকে টানে,
এক মন কোন্ দিকে যায়?
এককালে সবে টানে, গেল ঘোড়ার পরাণে,
এই দুঃখ সহন না যায় ॥ ১৭ ॥

eka aśva eka-kṣaṇe, pāṅca pāṅca dike ṭāne,
eka mana kon dike yāya?
eka-kāle sabe ṭāne, gela ghoḍāra parāṇe,
ei duḥkha sahana nā yāya

SYNONYMS

eka—one; *aśva*—horse; *eka-kṣaṇe*—at one time; *pāṅca*—five men; *pāṅca dike*—in five directions; *ṭāne*—pull; *eka*—one; *mana*—mind; *kon dike*—in what direction; *yāya*—will go; *eka-kāle*—at one time; *sabe*—all; *ṭāne*—pull; *gela*—will go; *ghoḍāra*—of the horse; *parāṇe*—life; *ei*—this; *duḥkha*—unhappiness; *sahana*—tolerating; *nā yāya*—is not possible.

TRANSLATION

"My mind is just like a single horse being ridden by the five senses of perception, headed by sight. Each sense wants to ride that horse, and thus they pull My mind in five directions simultaneously. In what direction will it go? If they all pull at one time, certainly the horse will lose its life. How can I tolerate this atrocity?

TEXT 18

ইন্দ্রিয়ে না করি রোষ, ইঁহা-সবার কাহাঁ দোষ,
কৃষ্ণরূপাদির মহা আকর্ষণ ।
রূপাদি পাঁচ পাঁচে টানে, গেল ঘোড়ার পরাণে,
মোর দেহে না রহে জীবন ॥ ১৮ ॥

indriye nā kari roṣa, iṅhā-sabāra kāhāṅ doṣa,
kṛṣṇa-rūpādira mahā ākarṣaṇa
rūpādi pāṅca pāṅce ṭāne, gela ghoḍāra parāṇe,
mora dehe nā rahe jīvana

SYNONYMS

indriye—at the senses; *nā*—not; *kari roṣa*—I can be angry; *iṅhā-sabāra*—of all of them; *kāhāṅ*—where; *doṣa*—fault; *kṛṣṇa-rūpa-ādira*—of Lord Kṛṣṇa's beauty, sounds, touch, fragrance and taste; *mahā*—very great; *ākarṣaṇa*—attraction; *rūpa-ādi*—the beauty and so on; *pāṅca*—five; *pāṅce*—the five senses; *ṭāne*—drag; *gela*—is going away; *ghoḍāra*—of the horse; *parāṇe*—life; *mora*—My; *dehe*—in the body; *nā*—not; *rahe*—remains; *jīvana*—life.

TRANSLATION

"My dear friend, if you say, 'Just try to control Your senses,' what shall I say? I cannot become angry at My senses. Is it their fault? Kṛṣṇa's beauty, sounds, touch, fragrance and taste are by nature extremely attractive. These five features are attracting My senses, and each wants to drag My mind in a different direction. Thus the life of My mind is in great danger, just like a horse ridden in five directions at once. Thus I am also in danger of dying.

TEXT 19

কৃষ্ণরূপামৃতসিন্ধু, তাহার তরঙ্গ-বিন্দু,
একবিন্দু জগৎ ডুবায়।
ত্রিজগতে যত নারী, তার চিত্ত-উচ্চগিরি,
তাহা ডুবাই আগে উঠি' ধায় ॥ ১৯ ॥

kṛṣṇa-rūpāmṛta-sindhu, tāhāra taraṅga-bindu,
eka-bindu jagat ḍubāya
trijagate yata nārī, tāra citta-ucca-giri,
tāhā ḍubāi āge uṭhi' dhāya

SYNONYMS

kṛṣṇa-rūpa—of Kṛṣṇa's transcendental beauty; *amṛta-sindhu*—the ocean of nectar; *tāhāra*—of that; *taraṅga-bindu*—a drop of a wave; *eka-bindu*—one drop; *jagat*—the whole world; *ḍubāya*—can flood; *tri-jagate*—in the three worlds; *yata nārī*—all women; *tāra citta*—their consciousness; *ucca-giri*—high hills; *tāhā*—that; *ḍubāi*—drowning; *āge*—forward; *uṭhi'*—raising; *dhāya*—runs.

TRANSLATION

"The consciousness of each woman within the three worlds is certainly like a high hill, but the sweetness of Kṛṣṇa's beauty is like an ocean. Even a drop of water from that ocean can flood the entire world and submerge all the high hills of consciousness.

TEXT 20

কৃষ্ণের বচন-মাধুরী, নানা-রস-নর্মধারী,
তার অন্যায় কথন না যায়।
জগতের নারীর কাণে, মাধুরীগুণে বান্ধি' টানে,
টানাটানি কাণের প্রাণ যায় ॥ ২০ ॥

kṛṣṇera vacana-mādhurī, nānā-rasa-narma-dhārī,
tāra anyāya kathana nā yāya
jagatera nārīra kāṇe, mādhurī-guṇe bāndhi' ṭāne,
ṭānāṭāni kāṇera prāṇa yāya

SYNONYMS

kṛṣṇera—of Lord Kṛṣṇa; *vacana-mādhurī*—the sweetness of speaking; *nānā*—various; *rasa-narma-dhārī*—full of joking words; *tāra*—of that; *anyāya*—atrocities;

kathana—description; *nā yāya*—cannot be made; *jagatera*—of the world; *nārīra*—of women; *kāṇe*—in the ear; *mādhurī-guṇe*—to the attributes of sweetness; *bāndhi'*—binding; *ṭāne*—pulls; *ṭānāṭāni*—tug-of-war; *kāṇera*—of the ear; *prāṇa yāya*—the life departs.

TRANSLATION

"The sweetness of Kṛṣṇa's joking words plays indescribable havoc with the hearts of all women. His words bind a woman's ear to the qualities of their sweetness. Thus there is a tug-of-war, and the life of the ear departs.

TEXT 21

কৃষ্ণ-অঙ্গ সুশীতল, কি কহিমু তার বল,
ছটায় জিনে কোটীন্দু-চন্দন ।
সশৈল নারীর বক্ষ, তাহা আকর্ষিতে দক্ষ,
আকর্ষয়ে নারীগণ-মন ॥ ২১ ॥

kṛṣṇa-aṅga suśītala, ki kahimu tāra bala,
chaṭāya jine koṭīndu-candana
saśaila nārīra vakṣa, tāhā ākarṣite dakṣa,
ākarṣaye nārī-gaṇa-mana

SYNONYMS

kṛṣṇa-aṅga—the body of Kṛṣṇa; *su-śītala*—very cool; *ki kahimu*—what shall I say; *tāra*—of that; *bala*—the strength; *chaṭāya*—by the rays; *jine*—surpasses; *koṭi-indu*—millions upon millions of moons; *candana*—sandalwood pulp; *sa-śaila*—like raised hills; *nārīra*—of a woman; *vakṣa*—breasts; *tāhā*—that; *ākarṣite*—to attract; *dakṣa*—very expert; *ākarṣaye*—attracts; *nārī-gaṇa-mana*—the minds of all women.

TRANSLATION

"Kṛṣṇa's transcendental body is so cool that it cannot be compared even to sandalwood pulp or to millions upon millions of moons. It expertly attracts the breasts of all women, which resemble high hills. Indeed, the transcendental body of Kṛṣṇa attracts the minds of all women within the three worlds.

TEXT 22

কৃষ্ণাঙ্গ—সৌরভ্যভর, মৃগমদ-মদহর,
নীলোৎপলের হরে গর্ব-ধন ।

জগৎ-নারীর নাসা, তার ভিতর পাতে বাসা,
নারীগণে করে আকর্ষণ ॥ ২২ ॥

kṛṣṇāṅga——saurabhya-bhara, mṛga-mada-mada-hara,
nīlotpalera hare garva-dhana
jagat-nārīra nāsā, tāra bhitara pāte vāsā,
nārī-gaṇe kare ākarṣaṇa

SYNONYMS

kṛṣṇa-aṅga—the body of Kṛṣṇa; *saurabhya-bhara*—full of fragrance; *mṛga-mada*—of musk; *mada-hara*—intoxicating power; *nīlotpalera*—of the bluish lotus flower; *hare*—takes away; *garva-dhana*—the pride of the treasure; *jagat-nārīra*—of the women in the world; *nāsā*—nostrils; *tāra bhitara*—within them; *pāte vāsā*—constructs a residence; *nārī-gaṇe*—women; *kare ākarṣaṇa*—attracts.

TRANSLATION

"The fragrance of Kṛṣṇa's body is more maddening than the aroma of musk, and it surpasses the fragrance of the bluish lotus flower. It enters the nostrils of all the women of the world and, making a nest there, thus attracts them.

TEXT 23

কৃষ্ণের অধরামৃত, তাতে কর্পূর মন্দস্মিত,
স্ব-মাধুর্যে হরে নারীর মন।
অন্যত্র ছাড়ায় লোভ, না পাইলে মনে ক্ষোভ,
ব্রজনারীগণের মূলধন ॥"২৩ ॥

kṛṣṇera adharāmṛta, tāte karpūra manda-smita,
sva-mādhurye hare nārīra mana
anyatra chāḍāya lobha, nā pāile mane kṣobha,
vraja-nārī-gaṇera mūla-dhana"

SYNONYMS

kṛṣṇera—of Lord Kṛṣṇa; *adhara-amṛta*—the sweetness of the lips; *tāte*—with that; *karpūra*—camphor; *manda-smita*—gentle smile; *sva-mādhurye*—by His sweetness; *hare*—attracts; *nārīra mana*—the minds of all women; *anyatra*—anywhere else; *chāḍāya*—vanquishes; *lobha*—greed; *nā pāile*—without getting; *mane*—in the mind; *kṣobha*—great agitation; *vraja-nārī-gaṇera*—of all the *gopīs* of Vṛndāvana; *mūla-dhana*—wealth.

TRANSLATION

"Kṛṣṇa's lips are so sweet when combined with the camphor of His gentle smile that they attract the minds of all women, forcing them to give up all other attractions. If the sweetness of Kṛṣṇa's smile is unobtainable, great mental difficulties and lamentation result. That sweetness is the only wealth of the gopīs of Vṛndāvana."

TEXT 24

এত কহি' গৌরহরি, দুইজনার কণ্ঠ ধরি',
কহে,—'শুন, স্বরূপ-রামরায়।
কাহাঁ করোঁ, কাহাঁ যাঙ, কাহাঁ গেলে কৃষ্ণ পাঙ,
দুঁহে মোরে কহ সে উপায়' ॥ ২৪ ॥

eta kahi' gaurahari, dui-janāra kaṇṭha dhari',
kahe,—'śuna, svarūpa-rāmarāya
kāhāṅ karoṅ, kāhāṅ yāṅa, kāhāṅ gele kṛṣṇa pāṅa,
duṅhe more kaha se upāya'

SYNONYMS

eta kahi'—saying this; *gaurahari*—Śrī Caitanya Mahāprabhu; *dui-janāra*—of the two persons; *kaṇṭha dhari'*—catching the necks; *kahe*—said; *śuna*—please hear; *svarūpa-rāma-rāya*—Svarūpa Dāmodara and Rāmānanda Rāya; *kāhāṅ karoṅ*—what shall I do; *kāhāṅ yāṅa*—where shall I go; *kāhāṅ gele*—going where; *kṛṣṇa pāṅa*—I can get Kṛṣṇa; *duṅhe*—both of you; *more*—unto Me; *kaha*—please say; *se upāya*—such a means.

TRANSLATION

After speaking in this way, Śrī Caitanya Mahāprabhu caught hold of the necks of Rāmānanda Rāya and Svarūpa Dāmodara. Then the Lord said, "My dear friends, please listen to Me. What shall I do? Where shall I go? Where can I go to get Kṛṣṇa? Please, both of you, tell Me how I can find Him."

TEXT 25

এইমত গৌরপ্রভু প্রতি দিনে-দিনে।
বিলাপ করেন স্বরূপ-রামানন্দ-সনে ॥ ২৫ ॥

ei-mata gaura-prabhu prati dine-dine
vilāpa karena svarūpa-rāmānanda-sane

SYNONYMS

ei-mata—in this way; *gaura-prabhu*—Śrī Caitanya Mahāprabhu; *prati dine-dine*—day after day; *vilāpa karena*—laments; *svarūpa-rāmānanda-sane*—in the company of Svarūpa Dāmodara Gosvāmī and Rāmānanda Rāya.

TRANSLATION

Thus absorbed in transcendental pain, Śrī Caitanya Mahāprabhu lamented day after day in the company of Svarūpa Dāmodara Gosvāmī and Rāmānanda Rāya.

TEXT 26

সেই দুইজন প্রভুরে করে আশ্বাসন ।
স্বরূপ গায়, রায় করে শ্লোক পঠন ॥ ২৬ ॥

sei dui-jana prabhure kare āśvāsana
svarūpa gāya, rāya kare śloka paṭhana

SYNONYMS

sei—those; *dui-jana*—two persons; *prabhure*—to Śrī Caitanya Mahāprabhu; *kare*—do; *āśvāsana*—pacification; *svarūpa gāya*—Svarūpa Dāmodara sings; *rāya*—Rāmānanda Rāya; *kare*—does; *śloka paṭhana*—recitation of verses.

TRANSLATION

Svarūpa Dāmodara Gosvāmī would sing appropriate songs, and Rāmānanda Rāya would recite suitable verses to enhance the ecstatic mood of the Lord. In this way they were able to pacify Him.

TEXT 27

কর্ণামৃত, বিদ্যাপতি, শ্রীগীতগোবিন্দ ।
ইহার শ্লোক-গীতে প্রভুর করায় আনন্দ ॥ ২৭ ॥

karṇāmṛta, vidyāpati, śrī-gīta-govinda
ihāra śloka-gīte prabhura karāya ānanda

SYNONYMS

karṇāmṛta—the book *Kṛṣṇa-karṇāmṛta; vidyāpati*—the author Vidyāpati; *śrī-gīta-govinda*—the book *Śrī Gīta-govinda* by Jayadeva Gosvāmī; *ihāra*—of these; *śloka-gīte*—verses and songs; *prabhura*—for Śrī Caitanya Mahāprabhu; *karāya*—create; *ānanda*—happiness.

TRANSLATION

The Lord especially liked to hear Bilvamaṅgala Ṭhākura's Kṛṣṇa-karṇāmṛta, the poetry of Vidyāpati and Śrī Gīta-govinda by Jayadeva Gosvāmī. Śrī Caitanya Mahāprabhu felt great pleasure in His heart when His associates chanted verses from these books.

TEXT 28

একদিন মহাপ্রভু সমুদ্র-তীরে যাইতে।
পুষ্পের উদ্যান তথা দেখেন আচম্বিতে ॥ ২৮ ॥

eka-dina mahāprabhu samudra-tīre yāite
puṣpera udyāna tathā dekhena ācambite

SYNONYMS

eka-dina—one day; *mahāprabhu*—Śrī Caitanya Mahāprabhu; *samudra-tīre*—to the seashore; *yāite*—while going; *puṣpera udyāna*—a flower garden; *tathā*—there; *dekhena*—sees; *ācambite*—suddenly.

TRANSLATION

One day, while going to the beach by the sea, Śrī Caitanya Mahāprabhu suddenly saw a flower garden.

TEXT 29

বৃন্দাবন-ভ্রমে তাহাঁ পশিলা ধাঞা।
প্রেমাবেশে বুলে তাহাঁ কৃষ্ণ অন্বেষিয়া ॥ ২৯ ॥

vṛndāvana-bhrame tāhāṅ paśilā dhāñā
premāveśe bule tāhāṅ kṛṣṇa anveṣiyā

SYNONYMS

vṛndāvana-bhrame—taking it for Vṛndāvana; *tāhāṅ*—there; *paśilā*—entered; *dhāñā*—running; *prema-āveśe*—in ecstatic love of Kṛṣṇa; *bule*—wanders; *tāhāṅ*—there; *kṛṣṇa*—Lord Kṛṣṇa; *anveṣiyā*—searching for.

TRANSLATION

Lord Caitanya mistook that garden for Vṛndāvana and very quickly entered it. Absorbed in ecstatic love of Kṛṣṇa, He wandered throughout the garden, searching for Him.

TEXT 30

রাসে রাধা লঞা কৃষ্ণ অন্তর্ধান কৈলা ।
পাছে সখীগণ যৈছে চাহি' বেড়াইলা ॥ ৩০ ॥

rāse rādhā lañā kṛṣṇa antardhāna kailā
pāche sakhī-gaṇa yaiche cāhi' beḍāilā

SYNONYMS

rāse—in the *rāsa* dance; *rādhā*—Śrīmatī Rādhārāṇī; *lañā*—taking; *kṛṣṇa*—Lord Kṛṣṇa; *antardhāna kailā*—disappeared; *pāche*—afterward; *sakhī-gaṇa*—all the *gopīs; yaiche*—as; *cāhi'*—looking; *beḍāilā*—wandered.

TRANSLATION

After Kṛṣṇa disappeared with Rādhārāṇī during the rāsa dance, the gopīs wandered in the forest looking for Him. In the same way, Śrī Caitanya Mahāprabhu wandered in that garden by the sea.

TEXT 31

সেই ভাবাবেশে প্রভু প্রতি-তরুলতা ।
শ্লোক পড়ি' পড়ি' চাহি' বুলে যথা তথা ॥ ৩১ ॥

sei bhāvāveśe prabhu prati-taru-latā
śloka paḍi' paḍi' cāhi' bule yathā tathā

SYNONYMS

sei—that; *bhāva-āveśe*—in ecstasy; *prabhu*—Lord Caitanya Mahāprabhu; *prati-taru-latā*—each tree and creeper; *śloka paḍi' paḍi'*—reciting verses; *cāhi'*—inquiring; *bule*—wanders; *yathā tathā*—here and there.

TRANSLATION

Absorbed in the ecstatic mood of the gopīs, Śrī Caitanya Mahāprabhu wandered here and there. He began to inquire after Kṛṣṇa by quoting verses to all the trees and creepers.

PURPORT

Śrī Caitanya Mahāprabhu then quoted the following three verses from *Śrīmad-Bhāgavatam* (10.30.9,7,8).

TEXT 32

চূতপ্রিয়াল-পনসাসনকোবিদার-
জম্ব্বর্কবিল্ববকুলাম্রকদম্বনীপাঃ ।
যেঽন্যে পরার্থভবকা যমুনোপকূলাঃ
শংসন্তু কৃষ্ণপদবীং রহিতাত্মনাং নঃ ॥ ৩২ ॥

cūta-priyāla-panasāsana-kovidāra-
jambv-arka-bilva-bakulāmra-kadamba-nīpāḥ
ye 'nye parārtha-bhavakā yamunopakūlāḥ
śaṁsantu kṛṣṇa-padavīṁ rahitātmanāṁ naḥ

SYNONYMS

cūta—O *cūta* tree (a kind of mango tree); *priyāla*—O *priyāla* tree; *panasa*—O jackfruit tree; *āsana*—O *āsana* tree; *kovidāra*—O *kovidāra* tree; *jambu*—O *jambu* tree; *arka*—O *arka* tree; *bilva*—O belfruit tree; *bakula*—O *bakula* tree; *āmra*—O mango tree; *kadamba*—O *kadamba* tree; *nīpāḥ*—O *nīpa* tree; *ye*—which; *anye*—others; *para-artha-bhavakāḥ*—very beneficial to others; *yamunā-upakūlāḥ*—on the bank of the Yamunā; *śaṁsantu*—please tell; *kṛṣṇa-padavīm*—where Kṛṣṇa has gone; *rahita-ātmanām*—who have lost our minds; *naḥ*—us.

TRANSLATION

"[The gopīs said:] 'O cūta tree, priyāla tree, panasa, āsana and kovidāra! O jambu tree, O arka tree, O bel, bakula and mango! O kadamba tree, O nīpa tree and all other trees living on the bank of the Yamunā for the welfare of others, please let us know where Kṛṣṇa has gone. We have lost our minds and are almost dead.

TEXT 33

কচ্চিত্তুলসি কল্যাণি গোবিন্দচরণপ্রিয়ে ।
সহ ত্বালিকুলৈর্বিভ্রদ্দৃষ্টস্তেঽতিপ্রিয়োঽচ্যুতঃ ॥ ৩৩ ॥

kaccit tulasi kalyāṇi
govinda-caraṇa-priye
saha tvāli-kulair bibhrad
dṛṣṭas te 'ti-priyo 'cyutaḥ

SYNONYMS

kaccit—whether; *tulasi*—O *tulasī* plant; *kalyāṇi*—all-auspicious; *govinda-caraṇa*—to Govinda's lotus feet; *priye*—very dear; *saha*—with; *tvā*—you; *ali-*

kulaiḥ—bumblebees; *bibhrat*—bearing; *dṛṣṭaḥ*—has been seen; *te*—your; *ati-priyaḥ*—very dear; *acyutaḥ*—Lord Kṛṣṇa.

TRANSLATION

" 'O all-auspicious tulasī plant, you are very dear to Govinda's lotus feet, and He is very dear to you. Have you seen Kṛṣṇa walking here wearing a garland of your leaves, surrounded by a swarm of bumblebees?

TEXT 34

মালত্যদর্শি বঃ কচ্চিন্মল্লিকে জাতি যূথিকে ।
প্রীতিং বো জনয়ন্ যাতঃ করস্পর্শেন মাধবঃ ॥ ৩৪ ॥

mālaty adarśi vaḥ kaccin
mallike jāti yūthike
prītiṁ vo janayan yātaḥ
kara-sparśena mādhavaḥ

SYNONYMS

mālati—O plant of *mālatī* flowers; *adarśi*—was seen; *vaḥ*—by you; *kaccit*—whether; *mallike*—O plant of *mallikā* flowers; *jāti*—O plant of *jātī* flowers; *yūthike*—O plant of *yūthikā* flowers; *prītim*—pleasure; *vaḥ*—your; *janayan*—creating; *yātaḥ*—passed by; *kara-sparśena*—by the touch of His hand; *mādhavaḥ*—Śrī Kṛṣṇa.

TRANSLATION

" 'O plants of mālatī flowers, mallikā flowers, jātī and yūthikā flowers, have you seen Kṛṣṇa passing this way, touching you with His hand to give you pleasure?' "

TEXT 35

আম্র, পনস, পিয়াল, জম্বু, কোবিদার ।
তীর্থবাসী সবে, কর পর-উপকার ॥ ৩৫ ॥

āmra, panasa, piyāla, jambu, kovidāra
tīrtha-vāsī sabe, kara para-upakāra

SYNONYMS

āmra—O mango tree; *panasa*—O jackfruit tree; *piyāla*—O *piyāla* tree; *jambu*—O *jambu* tree; *kovidāra*—O *kovidāra* tree; *tīrtha-vāsī*—inhabitants of a holy place; *sabe*—all; *kara*—please do; *para-upakāra*—others' benefit.

TRANSLATION

Śrī Caitanya Mahāprabhu continued: " 'O mango tree, O jackfruit tree, O piyāla, jambu and kovidāra trees, you are all inhabitants of a holy place. Therefore kindly act for the welfare of others.

TEXT 36

কৃষ্ণ তোমার ইহাঁ আইলা, পাইলা দরশন ?
কৃষ্ণের উদ্দেশ কহি' রাখহ জীবন ॥ ৩৬ ॥

kṛṣṇa tomāra ihāṅ āilā, pāilā daraśana?
kṛṣṇera uddeśa kahi' rākhaha jīvana

SYNONYMS

kṛṣṇa—Lord Kṛṣṇa; *tomāra*—your; *ihāṅ*—here; *āilā*—came; *pāilā daraśana*—you have seen; *kṛṣṇera*—of Lord Kṛṣṇa; *uddeśa*—the direction; *kahi'*—by telling; *rākhaha jīvana*—kindly save our lives.

TRANSLATION

" 'Have you seen Kṛṣṇa coming this way? Kindly tell us which way He has gone and save our lives.'

TEXT 37

উত্তর না পাঞা পুনঃ করে অনুমান ।
এই সব—পুরুষ-জাতি, কৃষ্ণের সখার সমান ॥৩৭॥

uttara nā pāñā punaḥ kare anumāna
ei saba——puruṣa-jāti, kṛṣṇera sakhāra samāna

SYNONYMS

uttara—answer; *nā*—not; *pāñā*—getting; *punaḥ*—again; *kare*—do; *anumāna*—guess; *ei saba*—all these; *puruṣa-jāti*—belonging to the male class; *kṛṣṇera*—of Kṛṣṇa; *sakhāra samāna*—as good as friends.

TRANSLATION

"When the trees did not reply, the gopīs guessed, 'Since all of these trees belong to the male class, all of them must be friends of Kṛṣṇa.

TEXT 38

এ কেনে কহিবে কৃষ্ণের উদ্দেশ আমায় ?
এ—স্ত্রীজাতি লতা, আমার সখীপ্রায় ॥ ৩৮ ॥

e kene kahibe kṛṣṇera uddeśa āmāya?
e——strī-jāti latā, āmāra sakhī-prāya

SYNONYMS

e—these; *kene*—why; *kahibe*—will say; *kṛṣṇera*—of Lord Kṛṣṇa; *uddeśa*—direction; *āmāya*—to us; e—these; *strī-jāti*—belonging to the class of women; *latā*—creepers; *āmāra*—our; *sakhī-prāya*—like friends.

TRANSLATION

" 'Why should the trees tell us where Kṛṣṇa has gone? Let us rather inquire from the creepers; they are female and therefore are like friends to us.

TEXT 39

অবশ্য কহিবে,—পাঞাছে কৃষ্ণের দর্শনে ।
এত অনুমানি' পুছে তুলস্যাদি-গণে ॥ ৩৯ ॥

avaśya kahibe,——pāñāche kṛṣṇera darśane
eta anumāni' puche tulasy-ādi-gaṇe

SYNONYMS

avaśya—certainly; *kahibe*—they will say; *pāñāche*—they have gotten; *kṛṣṇera*—of Lord Kṛṣṇa; *darśane*—audience; *eta*—this; *anumāni'*—guessing; *puche*—inquire from; *tulasī-ādi-gaṇe*—the plants and creepers, headed by the *tulasī* plant.

TRANSLATION

" 'They will certainly tell us where Kṛṣṇa has gone, since they have seen Him personally.' Guessing in this way, the gopīs inquired from the plants and creepers, headed by tulasī.

TEXT 40

"তুলসি, মালতি, যূথি, মাধবি, মল্লিকে ।
তোমার প্রিয় কৃষ্ণ আইলা তোমার অন্তিকে ? ৪০ ॥

"tulasi, mālati, yūthi, mādhavi, mallike
tomāra priya kṛṣṇa āilā tomāra antike?

SYNONYMS

tulasi—O tulasī; *mālati*—O mālatī; *yūthi*—O yūthī; *mādhavi*—O mādhavī; *mallike*—O mallikā; *tomāra*—your; *priya*—very dear; *kṛṣṇa*—Lord Kṛṣṇa; *āilā*—came; *tomāra antike*—near you.

TRANSLATION

" 'O tulasī! O mālatī! O yūthī, mādhavī and mallikā! Kṛṣṇa is very dear to you. Therefore He must have come near you.

TEXT 41

তুমি-সব—হও আমার সখীর সমান ।
কৃষ্ণোদ্দেশ কহি' সবে রাখহ পরাণ ॥" ৪১ ॥

tumi-saba——hao āmāra sakhīra samāna
kṛṣṇoddeśa kahi' sabe rākhaha parāṇa"

SYNONYMS

tumi-saba—all of you; *hao*—are; *āmāra*—our; *sakhīra*—dear friends; *samāna*—equal to; *kṛṣṇa-uddeśa*—the direction in which Kṛṣṇa has gone; *kahi'*—speaking; *sabe*—all of you; *rākhaha parāṇa*—save our lives.

TRANSLATION

" 'You are all just like dear friends to us. Kindly tell us which way Kṛṣṇa has gone and save our lives.'

TEXT 42

উত্তর না পাঞা পুনঃ ভাবেন অন্তরে ।
'এহ—কৃষ্ণদাসী, ভয়ে না কহে আমারে' ॥ ৪২ ॥

uttara nā pāñā punaḥ bhāvena antare
'eha——kṛṣṇa-dāsī, bhaye nā kahe āmāre'

SYNONYMS

uttara—reply; *nā*—not; *pāñā*—getting; *punaḥ*—again; *bhāvena*—think; *antare*—within their minds; *eha*—these; *kṛṣṇa-dāsī*—maidservants of Kṛṣṇa; *bhaye*—out of fear; *nā kahe*—do not speak; *āmāre*—to us.

TRANSLATION

"When they still received no reply, the gopīs thought, 'These plants are all Kṛṣṇa's maidservants, and out of fear they will not speak to us.'

TEXT 43

আগে মৃগীগণ দেখি' কৃষ্ণাঙ্গগন্ধ পাঞা ।
তার মুখ দেখি' পুছেন নির্ণয় করিয়া ॥ ৪৩ ॥

āge mṛgī-gaṇa dekhi' kṛṣṇāṅga-gandha pāñā
tāra mukha dekhi' puchena nirṇaya kariyā

SYNONYMS

āge—in front; *mṛgī-gaṇa*—the deer; *dekhi'*—seeing; *kṛṣṇa-aṅga-gandha*—the aroma of Kṛṣṇa's body; *pāñā*—getting; *tāra mukha*—their faces; *dekhi'*—seeing; *puchena*—inquire; *nirṇaya kariyā*—making certain.

TRANSLATION

"The gopīs then came upon a group of she-deer. Smelling the aroma of Kṛṣṇa's body and seeing the faces of the deer, the gopīs inquired from them to ascertain if Kṛṣṇa was nearby.

TEXT 44

অপ্যেণ-পত্ন্যুপগতঃ প্রিয়য়েহ গাত্রৈ-
স্তন্বন্ দৃশাং সখি সুনির্বৃতিমচ্যুতো বঃ ।
কান্তাঙ্গসঙ্গকুচকুঙ্কুম-রঞ্জিতায়াঃ
কুন্দস্রজঃ কুলপতেরিহ বাতি গন্ধঃ ॥ ৪৪ ॥

apy eṇa-patny upagataḥ priyayeha gātrais
tanvan dṛśāṁ sakhi sunirvṛtim acyuto vaḥ
kāntāṅga-saṅga-kuca-kuṅkuma-rañjitāyāḥ
kunda-srajaḥ kula-pater iha vāti gandhaḥ

SYNONYMS

api—whether; *eṇa-patnī*—O she-deer; *upagataḥ*—has come; *priyayā*—along with His dearmost companion; *iha*—here; *gātraiḥ*—by the bodily limbs; *tanvan*—increasing; *dṛśām*—of the eyes; *sakhi*—O my dear friend; *su-nirvṛtim*—happiness; *acyutaḥ*—Kṛṣṇa; *vaḥ*—of all of you; *kānta-aṅga*—with the body of the beloved; *saṅga*—by association; *kuca-kuṅkuma*—with *kuṅkuma* powder from the breasts; *rañjitāyāḥ*—colored; *kunda-srajaḥ*—of the garland of *kunda* flowers; *kula-pateḥ*—of Kṛṣṇa; *iha*—here; *vāti*—flows; *gandhaḥ*—the fragrance.

TRANSLATION

" 'O wife of the deer, Lord Kṛṣṇa has been embracing His beloved, and thus the kuṅkuma powder on Her raised breasts has covered His garland of kunda flowers. The fragrance of this garland is flowing here. O my dear friend, have you seen Kṛṣṇa passing this way with His dearmost companion, increasing the pleasure of the eyes of all of you?'

PURPORT

This verse is quoted from *Śrīmad-Bhāgavatam* (10.30.11).

TEXT 45

"কহ, মৃগি, রাধা-সহ শ্রীকৃষ্ণ সর্বথা।
তোমায় সুখ দিতে আইলা? নাহিক অন্যথা ॥ ৪৫ ॥

"kaha, mṛgi, rādhā-saha śrī-kṛṣṇa sarvathā
tomāya sukha dite āilā? nāhika anyathā

SYNONYMS

kaha—please say; *mṛgi*—O she-deer; *rādhā-saha*—with Śrīmatī Rādhārāṇī; *śrī-kṛṣṇa*—Lord Śrī Kṛṣṇa; *sarvathā*—in all respects; *tomāya*—to you; *sukha dite*—to give pleasure; *āilā*—did come; *nāhika anyathā*—it is certain.

TRANSLATION

" 'O dear doe, Śrī Kṛṣṇa is always very pleased to give you pleasure. Kindly inform us whether He passed this way in the company of Śrīmatī Rādhārāṇī. We think They must certainly have come this way.

TEXT 46

রাধা-প্রিয়সখী আমরা, নহি বহিরঙ্গ।
দূর হৈতে জানি তার যৈছে অঙ্গ-গন্ধ ॥ ৪৬ ॥

rādhā-priya-sakhī āmarā, nahi bahiraṅga
dūra haite jāni tāra yaiche aṅga-gandha

SYNONYMS

rādhā—of Śrīmatī Rādhārāṇī; *priya-sakhī*—very dear friends; *āmarā*—we; *nahi bahiraṅga*—are not outsiders; *dūra haite*—from a distance; *jāni*—we know; *tāra*—of Lord Kṛṣṇa; *yaiche*—as; *aṅga-gandha*—bodily fragrance.

TRANSLATION

" 'We are not outsiders. Being very dear friends of Śrīmatī Rādhārāṇī, we can perceive the bodily fragrance of Kṛṣṇa from a distance.

TEXT 47

রাধা-অঙ্গ-সঙ্গে কুচকুঙ্কুম-ভূষিত ।
কৃষ্ণ-কুন্দমালা-গন্ধে বায়ু—সুবাসিত ॥ ৪৭ ॥

rādhā-aṅga-saṅge kuca-kuṅkuma-bhūṣita
kṛṣṇa-kunda-mālā-gandhe vāyu——suvāsita

SYNONYMS

rādhā-aṅga—the body of Śrīmatī Rādhārāṇī; *saṅge*—by embracing; *kuca-kuṅkuma*—with the *kuṅkuma* from the breasts; *bhūṣita*—decorated; *kṛṣṇa*—of Lord Kṛṣṇa; *kunda-mālā*—of the garland of *kunda* flowers; *gandhe*—by the fragrance; *vāyu*—the air; *su-vāsita*—aromatic.

TRANSLATION

" 'Kṛṣṇa has been embracing Śrīmatī Rādhārāṇī, and the kuṅkuma powder on Her breasts has mixed with the garland of kunda flowers decorating His body. The fragrance of the garland has scented the entire atmosphere.

TEXT 48

কৃষ্ণ ইহাঁ ছাড়ি' গেলা, ইহোঁ—বিরহিণী ।
কিবা উত্তর দিবে এই—না শুনে কাহিনী ॥" ৪৮ ॥

kṛṣṇa ihāṅ chāḍi' gelā, ihoṅ——virahiṇī
kibā uttara dibe ei——nā śune kāhinī"

SYNONYMS

kṛṣṇa—Lord Kṛṣṇa; *ihāṅ*—here; *chāḍi' gelā*—has left; *ihoṅ*—the deer; *virahiṇī*—feeling separation; *kibā*—what; *uttara*—reply; *dibe*—will they give; *ei*—these; *nā śune*—do not hear; *kāhinī*—our words.

TRANSLATION

"'Lord Kṛṣṇa has left this place, and therefore the deer are feeling separation. They do not hear our words; therefore how can they reply?'

TEXT 49

আগে বৃক্ষগণ দেখে পুষ্পফলভরে ।
শাখা সব পড়িয়াছে পৃথিবী-উপরে ॥ ৪৯ ॥

āge vṛkṣa-gaṇa dekhe puṣpa-phala-bhare
śākhā saba paḍiyāche pṛthivī-upare

SYNONYMS

āge—in front; *vṛkṣa-gaṇa*—the trees; *dekhe*—see; *puṣpa-phala-bhare*—because of the heavy burden of flowers and fruits; *śākhā saba*—all the branches; *paḍiyāche*—have bent down; *pṛthivī-upare*—to the ground.

TRANSLATION

"The gopīs then came upon many trees so laden with fruits and flowers that their branches bent down to the ground.

TEXT 50

কৃষ্ণে দেখি' এই সব করেন নমস্কার ।
কৃষ্ণগমন পুছে তারে করিয়া নির্ধার ॥ ৫০ ॥

kṛṣṇe dekhi' ei saba karena namaskāra
kṛṣṇa-gamana puche tāre kariyā nirdhāra

SYNONYMS

kṛṣṇe dekhi'—seeing Kṛṣṇa; *ei*—these; *saba*—all; *karena namaskāra*—offer respectful obeisances; *kṛṣṇa-gamana*—the passing of Kṛṣṇa; *puche*—inquire; *tāre*—from them; *kariyā nirdhāra*—making certain.

TRANSLATION

"The gopīs thought that because all the trees must have seen Kṛṣṇa pass by they were offering respectful obeisances to Him. To be certain, the gopīs inquired from the trees.

TEXT 51

বাহুং প্রিয়াংস উপধায় গৃহীতপদ্মো
রামানুজস্তুলসিকালিকুলৈর্মদান্ধৈঃ ।
অন্বীয়মান ইহ বস্তরবঃ প্রণামং
কিংবাভিনন্দতি চরন্ প্রণয়াবলোকৈঃ ॥ ৫১ ॥

bāhuṁ priyāṁsa upadhāya gṛhīta-padmo
rāmānujas tulasikāli-kulair madāndhaiḥ
anvīyamāna iha vas taravaḥ praṇāmaṁ
kiṁvābhinandati caran praṇayāvalokaiḥ

SYNONYMS

bāhum—arm; *priyā-aṁse*—on the shoulder of His beloved; *upadhāya*—placing; *gṛhīta*—having taken; *padmaḥ*—a lotus flower; *rāma-anujaḥ*—Lord Balarāma's younger brother (Kṛṣṇa); *tulasikā*—because of the garland of *tulasī* flowers; *ali-kulaiḥ*—by bumblebees; *mada-andhaiḥ*—blinded by the fragrance; *anvīyamānaḥ*—being followed; *iha*—here; *vaḥ*—of you; *taravaḥ*—O trees; *praṇāmam*—the obeisances; *kiṁvā*—whether; *abhinandati*—welcomes; *caran*—while passing; *praṇaya-avalokaiḥ*—with glances of love.

TRANSLATION

"'O trees, kindly tell us whether Balarāma's younger brother, Kṛṣṇa, welcomed your obeisances with loving glances as He passed this way, resting one hand on the shoulder of Śrīmatī Rādhārāṇī, holding a lotus flower in the other, and being followed by a swarm of bumblebees maddened by the fragrance of tulasī leaves.'

PURPORT

This verse is quoted from *Śrīmad-Bhāgavatam* (10.30.12).

TEXT 52

প্রিয়া-মুখে ভৃঙ্গ পড়ে, তাহা নিবারিতে ।
লীলাপদ্ম চালাইতে হৈল অন্যচিত্তে ॥ ৫২ ॥

priyā-mukhe bhṛṅga paḍe, tāhā nivārite
līlā-padma cālāite haila anya-citte

SYNONYMS

priyā-mukhe—on His beloved's face; *bhṛṅga*—the bumblebees; *paḍe*—fall; *tāhā*—that; *nivārite*—to prevent; *līlā*—the pastimes; *padma*—the lotus flower; *cālāite*—causing to move; *haila*—was; *anya-citte*—diverted in the mind.

TRANSLATION

" 'To stop the bumblebees from landing on the face of His beloved, He whisked them away with the lotus flower in His hand, and thus His mind was slightly diverted.

TEXT 53

তোমার প্রণামে কি কৈরাছেন অবধান ?
কিবা নাহি করেন, কহ বচনপ্রমাণ ॥ ৫৩ ॥

tomāra praṇāme ki kairāchena avadhāna?
kibā nāhi karena, kaha vacana-pramāṇa

SYNONYMS

tomāra—your; *praṇāme*—to the obeisances; *ki*—whether; *kairāchena*—has given; *avadhāna*—attention; *kibā*—or; *nāhi karena*—did not do so; *kaha*—kindly speak; *vacana*—words; *pramāṇa*—evidence.

TRANSLATION

" 'Did He or did He not pay attention while You offered Him obeisances? Kindly give evidence supporting your words.

TEXT 54

কৃষ্ণের বিয়োগে এই সেবক দুঃখিত ।
কিবা উত্তর দিবে ? ইহার নাহিক সম্বিৎ ॥" ৫৪ ॥

kṛṣṇera viyoge ei sevaka duḥkhita
kibā uttara dibe? ihāra nāhika samvit"

SYNONYMS

kṛṣṇera viyoge—by separation from Kṛṣṇa; *ei*—these; *sevaka*—servants; *duḥkhita*—very unhappy; *kibā*—what; *uttara*—reply; *dibe*—will they give; *ihāra*—of these; *nāhika*—there is not; *samvit*—consciousness.

TRANSLATION

"'Separation from Kṛṣṇa has made these servants very unhappy. Having lost consciousness, how can they answer us?'

TEXT 55

এত বলি' আগে চলে যমুনার কূলে ।
দেখে,—তাহাঁ কৃষ্ণ হয় কদম্বের তলে ॥ ৫৫ ॥

eta bali' āge cale yamunāra kūle
dekhe,——tāhāṅ kṛṣṇa haya kadambera tale

SYNONYMS

eta bali'—saying this; *āge cale*—go forward; *yamunāra kūle*—onto the beach by the Yamunā; *dekhe*—they see; *tāhāṅ*—there; *kṛṣṇa*—Lord Kṛṣṇa; *haya*—is present; *kadambera tale*—underneath a *kadamba* tree.

TRANSLATION

"Saying this, the gopīs stepped onto the beach by the Yamunā River. There they saw Lord Kṛṣṇa beneath a kadamba tree.

TEXT 56

কোটিমন্মথমোহন মুরলীবদন ।
অপার সৌন্দর্যে হরে জগন্নেত্র-মন ॥ ৫৬ ॥

koṭi-manmatha-mohana muralī-vadana
apāra saundarye hare jagan-netra-mana

SYNONYMS

koṭi—ten million; *manmatha*—Cupids; *mohana*—enchanting; *muralī-vadana*—with His flute to His lips; *apāra*—unlimited; *saundarye*—by the beauty; *hare*—enchants; *jagat*—of the whole world; *netra-mana*—the eyes and mind.

TRANSLATION

"Standing there with His flute to His lips, Kṛṣṇa, who enchants millions upon millions of Cupids, attracted the eyes and minds of all the world with His unlimited beauty."

TEXT 57

সৌন্দর্য দেখিয়া ভূমে পড়ে মূর্চ্ছা পাঞা ।
হেনকালে স্বরূপাদি মিলিলা আসিয়া ॥ ৫৭ ॥

saundarya dekhiyā bhūme paḍe mūrcchā pāñā
hena-kāle svarūpādi mililā āsiyā

SYNONYMS

saundarya—beauty; *dekhiyā*—seeing; *bhūme*—on the ground; *paḍe*—fell; *mūrcchā pāñā*—becoming unconscious; *hena-kāle*—at that time; *svarūpa-ādi*—the devotees, headed by Svarūpa Dāmodara Gosvāmī; *mililā āsiyā*—came there and met.

TRANSLATION

When Śrī Caitanya Mahāprabhu saw the transcendental beauty of Kṛṣṇa, He fell down on the ground unconscious. At that time, all the devotees, headed by Svarūpa Dāmodara Gosvāmī, joined Him in the garden.

TEXT 58

পূর্ববৎ সর্বাঙ্গে সাত্ত্বিকভাবসকল ।
অন্তরে আনন্দ-আস্বাদ, বাহিরে বিহ্বল ॥ ৫৮ ॥

pūrvavat sarvāṅge sāttvika-bhāva-sakala
antare ānanda-āsvāda, bāhire vihvala

SYNONYMS

pūrva-vat—as before; *sarva-aṅge*—all over the body; *sāttvika*—transcendental; *bhāva-sakala*—all the symptoms of ecstatic love; *antare*—within; *ānanda-āsvāda*—the taste of transcendental bliss; *bāhire*—externally; *vihvala*—bewildered.

TRANSLATION

Just as before, they saw all the symptoms of transcendental ecstatic love manifested in the body of Śrī Caitanya Mahāprabhu. Although externally He appeared bewildered, He was tasting transcendental bliss within.

TEXT 59

পূর্ববৎ সবে মিলি' করাইলা চেতন ।
উঠিয়া চৌদিকে প্রভু করেন দর্শন ॥ ৫৯ ॥

pūrvavat sabe mili' karāilā cetana
uṭhiyā caudike prabhu karena darśana

SYNONYMS

pūrva-vat—as before; *sabe*—all; *mili'*—coming together; *karāilā cetana*—brought to consciousness; *uṭhiyā*—standing up; *cau-dike*—all around; *prabhu*—Śrī Caitanya Mahāprabhu; *karena darśana*—was looking.

TRANSLATION

Once again all the devotees brought Śrī Caitanya Mahāprabhu back to consciousness by a concerted effort. Then the Lord got up and began wandering here and there, looking all around.

TEXT 60

"কাহাঁ গেলা কৃষ্ণ ? এখনি পাইনু দরশন !
তাঁহার সৌন্দর্য মোর হরিল নেত্র-মন ! ৬০ ॥

"kāhāṅ gelā kṛṣṇa? ekhani pāinu daraśana!
tāṅhāra saundarya mora harila netra-mana!

SYNONYMS

kāhāṅ—where; *gelā kṛṣṇa*—has Kṛṣṇa gone; *ekhani*—just now; *pāinu daraśana*—I saw; *tāṅhāra*—His; *saundarya*—beauty; *mora*—My; *harila*—has taken away; *netra-mana*—eyes and mind.

TRANSLATION

Caitanya Mahāprabhu said, "Where has My Kṛṣṇa gone? I saw Him just now, and His beauty has captured My eyes and mind.

TEXT 61

পুনঃ কেনে না দেখিয়ে মুরলী-বদন !
তাঁহার দর্শন-লোভে ভ্রময় নয়ন ॥" ৬১ ॥

punaḥ kene nā dekhiye muralī-vadana!
tāṅhāra darśana-lobhe bhramaya nayana"

SYNONYMS

punaḥ—again; *kene*—why; *nā dekhiye*—I do not see; *muralī-vadana*—with His flute to His lips; *tāṅhāra*—of Him; *darśana-lobhe*—in hopes of seeing; *bhramaya*—are wandering; *nayana*—My eyes.

TRANSLATION

"Why can't I again see Kṛṣṇa holding His flute to His lips? My eyes are wandering in hopes of seeing Him once more."

TEXT 62

বিশাখারে রাধা যৈছে শ্লোক কহিলা ।
সেই শ্লোক মহাপ্রভু পড়িতে লাগিলা ॥ ৬২ ॥

viśākhāre rādhā yaiche śloka kahilā
sei śloka mahāprabhu paḍite lāgilā

SYNONYMS

viśākhāre—to Viśākhā; *rādhā*—Śrīmatī Rādhārāṇī; *yaiche*—as; *śloka kahilā*—recited a verse; *sei*—that; *śloka*—verse; *mahāprabhu*—Śrī Caitanya Mahāprabhu; *paḍite lāgilā*—began to recite.

TRANSLATION

Śrī Caitanya Mahāprabhu then recited the following verse, which was spoken by Śrīmatī Rādhārāṇī to Her dear friend Viśākhā.

TEXT 63

নবাম্বুদ-লসদ্দ্যুতির্নবতড়িন্মনোজ্ঞাম্বরঃ
সুচিত্রমুরলীস্ফুরচ্ছরদমন্দচন্দ্রাননঃ ।
ময়ূরদলভূষিতঃ সুভগতারহারপ্রভঃ
স মে মদনমোহনঃ সখি তনোতি নেত্রস্পৃহাম্ ॥৬৩॥

navāmbuda-lasad-dyutir nava-taḍin-manojñāmbaraḥ
sucitra-muralī-sphurac-charad-amanda-candrānanaḥ
mayūra-dala-bhūṣitaḥ subhaga-tāra-hāra-prabhaḥ
sa me madana-mohanaḥ sakhi tanoti netra-spṛhām

SYNONYMS

nava-ambuda—a newly formed cloud; *lasat*—brilliant; *dyutiḥ*—whose luster; *nava*—new; *taḍit*—lightning; *manojña*—attractive; *ambaraḥ*—whose dress; *su-citra*—very charming; *muralī*—with a flute; *sphurat*—appearing beautiful; *śarat*—autumn; *amanda*—bright; *candra*—like the moon; *ānanaḥ*—whose face; *mayūra*—peacock; *dala*—with a feather; *bhūṣitaḥ*—decorated; *su-bhaga*—lovely; *tāra*—of pearls; *hāra*—of a necklace; *prabhaḥ*—with the effulgence; *saḥ*—

He; *me*—My; *madana-mohanaḥ*—Lord Kṛṣṇa, the enchanter of Cupid; *sakhi*—O My dear friend; *tanoti*—increases; *netra-spṛhām*—the desire of the eyes.

TRANSLATION

"My dear friend, the luster of Kṛṣṇa's body is more brilliant than a newly formed cloud, and His yellow dress is more attractive than newly arrived lightning. A peacock feather decorates His head, and on His neck hangs a lovely necklace of brilliant pearls. As He holds His charming flute to His lips, His face looks as beautiful as the full autumn moon. By such beauty, Madana-mohana, the enchanter of Cupid, is increasing the desire of my eyes to see Him."

PURPORT

This verse is also found in the *Govinda-līlāmṛta* (8.4).

TEXT 64

নবঘনস্নিগ্ধবর্ণ, দলিতাঞ্জন-চিক্কণ,
ইন্দীবর-নিন্দি সুকোমল ।
জিনি' উপমান-গণ, হরে সবার নেত্র-মন,
কৃষ্ণকান্তি পরম প্রবল ॥ ৬৪ ॥

nava-ghana-snigdha-varṇa, dalitāñjana-cikkaṇa,
indīvara-nindi sukomala
jini' upamāna-gaṇa, hare sabāra netra-mana,
kṛṣṇa-kānti parama prabala

SYNONYMS

nava-ghana—a newly formed cloud; *snigdha*—attractive; *varṇa*—bodily complexion; *dalita*—powdered; *añjana*—ointment; *cikkaṇa*—polished; *indīvara*—a blue lotus flower; *nindi*—defeating; *su-komala*—soft; *jini'*—surpassing; *upamāna-gaṇa*—all comparison; *hare*—attracts; *sabāra*—of all; *netra-mana*—the eyes and mind; *kṛṣṇa-kānti*—the complexion of Kṛṣṇa; *parama prabala*—supremely powerful.

TRANSLATION

Caitanya Mahāprabhu continued: "Śrī Kṛṣṇa's complexion is as polished as powdered eye ointment. It surpasses the beauty of a newly formed cloud and is softer than a blue lotus flower. Indeed, His complexion is so pleasing that it attracts the eyes and mind of everyone, and it is so powerful that it defies all comparison.

TEXT 65

কহ, সখি, কি করি উপায় ?
কৃষ্ণাদ্ভুত বলাহক, মোর নেত্র-চাতক,
না দেখি' পিয়াসে মরি' যায় ॥ ৬৫ ॥ ধ্রু ॥

kaha, sakhi, ki kari upāya?
kṛṣṇādbhuta balāhaka, mora netra-cātaka,
nā dekhi' piyāse mari' yāya

SYNONYMS

kaha—please tell; *sakhi*—My dear friend; *ki kari upāya*—what shall I do; *kṛṣṇa*—Kṛṣṇa; *adbhuta*—wonderful; *balāhaka*—cloud; *mora*—My; *netra*—eyes; *cātaka*—like *cātaka* birds; *nā dekhi'*—without seeing; *piyāse*—from thirst; *mari' yāya*—are dying.

TRANSLATION

"My dear friend, please tell me what I should do. Kṛṣṇa is as attractive as a wonderful cloud, and My eyes are just like cātaka birds, which are dying of thirst because they do not see such a cloud.

TEXT 66

সৌদামিনী পীতাম্বর, স্থির নহে নিরন্তর,
মুক্তাহার বকপাঁতি ভাল ।
ইন্দ্রধনু-শিখিপাখা, উপরে দিয়াছে দেখা,
আর ধনু বৈজয়ন্তী-মাল ॥ ৬৬ ॥

saudāminī pītāmbara, sthira nahe nirantara,
muktā-hāra baka-pāṅti bhāla
indra-dhanu śikhi-pākhā, upare diyāche dekhā,
āra dhanu vaijayantī-māla

SYNONYMS

saudāminī—lightning; *pīta-ambara*—the yellow dress; *sthira*—still; *nahe*—is not; *nirantara*—always; *muktā-hāra*—the necklace of pearls; *baka-pāṅti bhāla*—like a line of ducks; *indra-dhanu*—the bow of Indra (a rainbow); *śikhi-pākhā*—the peacock feather; *upare*—on the head; *diyāche dekhā*—is seen; *āra dhanu*—another rainbow; *vaijayantī-māla*—the *vaijayantī* garland.

TRANSLATION

"Kṛṣṇa's yellow dress looks exactly like restless lightning in the sky, and the pearl necklace on His neck appears like a line of ducks flying below a cloud. Both the peacock feather on His head and His vaijayantī garland [containing flowers of five colors] resemble rainbows.

TEXT 67

মুরলীর কলধ্বনি, মধুর গর্জন শুনি',
বৃন্দাবনে নাচে ময়ূরচয় ।
অকলঙ্ক পূর্ণকল, লাবণ্য-জ্যোৎস্না ঝলমল,
চিত্রচন্দ্রের তাহাতে উদয় ॥ ৬৭ ॥

muralīra kala-dhvani, madhura garjana śuni',
vṛndāvane nāce mayūra-caya
akalaṅka pūrṇa-kala, lāvaṇya-jyotsnā jhalamala,
citra-candrera tāhāte udaya

SYNONYMS

muralīra—of the flute; *kala-dhvani*—the low vibration; *madhura*—sweet; *garjana*—thundering; *śuni'*—hearing; *vṛndāvane*—in Vṛndāvana; *nāce*—dance; *mayūra-caya*—the peacocks; *akalaṅka*—spotless; *pūrṇa-kala*—the full moon; *lāvaṇya*—beauty; *jyotsnā*—light; *jhalamala*—glittering; *citra-candrera*—of the beautiful moon; *tāhāte*—in that; *udaya*—the rising.

TRANSLATION

"The luster of Kṛṣṇa's body is as beautiful as a spotless full moon that has just risen, and the vibration of His flute sounds exactly like the sweet thundering of a newly formed cloud. When the peacocks in Vṛndāvana hear that vibration, they all begin to dance.

TEXT 68

লীলামৃত-বরিষণে, সিঞ্চে চৌদ্দ ভুবনে,
হেন মেঘ যবে দেখা দিল ।
দুর্দৈব-ঝঞ্ঝাপবনে, মেঘে নিল অন্যস্থানে,
মরে চাতক, পিতে না পাইল ॥ ৬৮ ॥

līlāmṛta-variṣaṇe, siñce caudda bhuvane,
hena megha yabe dekhā dila

durdaiva-jhañjhā-pavane, meghe nila anya-sthāne,
mare cātaka, pite nā pāila

SYNONYMS

līlā—of the pastimes of Kṛṣṇa; *amṛta*—of nectar; *variṣaṇe*—the shower; *siñce*—drenches; *caudda bhuvane*—the fourteen worlds; *hena megha*—such a cloud; *yabe*—when; *dekhā dila*—was visible; *durdaiva*—misfortune; *jhañjhā-pavane*—a high wind; *meghe*—the cloud; *nila*—brought; *anya-sthāne*—to another place; *mare*—dies; *cātaka*—the *cātaka* bird; *pite nā pāila*—could not drink.

TRANSLATION

"The cloud of Kṛṣṇa's pastimes is drenching the fourteen worlds with a shower of nectar. Unfortunately, when that cloud appeared, a whirlwind arose and blew it away from Me. Being unable to see the cloud, the cātaka bird of My eyes is almost dead from thirst."

TEXT 69

পুনঃ কহে,—'হায় হায়, পড় পড় রামরায়',
কহে প্রভু গদ্গদ আখ্যানে ।
রামানন্দ পড়ে শ্লোক, শুনি' প্রভুর হর্ষ-শোক,
আপনে প্রভু করেন ব্যাখ্যানে ॥ ৬৯ ॥

punaḥ kahe,—'hāya hāya, paḍa paḍa rāma-rāya',
kahe prabhu gadgada ākhyāne
rāmānanda paḍe śloka, śuni' prabhura harṣa-śoka,
āpane prabhu karena vyākhyāne

SYNONYMS

punaḥ—again; *kahe*—says; *hāya hāya*—alas, alas; *paḍa paḍa*—go on reading; *rāma-rāya*—Rāmānanda Rāya; *kahe*—says; *prabhu*—Śrī Caitanya Mahāprabhu; *gadgada ākhyāne*—in a faltering voice; *rāmānanda*—Rāmānanda Rāya; *paḍe*—reads; *śloka*—a verse; *śuni'*—hearing; *prabhura*—of Śrī Caitanya Mahāprabhu; *harṣa-śoka*—jubilation and lamentation; *āpane*—personally; *prabhu*—Śrī Caitanya Mahāprabhu; *karena vyākhyāne*—explains.

TRANSLATION

In a faltering voice, Śrī Caitanya Mahāprabhu again said, "Alas, go on reading, Rāma Rāya." Thus Rāmānanda Rāya began to read a verse. While listening

to this verse, the Lord was sometimes very jubilant and sometimes overcome by lamentation. Afterwards the Lord personally explained the verse.

TEXT 70

বীক্ষ্যালকাবৃতমুখং তব কুণ্ডলশ্রি
গণ্ডস্থলাধরসুধং হসিতাবলোকম্।
দত্তাভয়ঞ্চ ভুজদণ্ডযুগং বিলোক্য
বক্ষঃ শ্রিয়ৈকরমণঞ্চ ভবাম দাস্যঃ॥ ৭০ ॥

vīkṣyālakāvṛta-mukhaṁ tava kuṇḍala-śri-
gaṇḍa-sthalādhara-sudhaṁ hasitāvalokam
dattābhayaṁ ca bhuja-daṇḍa-yugaṁ vilokya
vakṣaḥ śriyaika-ramaṇaṁ ca bhavāma dāsyaḥ

SYNONYMS

vīkṣya—seeing; *alaka-āvṛta*—decorated with curling tresses of hair; *mukham*—face; *tava*—Your; *kuṇḍala-śri*—the beauty of earrings; *gaṇḍa-sthala*—falling in Your cheeks; *adhara-sudham*—and the nectar of Your lips; *hasita-avalokam*—Your smiling glance; *datta-abhayam*—which assure fearlessness; *ca*—and; *bhuja-daṇḍa-yugam*—the two arms; *vilokya*—by seeing; *vakṣaḥ*—chest; *śriyā*—by the beauty; *eka-ramaṇam*—chiefly producing conjugal attraction; *ca*—and; *bhavāma*—we have become; *dāsyaḥ*—Your maidservants.

TRANSLATION

" 'Dear Kṛṣṇa, by seeing Your beautiful face decorated with tresses of hair, by seeing the beauty of Your earrings falling on Your cheeks, and by seeing the nectar of Your lips, the beauty of Your smiling glances, Your two arms, which assure complete fearlessness, and Your broad chest, whose beauty arouses conjugal attraction, we have simply surrendered ourselves to becoming Your maidservants.'

PURPORT

This verse quoted from *Śrīmad-Bhāgavatam* (10.29.39) was spoken by the *gopīs* when they arrived before Kṛṣṇa for the *rāsa* dance.

TEXT 71

কৃষ্ণ জিনি' পদ্ম-চান্দ, পাতিয়াছে মুখ ফান্দ,
তাতে অধর-মধুস্মিত চার ।

ব্রজনারী আসি' আসি', ফান্দে পড়ি' হয় দাসী,
ছাড়ি' লাজ-পতি-ঘর-দ্বার ॥৭১॥

kṛṣṇa jini' padma-cānda, pātiyāche mukha phānda,
tāte adhara-madhu-smita cāra
vraja-nārī āsi' āsi', phānde paḍi' haya dāsī,
chāḍi' lāja-pati-ghara-dvāra

SYNONYMS

kṛṣṇa—Lord Kṛṣṇa; *jini'*—surpassing; *padma-cānda*—the lotus flower and the moon; *pātiyāche*—has spread; *mukha*—the face; *phānda*—noose; *tāte*—in that; *adhara*—lips; *madhu-smita*—sweet smiling; *cāra*—bait; *vraja-nārī*—the damsels of Vraja; *āsi' āsi'*—approaching; *phānde*—in the network; *paḍi'*—falling; *haya dāsī*—become maidservants; *chāḍi'*—giving up; *lāja*—prestige; *pati*—husbands; *ghara*—home; *dvāra*—family.

TRANSLATION

"After conquering the moon and the lotus flower, Kṛṣṇa wished to capture the doelike gopīs. Thus He spread the noose of His beautiful face, and within that noose He placed the bait of His sweet smile to misguide the gopīs. The gopīs fell prey to that trap and became Kṛṣṇa's maidservants, giving up their homes, families, husbands and prestige.

TEXT 72

বান্ধব কৃষ্ণ করে ব্যাধের আচার।
নাহি মানে ধর্মাধর্ম, হরে নারী-মৃগী-মর্ম,
করে নানা উপায় তাহার ॥ ৭২ ॥ ধ্রু ॥

bāndhava kṛṣṇa kare vyādhera ācāra
nāhi māne dharmādharma, hare nārī-mṛgī-marma,
kare nānā upāya tāhāra

SYNONYMS

bāndhava—O friend; *kṛṣṇa*—Lord Kṛṣṇa; *kare*—does; *vyādhera ācāra*—the behavior of a hunter; *nāhi*—not; *māne*—cares for; *dharma-adharma*—piety and impiety; *hare*—attracts; *nārī*—of a woman; *mṛgī*—doe; *marma*—the core of the heart; *kare*—does; *nānā*—varieties of; *upāya*—means; *tāhāra*—for that purpose.

TRANSLATION

"My dear friend, Kṛṣṇa acts just like a hunter. This hunter does not care for piety or impiety; He simply creates many devices to conquer the cores of the hearts of the doelike gopīs.

TEXT 73

গণ্ডস্থল ঝলমল, নাচে মকর-কুণ্ডল,
সেই নৃত্যে হরে নারীচয়।
সস্মিত কটাক্ষ-বাণে, তা-সবার হৃদয়ে হানে,
নারী-বধে নাহি কিছু ভয় ॥ ৭৩ ॥

gaṇḍa-sthala jhalamala, nāce makara-kuṇḍala,
sei nṛtye hare nārī-caya
sasmita kaṭākṣa-bāṇe, tā-sabāra hṛdaye hāne,
nārī-vadhe nāhi kichu bhaya

SYNONYMS

gaṇḍa-sthala—on the cheeks; *jhalamala*—glittering; *nāce*—dance; *makara-kuṇḍala*—earrings shaped like sharks; *sei*—that; *nṛtye*—dancing; *hare*—attracts; *nārī-caya*—all the women; *sa-smita*—with smiles; *kaṭākṣa*—of glances; *bāṇe*—by the arrows; *tā-sabāra*—of all of them; *hṛdaye*—the hearts; *hāne*—pierces; *nārī-vadhe*—for killing women; *nāhi*—there is not; *kichu*—any; *bhaya*—fear.

TRANSLATION

"The earrings dancing on Kṛṣṇa's cheeks are shaped like sharks, and they shine very brightly. These dancing earrings attract the minds of all women. Over and above this, Kṛṣṇa pierces the hearts of women with the arrows of His sweetly smiling glances. He is not at all afraid to kill women in this way.

TEXT 74

অতি উচ্চ সুবিস্তার, লক্ষ্মী-শ্রীবৎস-অলঙ্কার,
কৃষ্ণের যে ডাকাতিয়া বক্ষ।
ব্রজদেবী লক্ষ লক্ষ, তা-সবার মনোবক্ষ,
হরিদাসী করিবারে দক্ষ ॥ ৭৪ ॥

ati ucca suvistāra, lakṣmī-śrīvatsa-alaṅkāra,
kṛṣṇera ye ḍākātiyā vakṣa

vraja-devī lakṣa lakṣa, tā-sabāra mano-vakṣa,
hari-dāsī karibāre dakṣa

SYNONYMS

ati—very; *ucca*—high; *su-vistāra*—broad; *lakṣmī*—a mark of golden lines on the left side of the chest of Śrī Kṛṣṇa, indicating the residence of the goddess of fortune; *śrīvatsa*—a mark of silver hairs on the right side of the Lord's chest; *alaṅkāra*—ornaments; *kṛṣṇera*—of Lord Kṛṣṇa; *ye*—that; *ḍākātiyā*—like a plunderer; *vakṣa*—chest; *vraja-devī*—the damsels of Vraja; *lakṣa lakṣa*—thousands upon thousands; *tā-sabāra*—of all of them; *manaḥ-vakṣa*—the minds and breasts; *hari-dāsī*—maidservants of the Supreme Lord; *karibāre*—to make; *dakṣa*—expert.

TRANSLATION

"On Kṛṣṇa's chest are the ornaments of Śrīvatsa and the mark indicating the residence of the goddess of fortune. His chest, which is as broad as a plunderer's, attracts thousands upon thousands of damsels of Vraja, conquering their minds and breasts by force. Thus they all become maidservants of the Supreme Personality of Godhead.

TEXT 75

সুললিত দীর্ঘার্গল, কৃষ্ণের ভুজযুগল,
ভুজ নহে,—কৃষ্ণসর্পকায় ।
দুই শৈল-ছিদ্রে পৈশে, নারীর হৃদয়ে দংশে,
মরে নারী সে বিষজ্বালায় ॥ ৭৫ ॥

sulalita dīrghārgala, kṛṣṇera bhuja-yugala,
bhuja nahe,——kṛṣṇa-sarpa-kāya
dui śaila-chidre paiśe, nārīra hṛdaye daṁśe,
mare nārī se viṣa-jvālāya

SYNONYMS

su-lalita—very beautiful; *dīrgha-argala*—long bolts; *kṛṣṇera*—of Kṛṣṇa; *bhuja-yugala*—two arms; *bhuja*—arms; *nahe*—not; *kṛṣṇa*—black; *sarpa*—of snakes; *kāya*—bodies; *dui*—two; *śaila-chidre*—in the space between the hills; *paiśe*—enter; *nārīra*—of women; *hṛdaye*—the hearts; *daṁśe*—bite; *mare*—die; *nārī*—women; *se*—that; *viṣa-jvālāya*—from the burning of the poison.

TRANSLATION

"The two very beautiful arms of Kṛṣṇa are just like long bolts. They also resemble the bodies of black snakes that enter the space between the two hill-

like breasts of women and bite their hearts. The women then die from the burning poison.

PURPORT

In other words, the *gopīs* become very agitated by lusty desires; they are burning due to the poisonous bite inflicted by the black snakes of Kṛṣṇa's beautiful arms.

TEXT 76

কৃষ্ণ-কর-পদতল, কোটিচন্দ্র-সুশীতল,
জিনি' কর্পূর-বেণামূল-চন্দন।
একবার যার স্পর্শে, স্মরজ্বালা-বিষ নাশে,
যার স্পর্শে লুব্ধ নারী-মন ॥ ৭৬ ॥

kṛṣṇa-kara-pada-tala, koṭi-candra-suśītala,
jini' karpūra-veṇā-mūla-candana
eka-bāra yāra sparśe, smara-jvālā-viṣa nāśe,
yāra sparśe lubdha nārī-mana

SYNONYMS

kṛṣṇa—of Lord Kṛṣṇa; *kara-pada-tala*—the palms and the soles of the feet; *koṭi-candra*—millions upon millions of moons; *su-śītala*—cool and pleasing; *jini'*—surpassing; *karpūra*—camphor; *veṇā-mūla*—roots of *khasakhasa; candana*—sandalwood pulp; *eka-bāra*—once; *yāra*—of which; *sparśe*—by the touch; *smara-jvālā*—the burning effect of remembering; *viṣa*—the poison; *nāśe*—becomes vanquished; *yāra*—of which; *sparśe*—by the touch; *lubdha*—enticed; *nārī-mana*—the minds of women.

TRANSLATION

"The combined cooling effect of camphor, roots of khasakhasa and sandalwood is surpassed by the coolness of Kṛṣṇa's palms and the soles of His feet, which are cooler and more pleasing than millions upon millions of moons. If women are touched by them even once, their minds are enticed, and the burning poison of lusty desire for Kṛṣṇa is immediately vanquished."

TEXT 77

এতেক বিলাপ করি' প্রেমাবেশে গৌরহরি,
এই অর্থে পড়ে এক শ্লোক।

যেই শ্লোক পড়ি' রাধা, বিশাখারে কহে বাধা,
উঘাড়িয়া হৃদয়ের শোক ॥ ৭৭ ॥

eteka vilāpa kari' premāveśe gaurahari,
ei arthe paḍe eka śloka
sei śloka paḍi' rādhā, viśākhāre kahe bādhā,
ughāḍiyā hṛdayera śoka

SYNONYMS

eteka—thus; *vilāpa kari'*—lamenting; *prema-āveśe*—in ecstatic love of Kṛṣṇa; *gaurahari*—Śrī Caitanya Mahāprabhu; *ei arthe*—in understanding the purpose; *paḍe*—recites; *eka śloka*—one verse; *sei śloka*—this verse; *paḍi'*—reading; *rādhā*—Śrīmatī Rādhārāṇī; *viśākhāre*—to Viśākhā; *kahe*—says; *bādhā*—obstacle; *ughāḍiyā*—exposing; *hṛdayera*—of the heart; *śoka*—lamentation.

TRANSLATION

Lamenting in ecstatic love, Śrī Caitanya Mahāprabhu then recited the following verse, which was spoken by Śrīmatī Rādhārāṇī while exposing the lamentation of Her heart to Her friend Śrīmatī Viśākhā.

TEXT 78

হরিণ্মণিকবাটিকাপ্রততহারিবক্ষঃস্থলঃ
স্মরার্ত্ততরুণীমনঃকলুষহারিদোরর্গলঃ।
সুধাংশুহরিচন্দনোৎপলসিতাভ্রশীতাঙ্গকঃ
স মে মদনমোহনঃ সখি তনোতি বক্ষঃস্পৃহাম্ ॥ ৭৮ ॥

harinmaṇi-kavāṭikā-pratata-hāri-vakṣaḥ-sthalaḥ
smarārta-taruṇī-manaḥ-kaluṣa-hāri-dor-argalaḥ
sudhāṁśu-hari-candanotpala-sitābhra-śītāṅgakaḥ
sa me madana-mohanaḥ sakhi tanoti vakṣaḥ-spṛhām

SYNONYMS

harit-maṇi—of *indranīla* gems; *kavāṭikā*—like a door; *pratata*—broad; *hāri*—attractive; *vakṣaḥ-sthalaḥ*—whose chest; *smara-ārta*—distressed by remembering; *taruṇī*—of young women; *manaḥ*—of the mind; *kaluṣa*—the pain; *hāri*—taking away; *doḥ*—whose two arms; *argalaḥ*—like bolts; *sudhāṁśu*—the moon; *hari-candana*—sandalwood; *utpala*—lotus flower; *sitābhra*—camphor; *śīta*—cool; *aṅgakaḥ*—whose body; *saḥ*—that; *me*—My; *madana-mohanaḥ*—Kṛṣṇa, who is more attractive than Cupid; *sakhi*—My friend; *tanoti*—expands; *vakṣaḥ-spṛhām*—the desire of the breasts.

TRANSLATION

"My dear friend, Kṛṣṇa's chest is as broad and attractive as a door made of indranīla gems, and His two arms, strong as bolts, can relieve the mental anguish of young girls distressed by lusty desires for Him. His body is cooler than the moon, sandalwood, the lotus flower and camphor. In this way, Madana-mohana, the attractor of Cupid, is increasing the desire of My breasts."

PURPORT

This verse is also found in the *Govinda-līlāmṛta* (8.7).

TEXT 79

প্রভু কহে,—"কৃষ্ণ মুঞি এখনই পাইনু।
আপনার দুর্দৈবে পুনঃ হারাইনু ॥ ৭৯ ॥

prabhu kahe,——"kṛṣṇa muñi ekhana-i pāinu
āpanāra durdaive punaḥ hārāinu

SYNONYMS

prabhu kahe—Śrī Caitanya Mahāprabhu said; *kṛṣṇa*—Lord Kṛṣṇa; *muñi*—I; *ekhana-i*—just now; *pāinu*—had; *āpanāra*—My own; *durdaive*—by misfortune; *punaḥ*—again; *hārāinu*—I have lost.

TRANSLATION

Śrī Caitanya Mahāprabhu then said, "I just now had Kṛṣṇa, but unfortunately I have lost Him again.

TEXT 80

চঞ্চল-স্বভাব কৃষ্ণের, না রয় একস্থানে।
দেখা দিয়া মন হরি' করে অন্তর্ধানে ॥ ৮০ ॥

cañcala-svabhāva kṛṣṇera, nā raya eka-sthāne
dekhā diyā mana hari' kare antardhāne

SYNONYMS

cañcala—restless; *svabhāva*—characteristic; *kṛṣṇera*—of Lord Kṛṣṇa; *nā*—does not; *raya*—stay; *eka-sthāne*—in one place; *dekhā diyā*—giving His audience; *mana*—mind; *hari'*—enchanting; *kare*—does; *antardhāne*—disappearance.

TRANSLATION

"By nature, Kṛṣṇa is very restless; He does not stay in one place. He meets with someone, enchants his mind and then disappears.

TEXT 81

তাসাং তৎসৌভগমদং বীক্ষ্য মানঞ্চ কেশবঃ ।
প্রশমায় প্রসাদায় তত্রৈবান্তরধীয়ত ॥ ৮১ ॥

tāsāṁ tat-saubhaga-madaṁ
vīkṣya mānaṁ ca keśavaḥ
praśamāya prasādāya
tatraivāntaradhīyata

SYNONYMS

tāsām—of the *gopīs; tat*—their; *saubhaga-madam*—pride due to great fortune; *vīkṣya*—seeing; *mānam*—conception of superiority; *ca*—and; *keśavaḥ*—Kṛṣṇa, who subdues even *ka* (Lord Brahmā) and *īśa* (Lord Śiva); *praśamāya*—to subdue; *prasādāya*—to show mercy; *tatra*—there; *eva*—certainly; *antaradhīyata*—disappeared.

TRANSLATION

" 'The gopīs became proud of their great fortune. To subdue their sense of superiority and show them special favor, Keśava, the subduer of even Lord Brahmā and Lord Śiva, disappeared from the rāsa dance.' "

PURPORT

This verse quoted from *Śrīmad-Bhāgavatam* (10.29.48) was spoken by Śukadeva Gosvāmī to Mahārāja Parīkṣit.

TEXT 82

স্বরূপ-গোসাঞিরে কহেন,—"গাও এক গীত ।
যাতে আমার হৃদয়ের হয়ে ত' 'সম্বিৎ' ॥" ৮২ ॥

svarūpa-gosāñire kahena,—"gāo eka gīta
yāte āmāra hṛdayera haye ta' 'samvit' "

SYNONYMS

svarūpa-gosāñire—to Svarūpa Dāmodara Gosvāmī; *kahena*—said; *gāo*—sing; *eka*—one; *gīta*—song; *yāte*—by which; *āmāra*—My; *hṛdayera*—of the heart; *haye*—there is; *ta'*—certainly; *samvit*—consciousness.

TRANSLATION

Śrī Caitanya Mahāprabhu then said to Svarūpa Dāmodara Gosvāmī: "Please sing a song that will bring consciousness to My heart."

TEXT 83

স্বরূপ-গোসাঞি তবে মধুর করিয়া ।
গীতগোবিন্দের পদ গায় প্রভুরে শুনাঞা ॥ ৮৩ ॥

svarūpa-gosāñi tabe madhura kariyā
gīta-govindera pada gāya prabhure śunāñā

SYNONYMS

svarūpa-gosāñi—Svarūpa Dāmodara Gosvāmī; *tabe*—thereafter; *madhura kariyā*—very sweetly; *gīta-govindera*—of the book *Gīta-govinda; pada*—one verse; *gāya*—sings; *prabhure*—Śrī Caitanya Mahāprabhu; *śunāñā*—making to hear.

TRANSLATION

Thus for the pleasure of Śrī Caitanya Mahāprabhu, Svarūpa Dāmodara Gosvāmī began very sweetly singing the following verse from Gīta-govinda.

TEXT 84

রাসে হরিমিহ বিহিতবিলাসম্ ।
স্মরতি মনো মম কৃতপরিহাসম্ ॥ ৮৪ ॥

rāse harim iha vihita-vilāsam
smarati mano mama kṛta-parihāsam

SYNONYMS

rāse—in the *rāsa* dance; *harim*—Śrī Kṛṣṇa; *iha*—here; *vihita-vilāsam*—performing pastimes; *smarati*—remembers; *manaḥ*—mind; *mama*—my; *kṛta-parihāsam*—fond of making jokes.

TRANSLATION

"Here in the arena of the rāsa dance, I remember Kṛṣṇa, who is always fond of joking and performing pastimes."

PURPORT

This verse is quoted from *Gīta-govinda* (2.3).

TEXT 85

স্বরূপ-গোসাঞি যবে এই পদ গাহিলা ।
উঠি' প্রেমাবেশে প্রভু নাচিতে লাগিলা ॥ ৮৫ ॥

svarūpa-gosāñi yabe ei pada gāhilā
uṭhi' premāveśe prabhu nācite lāgilā

SYNONYMS

svarūpa-gosāñi—Svarūpa Dāmodara Gosvāmī; *yabe*—when; *ei*—this; *pada*—verse; *gāhilā*—sang; *uṭhi'*—standing up; *prema-āveśe*—in ecstatic love of Kṛṣṇa; *prabhu*—Śrī Caitanya Mahāprabhu; *nācite lāgilā*—began to dance.

TRANSLATION

When Svarūpa Dāmodara Gosvāmī sang this special song, Śrī Caitanya Mahāprabhu immediately got up and began to dance in ecstatic love.

TEXT 86

'অষ্টসাত্ত্বিক' ভাব অঙ্গে প্রকট হইল ।
হর্ষাদি 'ব্যভিচারী' সব উথলিল ॥ ৮৬ ॥

'aṣṭa-sāttvika' bhāva aṅge prakaṭa ha-ila
harṣādi 'vyabhicārī' saba uthalila

SYNONYMS

aṣṭa-sāttvika—eight spiritual; *bhāva*—emotions; *aṅge*—on the body; *prakaṭa ha-ila*—became manifest; *harṣa-ādi*—beginning with jubilation; *vyabhicārī*—thirty-three changes of *vyabhicārī-bhāva; saba*—all; *uthalila*—were manifest.

TRANSLATION

At that time, all eight kinds of spiritual transformations became manifest in Lord Caitanya's body. The thirty-three symptoms of vyabhicārī-bhāva, beginning with lamentation and jubilation, became prominent as well.

TEXT 87

ভাবোদয়, ভাব-সন্ধি, ভাব-শাবল্য ।
ভাবে-ভাবে মহাযুদ্ধে সবার প্রাবল্য ॥ ৮৭ ॥

bhāvodaya, bhāva-sandhi, bhāva-śābalya
bhāve-bhāve mahā-yuddhe sabāra prābalya

SYNONYMS

bhāva-udaya—awakening of all the ecstatic symptoms; *bhāva-sandhi*—meeting of ecstatic symptoms; *bhāva-śābalya*—mixing of ecstatic symptoms; *bhāve-bhāve*—between one ecstasy and another; *mahā-yuddhe*—a great fight; *sabāra*—of all of them; *prābalya*—prominence.

TRANSLATION

All the ecstatic symptoms, such as bhāvodaya, bhāva-sandhi and bhāva-śābalya, awakened in the body of Śrī Caitanya Mahāprabhu. A great fight arose between one emotion and another, and each of them became prominent.

TEXT 88

সেই পদ পুনঃ পুনঃ করায় গায়ন।
পুনঃ পুনঃ আস্বাদয়ে, করেন নর্তন ॥ ৮৮ ॥

sei pada punaḥ punaḥ karāya gāyana
punaḥ punaḥ āsvādaye, karena nartana

SYNONYMS

sei pada—that verse; *punaḥ punaḥ*—again and again; *karāya gāyana*—made to sing; *punaḥ punaḥ*—again and again; *āsvādaye*—tastes; *karena nartana*—dances.

TRANSLATION

Lord Caitanya Mahāprabhu had Svarūpa Dāmodara sing the same verse again and again. Each time he sang it, the Lord tasted it anew, and thus He danced again and again.

TEXT 89

এইমত নৃত্য যদি হইল বহুক্ষণ।
স্বরূপ-গোসাঞি পদ কৈলা সমাপন ॥ ৮৯ ॥

ei-mata nṛtya yadi ha-ila bahu-kṣaṇa
svarūpa-gosāñi pada kailā samāpana

SYNONYMS

ei-mata—in this way; *nṛtya*—dancing; *yadi*—when; *ha-ila*—was; *bahu-kṣaṇa*—for a long time; *svarūpa-gosāñi*—Svarūpa Dāmodara Gosvāmī; *pada*—verse; *kailā samāpana*—stopped.

TRANSLATION

After the Lord had been dancing for a long time, Svarūpa Dāmodara Gosvāmī stopped singing the verse.

TEXT 90

'বল্' 'বল্' বলি' প্রভু কহেন বারবার।
না গায় স্বরূপ-গোসাঞি শ্রম দেখি' তাঁর ॥ ৯০ ॥

'bal' 'bal' bali' prabhu kahena bāra-bāra
nā gāya svarūpa-gosāñi śrama dekhi' tāṅra

SYNONYMS

bal—sing; *bal*—sing; *bali'*—uttering; *prabhu*—Śrī Caitanya Mahāprabhu; *kahena*—says; *bāra-bāra*—again and again; *nā*—not; *gāya*—sings; *svarūpa-gosāñi*—Svarūpa Dāmodara Gosvāmī; *śrama*—fatigue; *dekhi'*—seeing; *tāṅra*—of Lord Caitanya.

TRANSLATION

Over and over again Śrī Caitanya Mahāprabhu said, "Go on! Sing! Sing!" But Svarūpa Dāmodara, seeing the Lord's fatigue, did not resume singing.

TEXT 91

'বল্' 'বল্' প্রভু বলেন, ভক্তগণ শুনি'।
চৌদিকেতে সবে মেলি' করে হরিধ্বনি ॥ ৯১ ॥

'bal' 'bal' prabhu balena, bhakta-gaṇa śuni'
caudikete sabe meli' kare hari-dhvani

SYNONYMS

bal bal—go on singing, go on singing; *prabhu balena*—Śrī Caitanya Mahāprabhu said; *bhakta-gaṇa*—the devotees; *śuni'*—hearing; *cau-dikete*—all around; *sabe*—all; *meli'*—combining; *kare hari-dhvani*—vibrate the holy name of Hari.

TRANSLATION

When the devotees heard Śrī Caitanya Mahāprabhu say, "Go on singing!" they all gathered around Him and began to chant the holy name of Hari in unison.

TEXT 92

রামানন্দ-রায় তবে প্রভুরে বসাইলা ।
বীজনাদি করি' প্রভুর শ্রম ঘুচাইলা ॥ ৯২ ॥

rāmānanda-rāya tabe prabhure vasāilā
vījanādi kari' prabhura śrama ghucāilā

SYNONYMS

rāmānanda-rāya—Rāmānanda Rāya; *tabe*—at that time; *prabhure*—Śrī Caitanya Mahāprabhu; *vasāilā*—made to sit down; *vījana-ādi kari'*—fanning and so on; *prabhura*—of Śrī Caitanya Mahāprabhu; *śrama*—fatigue; *ghucāilā*—dissipated.

TRANSLATION

At that time, Rāmānanda Rāya made the Lord sit down and dissipated His fatigue by fanning Him.

TEXT 93

প্রভুরে লঞা গেলা সবে সমুদ্রের তীরে ।
স্নান করাঞা পুনঃ তাঁরে লঞা আইলা ঘরে ॥ ৯৩ ॥

prabhure lañā gelā sabe samudrera tīre
snāna karāñā punaḥ tāṅre lañā āilā ghare

SYNONYMS

prabhure—Śrī Caitanya Mahāprabhu; *lañā*—taking; *gelā*—went; *sabe*—all; *samudrera tīre*—to the beach by the sea; *snāna karāñā*—bathing Him; *punaḥ*—again; *tāṅre*—Him; *lañā āilā*—brought back; *ghare*—to His residence.

TRANSLATION

Then all the devotees took Śrī Caitanya Mahāprabhu to the beach and bathed Him. Finally they brought Him back home.

TEXT 94

ভোজন করাঞা প্রভুরে করাইলা শয়ন ।
রামানন্দ-আদি সবে গেলা নিজ-স্থান ॥ ৯৪ ॥

bhojana karāñā prabhure karāilā śayana
rāmānanda-ādi sabe gelā nija-sthāna

SYNONYMS

bhojana karāñā—feeding; *prabhure*—Śrī Caitanya Mahāprabhu; *karāilā śayana*—made to lie down; *rāmānanda-ādi*—headed by Rāmānanda Rāya; *sabe*—all of them; *gelā*—went; *nija-sthāna*—to their homes.

TRANSLATION

After they fed Him lunch, they made Him lie down. Then all the devotees, headed by Rāmānanda Rāya, returned to their respective homes.

TEXT 95

এই ত' কহিলুঁ প্রভুর উদ্যান-বিহার।
বৃন্দাবন-ভ্রমে যাহাঁ প্রবেশ তাঁহার ॥ ৯৫ ॥

ei ta' kahiluṅ prabhura udyāna-vihāra
vṛndāvana-bhrame yāhāṅ praveśa tāṅhāra

SYNONYMS

ei ta'—thus; *kahiluṅ*—I have described; *prabhura*—of Śrī Caitanya Mahāprabhu; *udyāna-vihāra*—pastimes in the garden; *vṛndāvana-bhrame*—mistaking for Vṛndāvana; *yāhāṅ*—where; *praveśa*—entrance; *tāṅhāra*—His.

TRANSLATION

Thus I have described Śrī Caitanya Mahāprabhu's pastimes in the garden, which He entered, mistaking it for Vṛndāvana.

TEXT 96

প্রলাপ সহিত এই উন্মাদ-বর্ণন।
শ্রীরূপ-গোসাঞি ইহা করিয়াছেন বর্ণন ॥ ৯৬ ॥

pralāpa sahita ei unmāda-varṇana
śrī-rūpa-gosāñi ihā kariyāchena varṇana

SYNONYMS

pralāpa—ecstatic ravings; *sahita*—with; *ei*—this; *unmāda*—of madness; *varṇana*—description; *śrī-rūpa-gosāñi*—Śrī Rūpa Gosvāmī; *ihā*—this; *kariyāchena varṇana*—has described.

TRANSLATION

There He exhibited transcendental madness and ecstatic ravings, which Śrī Rūpa Gosvāmī has described very nicely in his Stava-mālā as follows.

TEXT 97

পয়োরাশেস্তীরে স্ফুরদুপবনালীকলনয়া
মুহুর্বৃন্দারণ্যস্মরণজনিতপ্রেমবিবশঃ।
ক্বচিৎ কৃষ্ণাবৃত্তিপ্রচলরসনো ভক্তিরসিকঃ
স চৈতন্যঃ কিং মে পুনরপি দৃশোর্যাস্যতি পদম্ ॥৯৭॥

payorāśes tīre sphurad-upavanālī-kalanayā
muhur vṛndāraṇya-smaraṇa-janita-prema-vivaśaḥ
kvacit kṛṣṇāvṛtti-pracala-rasano bhakti-rasikaḥ
sa caitanyaḥ kiṁ me punarapi dṛśor yāsyati padam

SYNONYMS

payaḥ-rāśeḥ—by the sea; *tīre*—on the beach; *sphurat*—beautiful; *upavanālī*—garden; *kalanayā*—by seeing; *muhuḥ*—continuously; *vṛndāraṇya*—the forest of Vṛndāvana; *smaraṇa-janita*—by remembering; *prema-vivaśaḥ*—being overwhelmed by ecstatic love of Kṛṣṇa; *kvacit*—sometimes; *kṛṣṇa*—of the holy name of Kṛṣṇa; *āvṛtti*—repetition; *pracala*—busily engaged in; *rasanaḥ*—whose tongue; *bhakti-rasikaḥ*—expert in devotional service; *saḥ*—that; *caitanyaḥ*—Śrī Caitanya Mahāprabhu; *kim*—whether; *me*—my; *punarapi*—again; *dṛśoḥ*—of the eyes; *yāsyati*—will go; *padam*—in the path.

TRANSLATION

"Śrī Caitanya Mahāprabhu is the topmost of all devotees. Sometimes, while walking on the beach, He would see a beautiful garden nearby and mistake it for the forest of Vṛndāvana. Thus He would be completely overwhelmed by ecstatic love of Kṛṣṇa and begin to dance and chant the holy name. His tongue worked incessantly as He chanted, 'Kṛṣṇa! Kṛṣṇa!' Will He again become visible before the path of My eyes?"

PURPORT

This quotation is from the first *Caitanyāṣṭaka,* verse 6, in Śrīla Rūpa Gosvāmī's *Stava-mālā.*

TEXT 98

অনন্ত চৈতন্যলীলা না যায় লিখন।
দিঙ্মাত্র দেখাঞা তাহা করিয়ে সূচন ॥ ৯৮ ॥

ananta caitanya-līlā nā yāya likhana
diṅ-mātra dekhāñā tāhā kariye sūcana

SYNONYMS

ananta—endless; *caitanya-līlā*—the pastimes of Śrī Caitanya Mahāprabhu; *nā yāya likhana*—it is impossible to write; *dik-mātra*—only a direction; *dekhāñā*—showing; *tāhā*—them; *kariye sūcana*—I introduce.

TRANSLATION

The pastimes of Śrī Caitanya Mahāprabhu are unlimited; it is not possible to write of them properly. I can only give an indication of them as I try to introduce them.

TEXT 99

শ্রীরূপ-রঘুনাথ-পদে যার আশ।
চৈতন্যচরিতামৃত কহে কৃষ্ণদাস ॥ ৯৯ ॥

śrī-rūpa-raghunātha-pade yāra āśa
caitanya-caritāmṛta kahe kṛṣṇadāsa

SYNONYMS

śrī-rūpa—Śrīla Rūpa Gosvāmī; *raghunātha*—Śrīla Raghunātha dāsa Gosvāmī; *pade*—at the lotus feet; *yāra*—whose; *āśa*—expectation; *caitanya-caritāmṛta*—the book named *Caitanya-caritāmṛta; kahe*—describes; *kṛṣṇadāsa*—Śrīla Kṛṣṇadāsa Kavirāja Gosvāmī.

TRANSLATION

Praying at the lotus feet of Śrī Rūpa and Śrī Raghunātha, always desiring their mercy, I, Kṛṣṇadāsa, narrate Śrī Caitanya-caritāmṛta, following in their footsteps.

Thus end the Bhaktivedanta purports to the Śrī Caitanya-caritāmṛta, Antya-līlā, *Fifteenth Chapter, describing Śrī Caitanya Mahāprabhu's pastimes in the garden by the sea.*

References

The statements of *Śrī Caitanya-caritāmṛta* are all confirmed by standard Vedic authorities. The following authentic scriptures are quoted in this book on the pages listed. Numerals in bold type refer the reader to *Śrī Caitanya-caritāmṛta's* translations. Numerals in regular type are references to its purports.

Amṛta-pravāha-bhāṣya (Bhaktivinoda Ṭhākura), 1, 51, 119, 137

Bhakti-rasāmṛta-sindhu (Rūpa Gosvāmī), 170

Bhakti-ratnākara (Narahari Cakravartī), 46

Gaurāṅga-stava-kalpavṛkṣa (Raghunātha dāsa Gosvāmī), **226, 247-**248

Gīta-govinda (Jayadeva Gosvāmī), **295**

Govinda-līlāmṛta (Kṛṣṇadāsa Kavirāja), **258, 283, 293**

Padma Purāṇa, 171

Padyāvalī (Rūpa Gosvāmī), 215

Śrīmad-Bhāgavatam, 48, 233, **268-269, 274-276, 277, 278-279, 287, 294**

Stava-mālā (Rūpa Gosvāmī), **301**

Tithi-tattva, 98

Ujjvala-nīlamaṇi (Rūpa Gosvāmī), **194, 214**

Glossary

A

Ācārya—a spiritual master who teaches by example.
Ānanda—spiritual bliss.
Arcanā—worship of the Deity in the temple.
Ananta-caturdaśī—date of the yearly festival commemorating the passing away of Haridāsa Ṭhākura.
Avaiṣṇavas—those who are after material enjoyment and those who are against the supremacy of the Lord.

C

Cintā—the ecstatic symptom of anxiety.
Cit—Kṛṣṇa's spiritual knowledge potency.

D

Dārī sannyāsī—a bogus tantric *sannyāsī* who keeps women.
Deva-dāsī—a female servant in the Jagannātha temple.
Divyonmāda—transcendental madness in separation from Kṛṣṇa.

G

Gṛhasthas—householders who follow regulative principles.

H

Hari bol—"Chant the holy name of Hari."

J

Jāgara—the ecstatic symptom of wakefulness.
Japa—chanting Hare Kṛṣṇa softly and slowly.

K

Karaṅga—a water pot.
Kīrtana—chanting Hare Kṛṣṇa loudly.
Kṣatriyas—the warrior and administrative class.

M

Mahā-mantra—the great chant for deliverance; Hare Kṛṣṇa, Hare Kṛṣṇa, Kṛṣṇa Kṛṣṇa, Hare Hare/ Hare Rāma, Hare Rāma, Rāma Rāma, Hare Hare.
Malina-aṅgatā—the ecstatic symptom of uncleanliness.
Māyāvādī—an impersonalist or voidist adhering to the belief that ultimately God is formless and without personality.
Moha—the ecstatic symptom of illusion.
Mṛtyu—the ecstatic symptom of death.

N

Nadīyā-nāgarī—a so-called party of devotees who worship Viṣṇupriyā.
Nāmācārya—*ācārya* of the chanting of the holy names (Haridāsa Ṭhākura).

P

Pāñji-ṭīkā—further explanations of a subject.
Paramahaṁsa—a topmost swan-like devotee of the Lord.
Parama-vidvān—the most learned scholar.
Pralāpa—the ecstatic symptom of talking like a madman.
Prasāda—remnants of food which have been offered to the Lord.
Proṣita-bhartṛkā—a woman whose husband has left home and gone to a foreign country.
Purāṇas—the eighteen very old books which are histories of this and other planets.

R

Rāga-mārga—the path of devotional service in spontaneous love.
Rāmacandra—the incarnation of the Supreme Lord as a perfect king.

S

Saṅkīrtana—congregational chanting of the holy names of God.
Sannyāsa—the renounced order of life.
Śāstra—revealed scripture.
Siṁha-dvāra—the gate of the Jagannātha temple.
Śrāddha-pātra—remnants of *prasāda* offered to the forefathers.
Śūdra—the servant and laboring class of men.

T

Tānava—the ecstatic symptom of thinness.

U

Udvega—the ecstatic symptom of mental agitation.
Unmāda—the ecstatic symptom of madness.

V

Vaijayantī—a garland containing flowers of five colors.
Vaiṣṇava—a devotee of Viṣṇu.
Vaiṣṇava-aparādha—an offense to a Vaiṣṇava.
Vidhi-mārga—the path of regulative devotional principles.
Vṛndāvana—the village where Kṛṣṇa lived as a child; the topmost transcendental abode of the Supreme Lord.
Vyādhi—the ecstatic symptom of disease.

Bengali Pronunciation Guide

BENGALI DIACRITICAL EQUIVALENTS AND PRONUNCIATION

Vowels

অ a আ ā ই i ঈ ī উ u ঊ ū ঋ ṛ

ৠ ṝ এ e ঐ ai ও o ঔ au

ং ṁ *(anusvāra)* ঁ ṅ *(candra-bindu)* ঃ ḥ *(visarga)*

Consonants

Gutterals:	ক ka	খ kha	গ ga	ঘ gha	ঙ ṅa
Palatals:	চ ca	ছ cha	জ ja	ঝ jha	ঞ ña
Cerebrals:	ট ṭa	ঠ ṭha	ড ḍa	ঢ ḍha	ণ ṇa
Dentals:	ত ta	থ tha	দ da	ধ dha	ন na
Labials:	প pa	ফ pha	ব ba	ভ bha	ম ma
Semivowels:	য ya	র ra	ল la	ব va	
Sibilants:	শ śa	ষ ṣa	স sa	হ ha	

Vowel Symbols

The vowels are written as follows after a consonant:

া ā ি i ী ī ু u ূ ū ৃ ṛ ৄ ṝ ে e ৈ ai ো o ৌ au

For example: কা kā কি ki কী kī কু ku কূ kū কৃ kṛ

কৄ kṝ কে ke কৈ kai কো ko কৌ kau

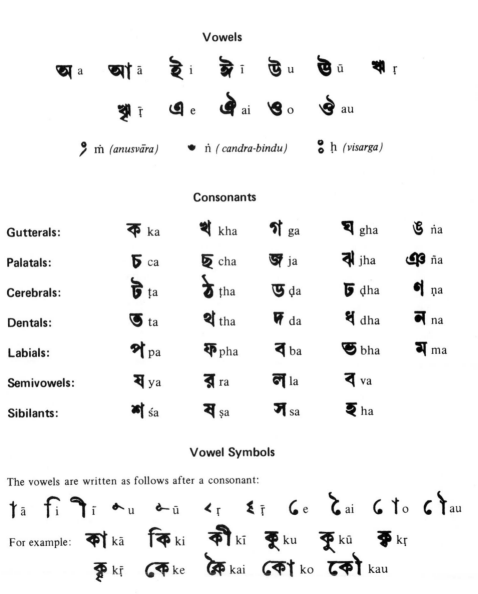

The letter *a* is implied after a consonant with no vowel symbol.

The symbol *virāma* (্) indicates that there is no final vowel. क् k

The letters above should be pronounced as follows:

a –like the *o* in hot; sometimes like the *o* in go; final *a* is usually silent.
ā –like the *a* in far.
i, ī –like the *ee* in meet.
u, ū –like the *u* in rule.
ṛ –like the *ri* in *ri*m.
ṝ –like the *ree* in *ree*d.
e –like the *ai* in pain; rarely like *e* in bet.
ai –like the *oi* in b*oi*l.
o –like the *o* in go.
au –like the *ow* in *ow*l.
ṁ –*(anusvāra)* like the *ng* in so*ng*.
ḥ –*(visarga)* a final *h* sound like in Ah.
ṅ –*(candra-bindu)* a nasal *n* sound like in the French word *bon*.
k –like the *k* in *k*ite.
kh –like the *kh* in Ec*kh*art.
g –like the *g* in *g*ot.
gh –like the *gh* in bi*g-h*ouse.
ṅ –like the *n* in ba*n*k.
c –like the *ch* in *ch*alk.
ch –like the *chh* in mu*ch-h*aste.
j –like the *j* in *j*oy.
jh –like the *geh* in colle*ge-h*all.
ñ –like the *n* in bu*n*ch.
ṭ –like the *t* in *t*alk.
ṭh –like the *th* in ho*t-h*ouse.
ḍ –like the *d* in *d*awn.
ḍh –like the *dh* in goo*d-h*ouse.
ṇ –like the *n* in g*n*aw.
t–as in *t*alk but with the tongue against the the teeth.
th–as in ho*t-h*ouse but with the tongue against the teeth.
d–as in *d*awn but with the tongue against the teeth.
dh–as in goo*d-h*ouse but with the tongue against the teeth.
n–as in *n*or but with the tongue against the teeth.
p –like the *p* in *p*ine.
ph –like the *ph* in *ph*ilosopher.
b –like the *b* in *b*ird.
bh –like the *bh* in ru*b-h*ard.
m –like the *m* in *m*other.
y –like the *j* in *j*aw. য
y –like the *y* in *y*ear. য়
r –like the *r* in *r*un.
l –like the *l* in *l*aw.
v –like the *b* in *b*ird or like the *w* in d*w*arf.
ś, ṣ –like the *sh* in *sh*op.
s –like the *s* in *s*un.
h–like the *h* in *h*ome.

This is a general guide to Bengali pronunciation. The Bengali transliterations in this book accurately show the original Bengali spelling of the text. One should note, however, that in Bengali, as in English, spelling is not always a true indication of how a word is pronounced. Tape recordings of His Divine Grace A. C. Bhaktivedanta Swami Prabhupāda chanting the original Bengali verses are available from the International Society for Krishna Consciousness, 3764 Watseka Ave., Los Angeles, California 90034.

Index of Bengali and Sanskrit Verses

This index constitutes a complete alphabetical listing of the first and third line of each four-line verse and both lines of each two-line verse in *Śrī Caitanya-caritāmṛta*. In the first column the transliteration is given, and in the second and third columns respectively the chapter-verse references and page number for each verse are to be found.

D

R

S

U

V

Y

General Index

Numerals in bold type indicate references to *Śrī Caitanya-caritāmṛta's* verses. Numerals in regular type are references to its purports.

A

B

S

T

U

V

W

Y

Z

The Author

His Divine Grace A. C. Bhaktivedanta Swami Prabhupāda appeared in this world in 1896 in Calcutta, India. He first met his spiritual master, Śrīla Bhaktisiddhānta Sarasvatī Gosvāmī, in Calcutta in 1922. Bhaktisiddhānta Sarasvatī, a prominent devotional scholar and the founder of sixty-four Gauḍīya Maṭhas (Vedic Institutes), liked this educated young man and convinced him to dedicate his life to teaching Vedic knowledge. Śrīla Prabhupāda became his student, and eleven years later (1933) at Allahabad he became his formally initiated disciple.

At their first meeting, in 1922, Śrīla Bhaktisiddhānta Sarasvatī Ṭhākura requested Śrīla Prabhupāda to broadcast Vedic knowledge through the English language. In the years that followed, Śrīla Prabhupāda wrote a commentary on the *Bhagavad-gītā,* assisted the Gauḍīya Maṭha in its work and, in 1944, without assistance, started an English fortnightly magazine, edited it, typed the manuscripts and checked the galley proofs. He even distributed the individual copies freely and struggled to maintain the publication. Once begun, the magazine never stopped; it is now being continued by his disciples in the West.

Recognizing Śrīla Prabhupāda's philosophical learning and devotion, the Gauḍīya Vaiṣṇava Society honored him in 1947 with the title "Bhaktivedanta." In 1950, at the age of fifty-four, Śrīla Prabhupāda retired from married life, and four years later he adopted the *vānaprastha* (retired) order to devote more time to his studies and writing. Śrīla Prabhupāda traveled to the holy city of Vṛndāvana, where he lived in very humble circumstances in the historic medieval temple of Rādhā-Dāmodara. There he engaged for several years in deep study and writing. He accepted the renounced order of life (*sannyāsa*) in 1959. At Rādhā-Dāmodara, Śrīla Prabhupāda began work on his life's masterpiece: a multivolume translation and commentary on the eighteen thousand verse *Śrīmad-Bhāgavatam* (*Bhāgavata Purāṇa*). He also wrote *Easy Journey to Other Planets.*

After publishing three volumes of *Bhāgavatam,* Śrīla Prabhupāda came to the United States, in 1965, to fulfill the mission of his spiritual master. Since that time, His Divine Grace has written over forty volumes of authoritative translations, commentaries and summary studies of the philosophical and religious classics of India.

In 1965, when he first arrived by freighter in New York City, Śrīla Prabhupāda was practically penniless. It was after almost a year of great difficulty that he established the International Society for Krishna Consciousness in July of 1966. Under his careful guidance, the Society has grown within a decade to a worldwide confederation of almost one hundred *āśramas,* schools, temples, institutes and farm communities.

In 1968, Śrīla Prabhupāda created New Vṛndāvana, an experimental Vedic community in the hills of West Virginia. Inspired by the success of New Vṛndāvana, now a thriving farm community of more than one thousand acres, his students have since founded several similar communities in the United States and abroad.

In 1972, His Divine Grace introduced the Vedic system of primary and secondary education in the West by founding the *Gurukula* school in Dallas, Texas. The school began with 3 children in 1972, and by the beginning of 1975 the enrollment had grown to 150.

Śrīla Prabhupāda has also inspired the construction of a large international center at Śrīdhāma Māyāpur in West Bengal, India, which is also the site for a planned Institute of Vedic Studies. A similar project is the magnificent Kṛṣṇa-Balarāma Temple and International Guest House in Vṛndāvana, India. These are centers where Westerners can live to gain firsthand experience of Vedic culture.

Śrīla Prabhupāda's most significant contribution, however, is his books. Highly respected by the academic community for their authoritativeness, depth and clarity, they are used as standard textbooks in numerous college courses. His writings have been translated into eleven languages. The Bhaktivedanta Book Trust, established in 1972 exclusively to publish the works of His Divine Grace, has thus become the world's largest publisher of books in the field of Indian religion and philosophy. Its latest project is the publishing of Śrīla Prabhupāda's most recent work: a seventeen-volume translation and commentary—completed by Śrīla Prabhupāda in only eighteen months—on the Bengali religious classic *Śrī Caitanya-caritāmṛta.*

In the past ten years, in spite of his advanced age, Śrīla Prabhupāda has circled the globe twelve times on lecture tours that have taken him to six continents. In spite of such a vigorous schedule, Śrīla Prabhupāda continues to write prolifically. His writings constitute a veritable library of Vedic philosophy, religion, literature and culture.

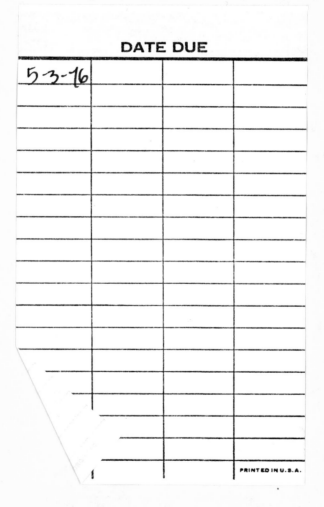